# THE POCKET LAWYER

*Solve Your Own*
*Legal Disputes*

Marilyn D. Sullivan, Attorney

Venture
2000 · Publishers

LARKSPUR, CALIFORNIA

**The Pocket Lawyer: Solve Your Own Legal Disputes**
Copyright 1997 Marilyn D. Sullivan

This publication is intended to provide guidance in regard to the subject matter covered. It is sold with the understanding that the author and publisher are not herein engaged in rendering legal or other professional services. If such services are required, professional services should be sought.

Quotations with permission from The Columbia Dictionary of Quotations, Columbia University Press.

Book cover design: Lightbourne Images, Ashland, OR

Printing: McNaughton and Gunn, Saline, Michigan

---

**Library of Congress Cataloging-in-Publication Data**
Sullivan, Marilyn D., 1950-
The pocket lawyer: solve your own legal disputes/ Marilyn D. Sullivan.
p.    cm.
Includes index.
ISBN 0-9629239-2-3
1.   Dispute resolution (Law)—United States—Popular works
2.   Attorney and client—United States—Popular works.   I. Title
KF9084.Z9S85     1997
347.73'9—dc21                                           96-49952
                                                        CIP

---

10  9  8 7 6 5 4 3 2 1

# Acknowledgments

As with all worthwhile endeavors, this book is the product of a cooperative effort. While the final product is my own, a team of legal and literary experts contributed their talents. Judge E. Warren McGuire, in all his judicial wisdom and humor, as Consulting Author, Jean Howard, chief editor and master wordsmith, as the polish behind the print, Lawrence Scancarelli, Esq., Charles Lewis, Esq. and John O'Reilly, Esq. as legal consultants, Cathy Baehler as copy editor, and Dorothy Omoth as proofreader. I thank them heartily for their valuable contributions. I also thank my husband for his love, patience, and support throughout.

# Dedication

This book is dedicated to empowering people beset by legal problems. The inflexible court system is intimidating and costly – but justice no longer needs to rob you of your time, emotions, and bankroll. Out-of-court dispute resolution systems are in place all over the country, ready for you to use.

With this book, you can finally handle your own legal problems – or if necessary, meaningfully join with your attorney in speedy, economic solutions outside the court system. Here you will find the tools and confidence to take the reins and bring your disputes to an end.

# Limits of Liability

# Marilyn D. Sullivan, Attorney
## Author

Marilyn D. Sullivan is an award-winning attorney and author of 3 prior books. Fifteen years of battles in the court system have made her determined to help you avoid it, if at all possible. Combining expertise as attorney, mediator and arbitrator, Marilyn is a recognized leader in promoting alternative dispute resolution to its present national popularity. An advocate for legal consumers, she has guided hundreds of disputes to mediated settlement or resolution by arbitration. A practicing attorney in Larkspur, California, Marilyn also directs The Dispute Resolution Forum, which provides arbitration and mediation services.

# Judge E. Warren McGuire, Ret.
## Consulting Author

Judge E. Warren McGuire brings a wealth of knowledge, experience and wisdom from a distinguished legal career spanning half a century. He served on the California Superior Court bench for 20 years. Before joining the bench, Judge McGuire practiced law from many different vantage points – as county counsel, deputy district attorney and private civil lawyer. For the past decade he has made a major contribution to alternative dispute resolution as a popular arbitrator and mediator in the San Francisco Bay Area.

# Resource Page

FOR INQUIRIES ABOUT THE AUTHOR'S SERVICES
CALL:
**LAW OFFICE OF MARILYN D. SULLIVAN**
415-461-2311

FOR BOOKS, FORMS AND SOFTWARE:
See Order Form at back of book
or contact:
**VENTURE 2000 PUBLISHERS**
100 Larkspur Landing Circle, Suite 112
Larkspur, California 94939
415-461-1470

FOR TRADE DISTRIBUTION:
**NATIONAL BOOK NETWORK**
4720 Boston Way
Lanham, Maryland 20706
1-800-462-6420

# Table of Contents

Self-Help Works! · The Costly Dump Truck Syndrome · Lawyers Cure Only Half the Problem · Legal Intimidation: How Much Justice Can You Afford? · Lady Justice and Her Scales · Justice Is Not Exact · Unpredictable Court Results · The Answer Is ADR

Why Use Alternative Dispute Resolution? · Complicated Rules and Regulations · Did You Know You Can Reduce Expenses in Your Case? · Two Popular Methods to Solve Your Legal Problem · The Difference Between Mediation and Arbitration · The Road After ADR

The Secret of Mediation's Success · Success Is a Matter of Timing · What is the Goal of Mediation? · The Mediator's Role · Why Mediate, If I'm Right? · When Should You Mediate? · How Do You Get to Mediation? · Should You Hire a Lawyer for Your Mediation?

Differences Between Mediation, Arbitration, and Court · Why Arbitrate? You'll Button Down Your Hearing Date · How Do You Arrive at the Arbitration Door? · How Do You Choose an Arbitrator? · What After Arbitration? · Which System Does Better?

# Foreword

During nearly fifty years in the daily pursuit of justice, I have seen its many faces. Throughout those years I served in many capacities: as deputy district attorney, county counsel, private practitioner, twenty years as Superior Court judge and most recently, almost a decade as mediator and arbitrator. Our legal system, unable to grow at the pace of its workload, has begun to falter in its mission to dispense justice.

My colleagues and I have seen the court system move out of reach for the average person: skyrocketing legal fees, facts upstaged by tactical maneuvers, court procedures becoming more complex, unreasonable delays. Disputants, nearly destroyed by their differences, work their way for years through the complex, expensive, overbooked legal system. We tried to find better ways, but our court system labors under the same conditions as all publicly funded services: it is overburdened and understaffed. There just aren't enough resources. The result: justice was no longer affordable, nor was it just.

Now, with *alternative dispute resolution,* popularly known as ADR, we finally have a system that *can* do the job – a civil justice system potentially more powerful than any we have ever known. ADR has such great power because it places *immediate* legal solutions squarely in your hands. Recognizing this, the courts have welcomed ADR into its highly respected role in the legal process. Mediation is the voluntary resolution method; arbitration provides a mini-trial.

ADR is a new kind of justice. You no longer have to live in conflict for years waiting to be heard. You don't need to spend all your savings on attorneys, strategy and costs in the pursuit of justice. ADR provides justice in a far more equitable way. It is available and affordable to *all* disputing parties, not just the affluent. Disputants can now access simple legal solutions for themselves – without lawyer representation, if they choose. These systems are cost-cutting, time saving and simple. In effect, they are *user friendly*. Now, with the agreement of your opponents, you can submit your dispute to mediation or arbitration – and have economical resolution in a matter of months.

Equipped with the tools in this book you will be able to intelligently handle your legal problems and make use of the ADR system yourself. Last, but not least, this book contains an indispensable aid never before available to the lay person – the tools of legal analysis. Of course, nothing is better for analysis than a formal legal education, but *The Pocket Lawyer Analyzer* comes very close. And the price is right.

A word about *truth*. In a dispute, there are at least two truths: one for each party. Each has its degree of merit. Our court system tends to drive a wedge between them. But alternative dispute resolution has another mission: to bring these truths and their parties together into something more satisfying and fair called *resolve*. If voluntary solution does not come about, the objective is to end the dispute quickly and efficiently with arbitration.

This timely book gives you all the tools you'll need to resolve your own dispute within this new user friendly forum. May it serve you well.

The Honorable
E. Warren McGuire (Ret.)

## — *Introduction* —

# WHY DO YOU NEED THIS BOOK?

A war is raging in this country. It's independent of the armed forces. We don't read about it in the daily news, or hear about it on television. The battlefield is in your own back yard: every courtroom in every city of the United States.

Each year, 14.5 million civil cases are filed nationwide. This creates well over *thirty million* plaintiffs and defendants. Each is a casualty – winners and losers alike – bearing financial and emotional scars. The cost in dollars: at least $88 billion a year to legal fees and expenses. The cost in quality time and energy: three to five years. The toll in stress and strain: several years of ongoing conflict and anxiety. The result:

> "THOSE DISPUTING, CONTRADICTING, AND CONFUTING PEOPLE ARE GENERALLY UNFORTUNATE IN THEIR AFFAIRS. THEY GET VICTORY, SOMETIMES, BUT THEY NEVER GET GOOD WILL, WHICH WOULD BE OF MORE USE TO THEM."
>
> —Benjamin Franklin

## Perfect Timing for This Book

Today's court system is a war fueled by conflict and destructive tactics. It strikes emotional and financial blows. It is a mix of inconsistent results for which disputing parties pay dearly. But our legal system has now begun to crack under these pressures. Overbooked, understaffed, and unable to keep pace, the courts now call upon alternative dispute resolution (ADR) for help.

This calling has been answered! For the first time in history, out-of-court systems are in place to effectively answer the needs of disputing parties. For centuries, all we had was the expensive, complicated, delay-plagued court system. At long last, the age of legal reform has arrived – and with it, powerful new alternative dispute resolution systems: mediation and arbitration.

## The Court System Turns a Page

We deal with our medical and emotional problems on an immediate basis. Generally, the problem comes up, we deal with it and move on. Legal problems have been different. Trapped in the court system, you were stuck in your dispute for the three to five years it took to get to trial. As time marched on, so did attorney fees. You couldn't get away from the escalating expense, delay, and stress.

On top of that, decisions received after years of waiting were inconsistent, at best. The court just didn't have the time or attention to produce a quality result. The end product: disputing parties spent valuable years and precious savings to obtain results that were less than equitable.

Time is of the essence with our legal problems, too. They need to be dealt with as they arise. Now, you have the option to resolve your dispute without waiting years for the court's attention. This book gives you a set of tools to resolve your dispute *now*, using these new out-of-court systems – and to get better results.

## YOU CAN HANDLE YOUR DISPUTE YOURSELF

With the tools in this book, you can resolve your legal problem *immediately* and *more effectively.* You no longer have to wait years for justice. These new out-of-court systems are built for simplicity, efficiency, and economy. They are designed for use by disputing parties *themselves.* We show you how to use them and what to expect.

What is it about the alternative dispute resolution process that gives you better results than the courts do? ADR systems have the time to fully hear and decide your case. They operate unimpaired by the restrictions of the publicly funded court system. There are no court calendar limits. And *you* control the funding. It makes a huge difference in the results.

Now, for the first time ever, you can *realistically* move ahead with your dispute without an attorney. Armed with these new and powerful legal tools, you will find rapid and better legal solutions. Indeed, you have more important things to do than to spend vast amounts of your time and energy consumed with your legal dispute!

It all sounds like a dream come true. The skeptic steps in and asks, "What about legal case evaluation? That's the one thing I can't do myself." With this book, that very important gap has been bridged. *The Pocket Lawyer Analyzer,* at Chapter 6 and available as software, evaluates your case for you.

### THE POCKET LAWYER ANALYZER

Whether you choose to represent yourself or not, you need the benefit of legal analysis. It's the key to your case, enabling you to make your best legal decisions. To this end we have developed an empowering system so that you, the reader, can analyze your own legal problem and take charge of it yourself. We have appropriately named our system *The Pocket Lawyer Analyzer.* This powerful interactive program applies a point system so you quickly and accurately assess the feasibility of your own potential legal problem. And our system is *the only one of its kind*!

Its seven easy steps provide you with a case assessment that will clearly spell out whether you should bring a legal action, and, if so, where you should bring it – in the court system, or outside it. *The Pocket Lawyer Analyzer* is easy to use and surprisingly accurate. In fact, some of the leading insurers may be using this program right now to value their insureds' cases. *The Pocket Lawyer Analyzer* can take the place of your lawyer, and the cost is a drop in the bucket when compared to just one hour of lawyer time. Of course, with some disputes you may still want to retain a lawyer – but with the aid of Chapter 13, *How to*

*Hire a Lawyer: Insider Tips,* you'll know exactly which questions to ask to hire the best representative for your case. You'll feel far more in charge of the meeting – you are the boss.

## THE AUTHORS

This book is written by a team with impressive credentials. Marilyn D. Sullivan is a lawyer meeting the challenge of solving legal problems in and out of court. She knows the legal system inside out and has seen it work, for better and for worse, for two decades. Our consultant is retired California Superior Court Judge E. Warren McGuire, who shares his unique and insightful perspective, derived from 20 years of experience on the bench and 18 years' prior experience as an attorney advocate. In recent years, both Ms. Sullivan and Retired Judge McGuire have helped litigants resolve their own disputes outside the courts through alternative dispute resolution. They join here together to pass on their wisdom from a half century of combined professional experience.

## THE SIMPSON TRIAL: A WARNING

Our introduction to this book would be incomplete without mention of the O. J. Simpson trial. Those unpalatable proceedings warn us of how expensive, tense, and drawn-out court proceedings can be – and how totally unpredictable.

Although it was a criminal case, the Simpson trial illustrates the complexities, frustrations, and costs of our legal system. It is a perfect example of the pressing need for another way to resolve legal conflict. We now offer a guide to all of the tools and skills you will need to do just that.

*— Chapter One —*

# SOLVING YOUR LEGAL PROBLEM: A BETTER ROUTE

Time is of the essence. Given the choice of traveling through a maze or moving in a straight line, we're sure to choose the direct route. And so it goes for legal matters. Only in this case the maze is the court system, and the new, direct route involves mediation and arbitration – the alternative dispute resolution methods popularly known as ADR. This chapter presents compelling reasons to resolve your legal disputes using ADR. It is the wave of the future.

## PLEASE, NOT A LEGAL PROBLEM

Staring the legal issue in the face often produces the flight syndrome.

As seekers of peace and pleasure, we invariably avoid or ignore problems when they arise. It's full speed ahead and we're flying carefree down the happy highway of life. Everything's going pretty much as we planned. Oops! One of those ornery obstacles ... an unplanned event. But please – don't let it be a legal problem.

As a society we have effective tools to deal with our emotional and medical problems. Apparently, to resolve them, we recognize the need to be personally involved. But for deep-rooted reasons, legal problems are handled differently. They are not managed in the creative, rational ways we handle other problems. Staring the legal issue in the face often produces the flight syndrome.

Consider some of the ways we respond to problems in other areas of life. How do we deal with an emotional problem, such as a phobia – an irrational fear? Do we hand the problem over to a psychologist and say, "Here, handle this for me and let me know when it's over?" No.

We spend weeks, sometimes months, pondering, discussing, and dealing with the problem, sometimes with the assistance of a therapist. Often we buy books, attend seminars, and explore any and all effective tools for problem solving. We realize we must get to the root of our emotional problem, understand it, and work on it. It can't be solved any other way.

### SELF HELP WORKS!

How do we respond to medical difficulties? Suppose you get the flu. Do you rely on your doctor for relief? No, indeed. You put on a pot of chicken soup, take two aspirin, and go to bed for the day. You give your body a rest. What about more chronic ailments, such as back pain or even arthritis? Would you depend solely on your medical practitioner? No. Knowing yourself – your limitations and symptoms – better than anyone, you can research the various solutions and work with the medical practitioner to bring about changes. We can have better health, control the problem, and even prevent the ailment from coming back.

Faced with emotional or medical problems, we seem to realize that identifying and treating the cause is the only way to a cure. Why then do we respond so differently to legal problems? If we are able to take responsibility for our medical and emotional woes, investigate their source, and propose solutions, why do we avoid our legal predicaments?

It's simple. We become intimidated and overwhelmed. We don't like legal issues. In fact, we abhor them. What do we do when a legal problem rears its ugly head? All too often we ignore it and refuse to acknowledge that it's there. Instead of meeting our legal problem head on and seeking a productive solution, we ignore it. We plow right over it. Or we fill up our dump truck and carefully drop it off at the fix-it center. With legal problems, that means the lawyer's door. Is this why so many lawyers set up offices by freeways?

> If we can be responsible for all of our medical and emotional woes, why avoid legal predicaments?

## THE COSTLY DUMP TRUCK SYNDROME

Saving lawyer time is in your best interest. Don't make the mistake of avoiding participation in your case.

Remember your last legal problem? When it surfaced, did you treat it like any other problem? Did you look at it, define it, analyze it, and then make a decision as to what to do about it? Or did you employ the dump truck method – carefully extracting all evidence of the problem, tucking it away in a file folder, plopping it down on some lawyer's desk with a hearty retainer, saying, "Here. Fix it and let me know when it's over"?

Did you hire your attorney by conducting interviews, asking the attorney candidates all the questions you had, until you decided your selected counsel was capable of representing your very important interests? Or did you drop it at the first law office you could find, glad to be rid of it, and run?

Meanwhile, an attorney's services are expensive. Remember how long it took you to read the stack you just dumped on the lawyer's desk? Well, for the lawyer's scrupulous review, multiply that by five. It becomes apparent that saving lawyer time is in your interest. And another more serious aspect of the situation hovers in the background: your opponent hopes you'll be the first to run out of funds to pay an attorney. And if you do ... all may be lost.

Many people adopt the dump truck plan. There's no real logic to it. It's more of an emergency disposal. The sooner you get rid of it, the sooner you forget it. Do you see yourself in the dump truck scenario? A legal problem – who, me? If I can't see it – it may just vanish. If I wait long enough – it will just go away. If I give it to a lawyer – I can just forget about it. Out of sight, out of mind.

> **Client participation benefits both clients and lawyers when clients are involved in their legal disputes.**

The dump truck method is an expensive way to go. Lawyers have a reputation for charging prohibitively expensive fees. Much of this bad press arises because attorney services are expensive, especially when they are not controlled. When the lawyer has to step in and do the whole job, the bill is out of reach to most people. But, it doesn't have to be that way anymore. There is a better way.

## BE THE DIRECTOR

People need to take a hands-on approach to legal problems. They need to step up to the batter's box and responsibly choose a course of action. That may be hiring a lawyer or it may be handling their dispute solo with or without intermittent lawyer consultation.

If your decision is to hire a lawyer, interview your candidates carefully. Do it with team work in mind. You will participate with this lawyer in achieving *your* legal solution. Client participation benefits both clients and lawyers when clients become responsibly involved in their legal disputes. It costs far less for the clients, and lawyers may be on their way to clearing their tainted reputations.

## WE ARE RESPONSIBLE FOR OUR LEGAL PROBLEMS

As with most of our difficulties, *we* are responsible for our legal problems. Indeed, legal predicaments arise and develop from our own actions, or lack of them, just as other problems

> If you don't control the details of your case you are faced with feeling powerless.

do. Most people don't view it this way. For the most part they feel that legal problems are obstacles that pop up randomly without cause. They refuse to acknowledge their part. When we avoid responsibility for a legal situation, we refuse to see our role in it. When this happens, we give up one of the most valuable tools to solve the problem: Our power to *affect the outcome.*

If someone else – like your attorney – controls the details of your case, you've lost control of your costs. You've also lost control of your ability to intelligently resolve the dispute before it becomes a major battle. The price: powerlessness.

## LAWYERS CURE ONLY HALF THE PROBLEM

Only by taking the bull by the horns can we affect the outcome of our legal disputes. And only through emotional resolution is lasting solution achieved. We may resolve the legal issues, but the underlying emotional mechanism remains in place – fertile ground for the seeds of future legal problems. As we detour past emotional resolution, potential conflict-escalating factors remain ready to take over once again.

For this reason, the legal system invariably fails to achieve full resolution. It skips right past emotional resolve. The attorney takes care of the legal aspect, but only half a solution has been found. The emotional element, if not addressed, remains. If change doesn't occur, the problem is sure to raise its ugly head – but next time, it will roar much louder.

We are not powerless to solve our legal problems. Indeed, we can help bring about better legal solutions if we involve ourselves responsibly in the legal process. What's more, we can prevent future problems when we address their source now.

### LEGAL INTIMIDATION

How did we become so overwhelmed by our legal problems? It began centuries ago when we were fooled into thinking the legal system is out of reach to ordinary folk. A privileged legal forum arose, using Latin terminology and complex, warlike tactics. This ivory tower was accessible only by scholarly doctors of jurisprudence. These first lawyers positioned themselves on pedestals and constructed the legal arena beyond the reach of the lay person. Lawyers were assured large fees and rising power. These arrogant ways and cryptically carved customs held reign far too long. They are now giving way to more democratic and enlightened methods.

For decades people have complained about the court system. The solutions handed down are not satisfactory. And *handed down* is precisely the right terminology. You sit there for the most part, powerless, waiting for the next round to mete out the next consequence. Downright disempowering and dictatorial!

Now it's your move. The legal system can't change; you can. The legal participants – the very people most interested in their disputes – have had very little to do with their case results. Attorneys scoop up the problems, dress them with legal jargon and offer them for legal determination. Then in comes Lady Justice to pick a winner and loser. The result – the disputing parties

> **The outdated customs of law are giving way to more democratic and enlightened methods.**

> **Most people are not heard, the court system is unduly complicated, and attorneys are expensive.**

are intimidated and often outraged by the process.

People report investing substantial sums in the court system, but their results don't justify the expense. They feel unheard and ripped off by a complicated legal system and by attorneys who charge too much. The fact is, most people are *not* heard, the court system *is* unduly complicated, and attorneys *are* expensive. Isn't it time to deal with our legal problems more effectively?

## HOW MUCH JUSTICE CAN YOU AFFORD?

Often, the result of your court case depends upon the work quality of the lawyer you hire and the amount of time assigned to your matter. Each factor depends on the supply of money you can spend on the case. If you have a sizable bankroll, you can hire the best attorneys and conduct voluminous investigations. You can literally outpaper your opponent and win a case not on its merits, but upon how much time your lawyer puts in and how many documents your lawyer can produce.

Understandably, this is a popular strategy in the legal community. Is it right that the winner is the one who has the most resources? Should our system operate this way? Should we do something to change it? This lopsided quality prompted British novelist William McIllvanney to write: "Who thinks the law has anything to do with justice? It's what we have because we can't have justice." When the results yielded by a system become sufficiently skewed, the system invariably gives way. And it has. This is one reason why our legal system is now undergoing major reform.

## TERRORS OF COURT TRIALS

Now to the decision makers. Although the judges are doing the best they can to dish out speedy and exact justice, they don't have sufficient time to dedicate to the increasing volume of cases before them. This sometimes affects their decisions. It has happened on a number of occasions. In one such case, the home seller concealed certain facts from the purchasers. The written contract between the parties contained an attorney fees provision, but no mediation or arbitration provision. The case went to trial after each side spent over $118,000 in attorney fees. The purchasers won the trial and the jury awarded money damages to them. The judge, however, awarded attorney fees to the *losing* defendants, labeling them the prevailing party. This is an extreme example of the injustice that can occur in our court system.

What about an appeal, you say? The U.S. Court of Appeals heard the case. This three-judge panel flatly stated that the determination as to who is the prevailing party lies solely within the discretion of the trial judge. The panel was unwilling to reverse his determination. Therefore the purchasers, who had won at trial, paid their own attorney fees of $118,000 and paid $76,000 of the defendants' attorney fees. In addition, the purchasers were assessed the defendants' attorney fees for the appeal, which brought their appellate fee tab to $21,000. Lady Justice's result: The purchasers prevailed at trial but were forced to pay $215,000 in attorney fees.

Although this example may be difficult to believe, it is true. And this is merely one example of the imperfections of the legal system. Most

> Judges don't have sufficient time to dedicate to the increasing volume of cases before them.

> The court sys-
> tem is open to
> anyone, without
> limitation. Any-
> one can file a
> lawsuit.

people who have had involvement with the court system have an example or two of their own – where Lady Justice has run amok.

## OVERBURDENED COURTS

Think about it. The court system is open to everyone – without limitation. Anyone can file a lawsuit: walk up to the court clerk's counter, pay a minimal filing fee, and away you go. You have yourself a lawsuit. There are no citizenship or residency requirements – you don't have to be an American citizen, or a resident of the district in which you file suit. There are no financial requirements – your income, or lack of it, doesn't matter. These days some courts even have form complaints – all you need do is fill in the blanks.

This open access to the courts brings mixed blessings. Anyone can use it, but increased use of the system has congested and overburdened it. Thus, entering the legal loop is not difficult. But after you pay your initial dues in the form of a filing fee, the process gets quite complicated. After you pass through the portals, survival within the legal system requires an endless supply of money and energy.

## LADY JUSTICE AND HER SCALES

Far too many people believe the court system always produces a just result. They *expect* justice – their version of justice. Because of the symbols selected to represent justice, they are convinced that the legal system is finely tuned, balanced, and invincible – until they have their first court experience.

Their vision is of two scales equitably weighing justice in perfectly balanced proportions. They see Lady Justice – so pure, blind to bias and partiality. Law libraries are brimming with legal books jam packed with carefully articulated black and white rules and regulations. A scrupulous system records volumes of decisions applying these rules and regulations.

> **When it comes to justice, there is no absolute right or wrong.**

### JUSTICE IS NOT EXACT

But the truth is, when it comes to justice, there is no absolute right or wrong. There are no rigid rules for people to judge one another's conduct – and that's what the justice system does. It decides whether people have done what they were supposed to do.

Justice is a hybrid of philosophy and morality. It is defined as "the use of authority to uphold what is right, just, or lawful." British author D.H. Lawrence summed it up: "The only justice is to follow the sincere intuition of the soul, angry or gentle. Anger is just, and pity is just, but judgment is never just."

Most people with at least one court litigation experience have observed the unpredictability of court decisions. There are many versions of justice – yours, your opponent's, the judge's, and each of the jurors'.

Thus, it follows that a system set up to evaluate and judge conduct can never be exact. Ideally, justice should be able to assign each person what he or she is due. But the problem lies in defining what is right and what is wrong. Criminal conduct is relatively easy to

> **The legal system strives to apply a myriad of complex standards to determine what is right and what is due.**

define, since it is so blatantly far afield of the norm. But civil conduct is not.

Civil conduct comes in many sizes, shapes and ranges, none of which are truly offensive. Civil conduct doesn't fall under any clear-cut law that says you strike your neighbor and you have committed battery, calling for a defined criminal penalty. The 14.5 million civil cases filed each year ask one question: "did the defendant violate a duty?"

## UNPREDICTABLE COURT RESULTS

The answer to this question is quite complex – it depends on a lot of varying factors. So the legal system strives to apply a myriad of standards to determine what is right and what is due. With such a mission, court decisions are unpredictable, to say the least.

So, yes, the halls are adorned with Lady Justice and equitable scales. But beyond mere symbols of purity and accuracy, law has no place for either of these qualities. It does the best it can to render everyone their due. But who's to say what the answer should be, when there really is no right answer. Invariably, when a system's task is to pick a winner and loser, the result is unpredictable. As litigants clamor for justice, the gavel falls sometimes here and sometimes there, and that's about as consistent as our court system gets.

## Is There Enough Justice to Go Around?

An analysis of the court system is not complete without reference to the inherent shortcomings of any publicly funded organization. The court system operates under the same deficits as any other public system that is accessible without limits: it is seriously underfunded, understaffed, and overburdened. Case filings are increasing each year while staff is downsizing. The job of meting out justice just can't be done well under these circumstances. With these restraints in place, no wonder the system's results are less than perfect.

> The court system operates under the same deficits as any other public system that is accessible without limits.

For these reasons, society demands better ways to facilitate our legal disputes. It has taken us a long time to implement these new ways. As Abraham Lincoln profoundly observed 150 years ago: "Mercy bears richer fruits than strict justice." We have borne the results of strict justice long enough. We now turn to alternative ways of resolving our legal disputes – mercy among them.

## The Answer Is in ADR

So, if there is no exact justice available, why spend years in a court system seeking it? Why not get your justice quickly and inexpensively? If our court system is so overbooked and underfunded that it can't do its job, why give it your case? These are the primary reasons to consider alternatives to the court system. And the timing is ideal!

Now, as we enter a new century, our bursting court system admits it can't do the job.

**Courts nationwide are setting hearings after cases are filed to refer their litigants to alternative dispute resolution (ADR).**

The court process can't address legal problems with current solutions. Many cases are not heard for a good five years after a dispute arises. By the time the case is heard, nobody has a clear recollection of the *actual* facts. But the litigants vividly remember the excessive time and money they spent getting there.

Acknowledging their shortcomings, the courts nationwide are setting hearings just after cases are filed for the purpose of referring their litigants to alternative dispute resolution (ADR) mechanisms, such as mediation and arbitration. All around the country, these alternative ways to resolve legal disputes out of court are becoming accepted, even preferred. In fact, some states now require litigants to mediate their case before gaining access to the courts.

The best news of all is that ADR is user friendly. Although the court system continues to be too complex for people to represent themselves, ADR was built to be available to the hands-on legal consumer. The pieces are all in place for you to be able to handle your case if you want to. If you don't, you still have the option of hiring an attorney. But at least you finally have the choice.

California, the leader in ADR programs, boasts that 85 percent of its court cases referred to mediation settle. And many other states log in with equally praiseworthy figures. The American Arbitration Association, the leading ADR provider in the country, vigorously supports mediation and arbitration. For attorneys, it means the end of laborious trials and substantial fees. But emerging client satisfaction is so great with these streamlined processes that it brings new meaning to their contributions as lawyers.

Public and private industry swell the ranks by including mediation and arbitration provisions in their contracts. Nearly every real estate contract, loan agreement, health care agreement, and labor contract now contain these provisions. Formal arbitration and mediation training is increasing in popularity among attorneys, and the legislature is responding, as well. Each state and federal court system is setting these alternative systems in place to help the general public resolve, rather than perpetuate, conflict.

> **Formal arbitration and mediation training is increasing in popularity among attorneys.**

## RESPONSIBILITY WILL SET YOU FREE

Now that the courts encourage outside methods of resolution and industry has demanded it, your voice can be heard – but only if you participate more fully in the legal process. This means you must take responsibility for your legal problem when it comes up. To do so, begin with a trip through *The Pocket Lawyer® Analyzer* program in Chapter 6. After using *The Pocket Lawyer Analyzer* you will know how to proceed with your dispute, and do so with confidence. Or you might interview an attorney for a more indepth review of your options, including alternatives to going to court. (See Chapter 13, *How to Hire a Lawyer,* which includes an Insider Checklist.)

In the chapters that follow, you will discover that being heard, simplifying the system, and cutting attorney fees can all happen. In fact, an attorney may not be necessary for your dispute. You have the ability to create these changes. This is an ideal time for change. At long last, our rigid court system is responding to public clamor for faster, easier and less costly ways to resolve disputes. Your participation is invited. This is a beginning, but it does not provide the complete answer to legal resolution. Each one of us must now take responsibility for our own legal problems: as participants and as solvers.

## CHANGE IS ON ITS WAY

It's the burgeoning Age of Personal Responsibility. The legal system is changing, opening its gates to new ways. The time is ripe for us to move forward and make a difference with our own legal problems. It's time to find a new way of justice.

***

We've described the current conditions. Now you're ready for solutions. Chapter 2 offers a powerful prescription for the legal system's ills – alternative dispute resolution. Then, in Chapters 3 and 4, we describe the ADR systems and how to use them to your advantage. Chapter 5 gives you your last chance to avoid formal resolution measures. Then, Chapters 6, 7, and 8 present The Pocket Lawyer Analyzer. This handy program will evaluate your dispute – and point you to the best methods for resolution. Welcome aboard!

*— Chapter Two —*

# ALTERNATIVE DISPUTE RESOLUTION: A BETTER WAY

Your legal education begins in earnest with this overview of alternatives to the court system. Riding the current wave of change in the legal field, alternative dispute resolution (ADR) avoids the shortcomings of the court system. What is this new program that serves up a potent prescription for the ailing courts? Does it provide better resolution of legal disputes? How is it different? What are its pros and cons? How do we shift into it? Here, we answer these questions – and many more – about ADR and its exciting new methods to end legal conflict.

## ADR: Relief for the Courts

Alternative dispute resolution is just that: ways to resolve legal disputes that bypass the court system. These alternative programs were developed to relieve the persistent problems of the traditional legal system – delay, expense, and complication. Alternative dispute resolution responds with quick, inexpensive methods that resolve legal issues. These methods can be set up in advance in a contract between parties, or selected by the parties when a dispute arises. Because you choose to bring these methods into play, you gain a sense of personal power over your legal dispute. No longer does an impersonal court system decide for you. *You* are in charge.

The two major ADR plans are mediation and binding arbitration. Binding arbitration entirely replaces the court system. By agreeing to binding arbitration, you and your opponent *give up your right* to access the court system. In return, you receive a quick, efficient verdict. Mediation, on the other hand, involves highly effective *cooperative* processes that do not interfere with your rights to trial and appeal in the courts. If a cooperative settlement is reached through mediation, there is no reason to take the dispute to court. If a settlement is not reached, you and your opponent can agree to submit your dispute to binding arbitration, or bring your dispute before the courts.

## Why Use Alternative Dispute Resolution?

The present legal system does not adequately address our problems. In virtually every part of our country, the legal process is far too

> You can gain a sense of personal power over your legal dispute with ADR.

complicated for an ordinary person to access *without* an attorney, and too expensive for access *with* an attorney. Legal consumers prefer to avoid personal responsibility and invoke the dump truck method. The end result: consumers are discouraged from representing themselves, despite the expense of retaining a lawyer.

> **If the stringent rules of the court system are not followed your case may be dismissed.**

### COMPLICATED RULES AND REGULATIONS

Recent attempts to streamline the legal system actually created more rules and structure. Around the country, court reforms have been labeled *delay reduction* and *fast track* programs. For the most part, delay has been reduced, but at a cost of *more* guidelines and *more* complexity. The added structure distances individuals even farther from the court system.

In the course of this overhaul, legal statutes and codes which guide a case through the legal system have been thoroughly revamped. Stringent regulations and time lines accompany the filing of each lawsuit. Each disputant, whether represented by counsel or not, is expected to follow the rules – or their cases will be dismissed.

### DID YOU KNOW YOU CAN REDUCE EXPENSES IN YOUR CASE?

Each case usually starts out as an emotional tug-of-war between two or more disputants. They haven't tried or haven't been able to resolve their matter – so they each bring in an attorney. The goal in bringing the matter to counsel is to terminate the dispute. However, at this point the typical dispute veers out of control – both emotionally and financially. Escalating

**You may be surprised to learn that a case can only be as expensive as you allow it to be.**

factors take over. Emotionally, your ego is inflated. You're fed up and you're going to make your opponent pay for it. Little do you realize that, in the long run, it is you who pays. Your opponent feels the same way. Your respective attorneys jump on the egotistical bandwagon. For them, it becomes a battle of wits. Who plays the game better? Emotions become highly charged. Egos rule. Paper generates. Calendars fill up. Expenses soar.

Our legal system's complexity virtually mandates that each disputant be represented by an attorney. Attorneys are expensive, but the structure of the system authorizes and supports that expense. You may be surprised to learn that a case can only be as expensive as you allow it to be. Yes, *you* – the disputant – can be in control, rather than the attorneys or the court system.

For instance, let's look at the process known as discovery. This is the set of pre-trial procedures that allows the parties to discover facts and evidence in a case. It consists of interrogatories (lists of questions posed to the parties, the answers to which become written testimony); demands for documents (which gather written evidence); and depositions (meetings where the attorneys obtain oral testimony under oath from witnesses, which is recorded for future use by the parties). As an example, one deposition can take a full 8-hour day, or multiple days. Charges for each attorney and the cost for court reporter services accompany these depositions. Obviously, attorney fees escalate as testimony is gathered, reviewed, and analyzed. However, a deposition can be completed in a few hours if the questions are carefully worded.

The *amount* of discovery conducted is actually up to you. For example, no rule requires that several sets of interrogatories must be served on an opponent, or that even one set be served. No rule dictates that lengthy document demands must be generated to each party in a case. There is no requirement that depositions of each witness or party – or any depositions at all – be taken. After thorough evaluation by you and your attorney of the merits of the dispute, the probability of success or failure, and the range of anticipated recovery, you and your attorney should discuss each discovery method in terms of potential cost and benefit. With these factors in mind, you can evaluate whether you want your case to take on this added expense. *You* are paying the cost and *you* should make the decision.

> **The amount of discovery is actually up to you.**

## PAPER WARS

Once the lawsuit begins, the attorneys check their arsenals for available weapons. Attorney weapons consist primarily of these expensive discovery procedures we've described. Drawing a weapon before your opponent does becomes a strategy. Each time one attorney unleashes a weapon, opposing counsel retaliates with a bigger, better, and more expensive weapon. A deposition notice summons up another deposition and an elaborate set of written interrogatories. The drums pound, the elaborate battle dance proceeds in stages, and each stage takes on grander proportions.

## LEGAL ANIMALS

The legal animal is a fighter – a fierce combination of high-level intensity and adversity. This is a powerful and infectious combination. The blend of conflict and attorneys who advocate it produces a combustible mixture. A step through the archway of litigation causes even the most introverted participant to take up armor and sword and adopt the *en garde* stance. Throughout the litigation process, the duel accelerates.

> **A step through the archway of litigation causes court participants to become warriors in an escalating war.**

## WHO REALLY WINS?

By the time you get to trial, you're drained from answering too many interrogatories, producing too many documents, and answering too many questions at deposition. The enormous amount of data generated is difficult and expensive to manage. At trial, it all begins again. Emotionally, you're depleted. Financially, what was once your nest egg is used by your attorney to conduct the battle. This is the climate that prompted poet Robert Frost to comment: "A jury consists of twelve persons chosen to decide who has the better lawyer."

Even if you did have the better lawyer – or at least you had more money to pay for one – you feel drained and ripped off by your trial win. When it's over, the warriors become humans again and shed their armor. We sit there in the courtroom, winners and losers, able to think rationally and breathe again – for the first time since the battle began years ago. And we ask ourselves, was all the time, money, and energy worth it? Usually the answer is a resounding *No* – even for those who prevailed at trial. It took too long, it cost too much, and the emotional commitment was exhausting.

### ADR: What's in It for Lawyers?

The answer for all of us, clients and lawyers alike, is not to litigate, but to resolve disputes by alternative, *independent* means. For the lawyer reading this book, I invite you to enhance the quality of your life and your law practice with alternative dispute resolution – both for your clients and yourself. Beside the fact that it's the wave of the future, it can be extremely rewarding.

For me, this shift to ADR transformed every aspect of my law practice. The level of satisfaction for my clients and myself has increased a hundred fold. ADR tools and techniques make it possible for me to offer my clients many more options as legal solutions. Legal remedies now come in assortments. I feel much more like a legal healer than a warrior. Read on to see how this came about for me.

### The New Attorney:
### A Personal Experience from Warrior
### to Peacemaker

Many attorneys, fed up with the aggressive, counter-productive roles they are expected to play, have at long last found meaning as providers of these new conciliatory services. Now, in the role of peacemakers, they at last see their clients achieving true resolution of their legal-based problems.

For me, providing these peacemaking services brought my first positive contribution

> The answer for all of us faced with the legal system is to resolve disputes by alternative, independent means.

| A journey from warrior to peacemaker. |
| --- |

through law. It was well over 20 years ago that I selected law as my profession. On a deep level, I was committed to serve humanity and enhance the quality of life through law. A little over ten years later the vision of such a purpose was lost. I had litigated a high volume of cases throughout many courts. Sharper and more alert than most, I was highly successful at being one up on my opponents. My clients loved that. Despite my weight of barely 100 pounds, my intense focus and high energy level made me a powerhouse. In fact, one opponent called me "the best-looking pit bull" he'd ever seen!

Yet feelings of loss and depression followed my biggest trial wins. Despite an enviable victory rate, I felt unsuccessful and depleted. It was as if I perpetuated a system with little or no merit. I was deeply dissatisfied with my participation in the legal system. My entry into a client's dispute would actually invigorate it, not defuse it. Each attorney coming on board in the case had a way of fueling the conflict. By the time we got to trial, the vigor was grand and the dispute was totally out of proportion. So were its costs.

## DEMOLITION, NOT RESTORATION

On the one hand, my clients realized they had won the battle they began many years earlier. They achieved their goal. But the winning felt hollow. Getting there robbed them of valuable resources: a wealth of precious energy and hard-earned money. The legal arena swallows up these resources. The legal system depletes energy and money without restoring them. Restoration isn't part of the legal system, but demolition is. Sounds a lot like war, doesn't it?

## ATTORNEY TRANSFORMED

Ten years ago was a pivotal time for me. I clearly saw litigation was not producing meaningful and lasting resolution for disputants. It was one avenue toward resolution, but only as a last resort. I began to work with clients in a completely different manner. Their legal problems became issues that could be examined and managed in many different ways.

My clients and I began to sit down and examine every conceivable way to resolve their disputes. We analyzed all potential solutions. Results were examined in terms of time, money, and energy. Level-headedness and common sense became important in deciding which course to take. In earlier years, I automatically directed clients through the portals of the court system. Now I found myself pointing them toward alternative methods to settle their disputes.

## EMPOWERMENT COMES WITH ADR

I became an arbitrator with the American Arbitration Association to help terminate disputes on a larger scale. I have since worn the arbitrator hat far more often than the litigator helmet. Upon completing extensive training, I also joined the ranks as mediator. Since then I have facilitated hundreds of mediations, the vast majority of which resulted in settlement. After many years as a litigation gladiator, my satisfaction from resolving disputes now tops the fulfillment charts.

> **Legal problems are issues that can be examined and managed in different ways than court litigation.**

> **Mediation and arbitration are the two most popular ADR forums for resolving legal disputes.**

Over this past decade I feel like I am making a truly meaningful contribution to law – and society. As is the case for many well-intentioned lawyers, my reason for entering the profession was to assist others with legal crisis. But it is impossible to tap any humanistic meaning from the adversarial nature of litigation. My new solution-finding strategies have transformed my practice from litigation to consultation. The many lawyers and their clients disillusioned with the legal system can turn it around for themselves with ADR. It's a brand new way of law with a brand new sense of fairness.

Now, with many alternatives to litigation, clients respond with an entirely different demeanor. They are interested in looking at all possibilities and are sometimes quite enthusiastic about their range of options. Instead of feeling overwhelmed and fearful, they feel in charge and ready to meet the challenge of meaningful solution. Now, they choose to enter the doors to mediation and arbitration far more often than climbing the courthouse steps. For them, the potential burdens of the court system outweigh its benefits.

## TWO POPULAR METHODS TO SOLVE YOUR LEGAL PROBLEM

What are these ADR procedures that provide relief to people burdened by legal problems? Provided to replace the overworked court system for a beleaguered public, mediation and arbitration are the two most popular forums for resolving legal disputes. Now, when you sign a contract, it often includes provisions for mediation and arbitration. Many courts across the United

States now require disputants to explore mediation or arbitration before they are allowed access.

On this wave of popularity, these out-of-court methods are easier for you to use. Packaged to avoid expense and complexities of filing a lawsuit, they are tailored to be accessible to you, so you can economically and promptly resolve your dispute.

> The purpose of mediation and arbitration is quick resolution and minimal expense.

The purpose of mediation and arbitration is quick resolution and minimal expense. Achieving these two goals is reason enough to join the ADR club. Time and money are two of our most valued commodities. But equally important is conservation of energy for our valued interests. If freed up, the vast amount of personal energy funneled into litigation can make a far more meaningful contribution to our lives. Thus, ADR serves a threefold purpose: saving time, money, and energy.

## THE DIFFERENCE BETWEEN MEDIATION AND ARBITRATION

Arbitration has been around for a long time. People know it. Mediation is relatively new. For this reason, these two processes are often confused – even by attorneys. The truth is, mediation and arbitration couldn't be more different.

The purpose of both processes is quick resolution and minimal expense. Mediation is a voluntary process; the parties make their own decisions. Binding arbitration is an adversarial process. An arbitrator, usually a lawyer, retired judge or industry expert well versed in the topic of the case, decides who wins and who loses and

**Arbitration streamlines the legal process and terminates the dispute quickly and economically.**

renders an award. Arbitration is a far better forum than the court system, because it streamlines the legal process. It terminates the dispute, one way or the other, quickly and at a relatively low expense. It allows the parties to move on.

The biggest difference between the two processes is that mediation does *not* result in a decision, order, or judgment *imposed* on the parties. Even when required by contract, mediation is a settlement process and involves no decision making, other than the parties' decision to settle or not. Mediation is a no-fault, voluntary process that leaves the parties in charge of their case. Therefore the mediation process does not place blame; it is a means to *settlement*. Arbitration, on the other hand, is combat. It yields a decision by the arbitrator against one party in the form of an *award*.

### WHEN YOU MEDIATE, YOU DETERMINE THE OUTCOME

Often, parties confusing mediation with arbitration arrive at the mediation session ready to do battle, when they should be prepared to work toward settlement. This combative attitude impedes the mediation process, which must be approached with conciliation and resolve to succeed.

With mediation, the participants create and abide by their *own* settlement. It is true that the mediator facilitates, encourages, and directs the process. But no one makes decisions for the parties as a judge, jury, or arbitrator would. Instead, with the mediator's assistance the parties cooperatively and voluntarily determine their own outcome. They walk away from a mediation session knowing they have made their own decisions and resolved their matter. They are doubly satisfied. And usually mediation occurs early on, before the money and energy drain of the legal process has left its mark.

**Mediation is a means to settlement; arbitration is combat.**

## THE ROAD AFTER ADR

Another distinction lies in the options available *after* ADR. With mediation, if the case doesn't settle you still have litigation ahead of you - either in the court system or by binding arbitration if you have a Binding Arbitration Agreement. Mediation does not replace any procedure; it just adds a valuable settlement step before litigation.

Arbitration, on the other hand, yields an award. It is an adversarial, mandatory process that puts the arbitrator in charge of the dispute. The parties give the arbitrator exclusive power to determine the winner and loser. The judge and jury of the court system is replaced with the arbitrator who makes a decision against one party and in favor of the other. The arbitrator's decision carries the same weight as a decision rendered in the court system. Thus, arbitration is combat in every sense. Each party is there to be determined winner or loser in legally enforceable black and white.

When the parties depart from the arbitration hearing, they leave with a judgment or receive it within a month. It is the ultimate and only decision. They are bound by it. When the mediation participants leave the mediation, hopefully they have signed a settlement agreement setting forth the terms they agreed to. Otherwise, they leave without a settlement, and with all their legal rights to proceed. One way or the other, their legal process is concluded or they are a step closer to conclusion.

ADR is a whole new way of rapid, targeted legal resolution.

\* \* \*

Attention, attorneys and clients alike: don't litigate – *mitigate*. Neutralize your war so you can work constructively toward a solution on your own or with ADR. Meanwhile, your tools to legal solution follow: mediation in Chapter 3, arbitration in Chapter 4 and your last chance settlement in Chapter 5. Turn the page to access these powerful tools.

# — *Chapter Three* —

# MEDIATION:
# THE WAVE OF THE
# FUTURE

---

Court battles will cost you your time, emotions, *and* money. Instead of fighting, suppose you could sit down with your opponent and work out an agreeable, reasonable, and equitable solution to your problem. Not only that – it would cost just a fraction of a court action. Well, you can! Mediation is your forum. This chapter introduces you to mediation – its advantages, how it came about, the philosophy behind it, when you should consider mediation, and how mediation brings the litigation juggernaut to a screeching halt.

It's never too late
to mediate ...

---

> Mediation em-
> powers people
> instead of
> breaking them
> down.

## The Secret of Mediation's Success

Mediation is the application of cooperative efforts between disagreeing parties. Because mediation is a *voluntary* legal process, it brings with it a promise of deep personal resolve. Imposed solutions, available through litigation and arbitration, never achieve the level of flexibility and satisfaction of voluntary solutions because someone else makes your decisions. Thus, the greatest reward and deepest resolve comes from mediation – when disagreeing parties create their own settlement with the skillful facilitation of a mediator.

Why has mediation become the hit parade of the legal repertoire? We'll cut to the chase and tell you why. Very simply – the process empowers people instead of breaking them down. In a strategic *about face*, disputing parties are encouraged to participate and find solution. Incredibly, they do. It's a process that restores, not destroys.

## To Cure, Get to the Cause

As with other problems, legal ills tend to surface again if they are not cured. In the litigation process you blame someone else and therefore avoid responsibility for your predicament. This is why litigants rarely get to the root of their disputes or effect any remedy for the forces which brought it about. Parties who enter the litigation and arbitration turnstiles often repeat their experiences, but with new people.

Mediation is an exploratory process that can reach the root and get to the cause of the problem. Because the parties must examine and work out their conflict, the hands-on personal involvement creates solutions that are often long lasting. Time and again, we find that those who successfully mediate do not see their legal problems resurface. Because of its reputation for achieving quick, lasting solution, mediation is often referred to as the holistic legal approach.

> **ADR methods are streamlined, relatively easy, inexpensive, and effective.**

Now that we've given away mediation's secret, let's take a look at the philosophy behind mediation, and the reasons why it works so well.

## THE EMERGENCE OF ADR

Invariably, when systems no longer work, new programs come along to take their place. Fortunately for the legal consumer, this quandary has created alternative methods for legal solution. These new methods are free of the ongoing costs, delays, and complications of the legal system. They are streamlined, relatively easy, inexpensive, and effective. Mediation and arbitration are the front runners of these new ADR procedures. The American Arbitration Association is the national leader in providing ADR services. For over ten years their mediation services have settled hundreds of thousands of disputes.

Alternative Dispute Resolution (ADR) emerged as the answer to a court system that is excessively warlike, unreasonably expensive, and unduly drawn out. Due to an enormously overbooked court system, the results are highly unpredictable. Judges just don't have the time to give sufficient attention to the cases

In order for settlement negotiations to have the best chance of success, they must come at the beginning of the case.

they hear. The case that consumed so much of your time and attention doesn't get the level of scrutiny it deserves. There isn't time, nor is there interest. To the court, it's just another case in a backlog.

## SUCCESS IS A MATTER OF TIMING

Mediation has been around for a long time, under the labels of *settlement conference* and *conciliation proceedings*. In the court system, the settlement conference immediately precedes trial. Conciliation is designed as a cooperative deterrent to couples contemplating dissolution of marriage. It attempts to heal the differences between the parties. Both the settlement conference and conciliation are alternative means to resolve legal disputes.

In court proceedings, the settlement conference typically takes place only after the parties are involved in expensive and time-consuming litigation. It is the step right before trial. Most often, it fails to produce resolve because it comes too late. At this late date, resolution is improbable; there's too much blood on the litigation battlefield. The litigation frenzy has taken hold. The parties have each spent so much in attorney fees they can't recoup this loss through settlement. Emotions reign, egos are high, and rigid legal positions rule. It's too late in the game for compromise. Nobody can realistically budge. It's on to battle. Each intends to be the grand victor.

In revamping its system, the courts have taken a good hard look at resolving cases early. It became apparent that in order for settlement negotiations to have the very best chance of

success, they must come at the beginning of
the case – before the battle begins. Mediation
was created to meet this need. In court proceedings it now comes at the beginning of your
case. It precedes the war – and hopefully takes
its place. For disputes that haven't yet found
their way to court, mediation now heads off
hundreds of thousands of lawsuits.

Although mediation as a settlement
conference has been around for quite some
time, mediation in its current format is quite
new. But it is here to stay. Even courts now
recognize its value as the best way to solve
your legal dispute.

## THE EVOLUTION OF MEDIATION

Mediation among agreeing parties is
relatively new to the legal profession, and is
unconventional in its departure from the cen-
turies-old rival scenario characterizing our legal process. Mediation is a new way to legal
solution through facilitated meetings at the negotiation table. It completely discards the warlike practices of our traditional court system.
Litigation is intimidating. The mediation process is highly empowering.

For these reasons, mediation is ac-
claimed as the cutting edge for resolving legal
disputes with a minimum investment of time,
energy, and money. The parties agree to their
own solutions. The trained mediator may be
the facilitator or even the creator of the solution, but it is only with the parties' agreement
that a successful settlement can be reached.

> **With disputes that haven't yet found their way to court, mediation is now heading off hundreds of thousands of court filings.**

## IT'S BECOMING COURT POLICY

> Easily 85 percent of court cases resolve with ADR and make court access unnecessary.

Now, across the nation, courts are implementing their reorganization plans. They've established a status conference program early in each case – usually within three months of filing. At this conference the parties must select a form of alternative dispute resolution before they move forward with their court battle. The parties agree to either mediate their dispute or submit it to binding arbitration. In some courts, this step is mandatory. These courts block access to the court system until the parties arrange for alternative dispute resolution services. Easily 85 percent of cases resolve at this stage and make court access unnecessary.

In California the court rule requiring mediation reads as follows:

"IN THE CASE OF MANY DISPUTES, LITIGATION CULMINATING IN A TRIAL IS COSTLY, TIME CONSUMING, AND STRESSFUL FOR THE PARTIES INVOLVED. MANY DISPUTES CAN BE RESOLVED IN A FAIR AND EQUITABLE MANNER THROUGH LESS FORMAL PROCESSES. ALTERNATIVE PROCESSES FOR REDUCING THE COST, TIME, AND STRESS OF DISPUTE RESOLUTION, SUCH AS MEDIATION, HAVE BEEN EFFECTIVELY USED IN CALIFORNIA AND ELSEWHERE. IN APPROPRIATE CASES, MEDIATION PROVIDES PARTIES WITH A SIMPLIFIED AND ECONOMICAL PROCEDURE FOR OBTAINING PROMPT AND EQUITABLE RESOLUTION OF THEIR DISPUTES AND A GREATER OPPORTUNITY TO PARTICIPATE DIRECTLY IN RESOLVING THESE DISPUTES."

The courts now acknowledge the importance of the parties' direct participation in resolving their disputes.

### IT'S A NO-FAULT PROCESS

Mediation's legal pioneers were not trained until the mid-80s. The American Arbitration Association was the first nationwide mediation trainer. Today's mediation training involves psychological principles, perhaps even more than legal principles. The mediator skilled in facilitation makes all the difference. The combination of a masterful mediator, willing parties, and a no fault attitude has popularized mediation and made it the cutting edge for resolving legal disputes.

Mediation has caught on with such high acclaim that many people choose it before they access the court system. It only makes sense. Why spend the time and money to file a lawsuit just so the court can send you through the mediation door? If you succeed with mediation, you've spent litigation fees for no reason. Savvy people are catching on by entering the ADR door before they climb the stairs to the courthouse.

### WHAT IS THE GOAL OF MEDIATION?

You come to mediation in one of two ways: as a lawsuit participant who is routed there by the court, or by your own choice. Whichever method brings you to mediation, the goal is always the same: to find rapid, effective resolution of your legal issue. Participants are well aware of the pitfalls of litigation and are motivated by that knowledge. They

> Savvy people are catching on by entering the ADR door before they climb the stairs to the courthouse.

| The trained mediator stimulates negotiation and facilitates you and your foes to reach your settlement. |

want to get past the conflict. They want to be in charge and make the decisions themselves. They want results *now*. Mediation serves that purpose. It's quick, and the parties make their own decisions with the mediator's invaluable guidance.

## THE MEDIATOR'S ROLE

A masterful mediator is able to bring about settlement through skilled applications of reasoning, analysis, and exploration of options. This occurs through the mediator's mindful application of reframing and releasing techniques. The mediator's role is best described as that of a legal therapist or theorist. The mediator is usually a lawyer or retired judge experienced in the field of your dispute, and trained in principles of psychological intervention.

Because mediation's sole purpose is to settle your dispute, the trained mediator stimulates negotiation and *facilitates* you and your foes to reach your settlement. The process is an optimum blend of psychological processes. It's far less charged than one-on-one negotiation – by utilizing the mediator as intermediary and buffer. There's no direct contact without the presence of the mediator. All negotiations are undertaken with the mediator, who serves neutrally for all parties but effectively passes information back and forth in an atmosphere of conciliation.

The mediator's task is to encourage the parties to express their point of view, then carefully move them past the conflict through settlement. The purpose is not to change opinions or blame participants. No one is ever proven wrong in the mediation process. There is no finger-pointing. Instead, differing points of view are acknowledged and validated. Mediation is, in fact, a true behavioral process.

> **The answer in mediation is to acknowledge each party's point of view and find a mutually agreeable way to close the chapter.**

As long as we are human, we will always have differences of opinion. They are not right or wrong. They are opinions. Resolution does not come about because opinions change. The answer in mediation is to acknowledge each party's point of view and find a mutually agreeable way to close the chapter. Nobody's right and nobody's wrong.

Because of the psychological intervention inherent in the process, mediation will never work without qualified mediator participation. In the midst of conflict we're unable to achieve the arms-length, objective attitude required for resolution. If you follow our recommendations in this book, before reaching formal mediation you've exhausted your own conflict-resolving tools. Chapter 5 on *Last Chance* presents procedures for resolving conflict on your own. Thus, we presume you've tapped your own resolution resources prior to selecting mediation. At the mediation juncture, you've been unable to resolve the issue on your own. Now, you need the mediator to break the ice.

## MEDIATION ADDRESSES THE NEEDS OF THE PARTIES

Mediation also achieves its role as the cutting edge for solution because it targets and attempts to meet the complaining party's needs. One of the most important roles of the mediator is to discover the unique needs of the

> **Once the underlying emotion is gone, the parties can see what they need to solve this dispute.**

parties and tailor a creative way to meet those needs. Yes, the mediation hearing considers the case facts and applicable law, but success comes when each parties' needs are met.

Getting to the parties' needs means getting them past their issue. Usually, participants can't describe their important needs if they are entrenched in emotion. For example, feeling like a victim continually blocks any objective view. So, if there is still strong emotion about the matter, the mediator's goal is to assist the involved party through and past this emotional state.

The mediator accomplishes this by separately caucusing with the stuck party to defuse emotion, guiding them one-on-one through a series of psychological steps. In some disputes, I find that the only way to truly release the emotion is to get the disputing parties together with careful facilitation from a mediator. This is why the mediator must be well trained in psychological principles.

Once the underlying emotion is gone, the parties can see what they need to solve this dispute. It feels as if a curtain has lifted and this is where the *real* work begins. The mediator discovers what the injured party wants, then researches how the responding party may fill this goal. It may not take the same form as the injured party wants, but it will still work. Creative packaging of settlements can be more fun than a day at the granddaddy of all estate sales.

## ANOTHER COMPELLING REASON TO AVOID THE COURTS

There's nothing like a horror story to motivate you to consider the alternatives. These days, horror stories abound of the unexpected results received from Lady Justice. People are beginning to realize that when it comes to law, there is no absolute right or wrong. In fact, nothing is exact in a system set up to evaluate and judge human conduct.

Litigants have learned that Lady Justice and the finely balanced scales have little to do with the litigation process. Symbols of law such as Lady Justice and the balanced scales lead people to believe our court system balances truth, justice, and the American way. This statement is true, in part. The court system does mete out justice, but justice is about as vague as truth. Everyone has a different definition. Because litigants now recognize these imperfections, they are willing to measure out their own results in mediation.

## WHY MEDIATE, IF I'M RIGHT?

Right and wrong has no place in mediation. In fact, gaming tactics have no place whatsoever at the mediation bargaining table. Mediation never judges, never determines winners and losers. There is one objective – to resolve your dispute no matter what it takes. The weapons and tricks of the litigation arsenal just don't apply.

At mediation, everyone is a winner by making a choice to resolve their dispute. If you participate in the "Right and Wrong Game,"

> Litigants have learned that Lady Justice and the finely balanced scales have little to do with the litigation process.

you will find plenty of players. You present an argument and so does your foe. Everyone has a reason for being right. Generally, your foe will have an argument just as compelling as you do. Before a judge or a jury, or even before an arbitrator, these arguments might carry equal weight. Or they might not. It's a gamble! You're at mediation because you are not willing to risk such an undefined territory – right?

People sometimes come to mediation with the stance: "But I'm right and he's wrong. Why should I compromise?" We head off this mediation impediment at the pass. Why should you compromise? Because you don't want to spend your savings proving you're right, especially in a system where there is no absolute right. You don't want to carry this dispute around with you for years like a heavy coat until the court system's alarm finally sounds for your battle to begin. You have better things to do. The case for right and wrong gets lost in the litigation shuffle; the case for mediation is a powerful one.

### Is Mediation Favored by Everyone?

We find potential litigants quite open to the alternative methods of ADR. As they become more familiar with mediation, it's their preference. Objections come from attorneys in ivory towers, making an excellent living from the litigation game of right and wrong. Litigation is a highly lucrative playground. The adversarial frenzy generated by right and wrong is expensive, indeed.

The frenzy begins with discovery devices and fishing expeditions. Each revelation is met by an investigation of grander proportions. The stacks of documents to be reviewed and analyzed get taller and taller. Issues that once seemed clear and straightforward become extremely complex. The more issues are raised, the more your attorney is raking in your savings.

It's not really the attorney's fault. Litigation combat is tough. It takes a lot of work and staying power. And you did hire counsel to wage *your* war. That's exactly what litigation attorneys do. At the same time, these attorneys make a good living in the litigation pit. Some of these litigators are hesitant to give up that income in favor of alternative dispute resolution – which they see as a serious threat to their lifestyles. Leaving the pit in favor of mediation is actually like changing careers. It takes a strong dose of humanistic motivation for the litigation lawyer to cross the bridge to mediation peacemaking.

If you meet with counsel who opposes or objects to mediation, or even arbitration, remember *you* are the boss. Which route to travel is entirely your decision. You may find that attorneys who serve as mediators and arbitrators are the best choice to represent or advise you.

## WHEN SHOULD YOU MEDIATE?

If there is no written mediation provision between you and your opponent, you do not have to mediate before seeking legal redress. Nevertheless, remember that you both may agree to mediate at any time. As a mediator who sees its 85% success rate, I feel that *all*

> It's never too late to mediate. All parties should engage in mediation before moving forward with their dispute.

> **The mediation process can't hurt your case – and if settlement occurs, it can save you a lot of money and headaches.**

parties should engage in mediation before moving forward with their dispute. The mediation process can't hurt your case – and if settlement occurs, it can save you a lot of money and headaches.

It's never too late to mediate. Even if you've come through the court system, and trial is lurking around the corner, consider mediation. In fact, this is an ideal time for it. Incentives couldn't be higher. Each party faces hefty lawyer deposits and the gavel's final verdict is just around the bend. Similarly, if arbitration is your next step, an ideal time out presents itself in mediation.

## CONTINUALLY PROPOSE MEDIATION

At any stage of your legal process, you can offer mediation as a method of getting past your dispute. This can occur when the dispute first arises or following years of court litigation. Mediation isn't something you consider only once. In fact, you might have an unsuccessful mediation early on. Later, when the legal system has zapped your energy and your nest egg, you may want to try mediation again. We find that after the parties have had a taste of litigation, they are far more willing to compromise.

## HOW DO YOU GET TO MEDIATION?

The mediation process is accessed in many ways. Some parties are litigants just beginning their court battle and directed by the court to mediate at their status conference. Others signed an agreement to mediate before their dispute arose. Others decided to invoke mediation after their dispute arose, hoping to make arbitration or court unnecessary. Chapter 10 entitled *Mediation Mechanics* details mediation's procedures and protocol.

## A Written Contract to Mediate

Have you and your foe previously signed a contract which required mediation to settle any dispute which might arise? When you use *The Pocket Lawyer Analyzer* in Chapter 6, you will review your written agreement to determine if there is such a provision. Mediation provisions are now common in many contracts, ranging from real estate purchases to health care provider agreements. In fact, it is becoming more and more common for mediation provisions to be included in contracts encountered in all facets of life. Some sample mediation provisions are included in Chapter 12 entitled *Loss Prevention* and in the Appendix.

## A Mediation Agreement After the Dispute Begins

Another way to arrive at mediation is for the disputing parties to agree to mediation without having a prior agreement to do so. You can initiate such a plan. See the sample Mediation Agreement in the Appendix. In other words, when the dispute arises, you and your foe can agree to mediate your dispute. Mediation does not interfere with any legal rights. All options are still available to you if mediation doesn't resolve your dispute. It can't hurt; it can only help.

> **Mediation does not interfere with any legal rights.**

> Mediation succeeds because the parties arrive empowered to reach their own solutions.

## SHOULD YOU HIRE A LAWYER FOR YOUR MEDIATION?

Must you hire a lawyer for the mediation? No. But if you already hired one and the adversarial process has begun, it is a good idea to include your lawyer. Just let your lawyer know you want to mediate. If you have not hired a lawyer and you feel competent to present your side of the case, you are free to do so. Remember, mediation is not an adversarial process – so you don't need a lawyer to act on your behalf. If you select a mediator who knows a lot about the type of law involving your case, then you have the necessary legal knowledge on board. However, you may want to consult with a lawyer in advance of the mediation to obtain a legal opinion of your case and a summary of the applicable law. *The Pocket Lawyer Analyzer* presented in Chapter 6 will also provide you with a wealth of legal analysis.

## WHY DOES MEDIATION WORK WHEN OTHER PROCESSES FAIL?

Mediation succeeds because the parties arrive empowered to reach their own solutions. By choosing to mediate, they now take the reins. These parties gather with a single intent: to settle their dispute. They are in the ideal state of mind and have hired a professional to facilitate them to close the chapter. With the assistance of the mediator, these parties create an optimum success rate.

Mediation participants want to find quick, effective resolve to their legal issue. The secret to the success of mediation is that it permits the parties to control their own destiny. For this reason and this reason alone, we find mediation produces a degree of resolve that is never achieved when a third party makes the decision. It makes no difference whether a judge or jury has pronounced the winner. When someone else makes the decision, there is never a deeply felt resolve. It is only when the disputants themselves decide to resolve the dispute that they get a feeling of satisfaction and completion.

The mediation settler, though perhaps not receiving everything requested, feels relieved and successful. Empowered by the contributions he made to the settlement solution, he realizes it could not have occurred without him. There is little recovering to do, since the dispute has not been going on very long. There was no litigation frenzy, no unreasonable costs of money, time, and energy. It's clear that mediation brings emotional and legal resolve. Litigation produces only legal resolve, and that result may not be satisfying.

We have compared people walking away from mediated settlements with winners coming out of court. We invariably find that the parties who have settled at mediation are in a far better place. Recovery for the winning litigation survivor usually takes a long time, and is never complete. He may have won but it doesn't feel as if he brought it about. He feels disempowered because the courts and his attorney have made the decisions in the case. Until the moment of the verdict, he knew it

> **Recovery for the winning litigation survivor usually takes a long time, and is never complete.**

could go either way. For these reasons, he doesn't feel victorious. Prolonged litigation takes its toll. The win comes up short. All the time, money, and energy spent along the way can't be restored.

For all these reasons, mediation has reached high public acclaim as the cutting edge for solving legal disputes. See Chapter 10, *Mediation Mechanics*, for more detail on this powerful process.

★★★

The companion star to mediation is arbitration. We call mediation and arbitration companions because they are the perfect team to a quick, effective legal solution. Mediation is the settlement step, while arbitration is the final determination. Move on to Chapter 4 for more on Arbitration: Justice at a Fraction of the Cost.

# Chapter Four

# ARBITRATION: JUSTICE AT A FRACTION OF THE COST

Imagine you are faced with a long, expensive court trial with an uncertain date some time in the next few years. What if you could move this trial to a month from now and know you will receive a verdict after only two days? You can! All you have to do is give up your right to be heard in court and your right to appeal. Arbitration, the swiftest justice in town, works just that way. Whether you are a plaintiff or a defendant, learn what you need to know to choose arbitration as your forum – the only forum to guarantee a judgment quickly and inexpensively. On top of that, the result can be far better than in the court system.

**Time is our most valuable commodity and arbitration uses it wisely.**

## ARBITRATION'S GOAL

The goal of arbitration, like that of a court trial, is to terminate a dispute and provide relief (usually a money judgment) to the complaining party. Unlike its court counterpart, arbitration achieves this result quickly and with a minimum of expense. In these times of high technology, people just don't want to be embroiled in disputes for years. Time is our most valuable commodity, and arbitration uses it wisely. Disputing parties appear before the arbitrator, each given ample opportunity to be heard, then they receive an answer based on evidence and testimony. Unlike a trial verdict, the arbitrator's judgment cannot be appealed – but this is the cost of swift justice. The arbitration process is quick, forward moving, and intelligent.

## WHY DO PEOPLE ARBITRATE?

People choose arbitration to get their legal dispute determined quickly and inexpensively – at least when compared with the court system. Disputants can obtain a binding judgment for a fraction of the time and cost of maneuvering through the massive court maze. When parties agree to binding arbitration, they forego the cost and delay of the court system. They also forego their legal right to appeal, with its own attending costs and delay.

## Differences Between Mediation, Arbitration, and Court

Mediation, arbitration, and court litigation are three entirely different processes. They are easily distinguished.

Mediation is generally used as an early remedy in your dispute. If successful, your matter is settled with no need to go further. If mediation does not result in settlement, you still have your adversarial procedures intact – arbitration or court litigation.

Arbitration can be binding or non-binding. Non-binding arbitration is just an advisory arbitration. The arbitrator makes his decision, but the parties are still free to continue on with their dispute in the court system, despite the arbitrator's ruling. For purposes of this book, when we refer to arbitration, we mean binding arbitration, not non-binding arbitration.

Binding arbitration takes the place of the court system. When parties agree to binding arbitration they are giving up their right to have their dispute decided in court. You can agree to binding arbitration in an agreement before the dispute begins or at any time after you enter the court system. If you've decided upon binding arbitration, the court won't let you in the door. And if you're already in the court system, you'll be swiftly escorted out. Binding arbitration has no place in the courts!

If the disputing parties do not make a Binding Arbitration Agreement, the courthouse is their forum. The courts are available to all.

> When people agree to binding arbitration they are giving up their right to have their dispute heard in court.

**Arbitration is far more expedient and cost-effective than a court trial.**

You don't have to be an American. You don't have to be a voter. You can even be a felon. The United States court system was established as the means for terminating legal disputes. Thus, no one is denied access.

With these differences in mind, binding arbitration is featured here as a valuable alternative to the courts. Actually, arbitration's value is obvious only by comparing it to the court system. These two processes are similar in that they are both adversarial. A winner and a loser are selected in a contest. Other than that, these two processes differ greatly, especially in matters of time, expense, and litigant control.

## THE SECRETS OF ARBITRATION'S VALUE

Arbitration is far more expedient and cost-effective than a court trial. Typically, you get to an arbitration hearing in one to three months. Through the court system, it could be one to five years before you go to trial.

The value of having your dispute decided quickly and inexpensively is enormous. Spend a year or two in the court system and you'll know what we mean. Prolonged participation in a lawsuit has a profound effect on your life. It just gets you down. You relive the experience that brought you to this dispute over and over again and become more negative about the wrong that's been done. The dispute escalates and drains much of your energy.

Although you typically have an attorney representing you, you're still involved in the case. Your deposition is taken and questions are asked in written form. You're getting huge attorney bills each month. You can't get away from it. Your case takes on a life of its own. Thus, the foremost importance of arbitration is its swiftness. It gets you past your dispute within a matter of months and gives you the freedom to move forward.

## THE EVOLUTION OF ARBITRATION

Arbitration was created about 70 years ago to avoid the costs, delays, and risks of a litigation system unresponsive to the needs of the industrial age. The American Arbitration Association (AAA) was formed in 1926 to advance the use of arbitration nationwide. Since that time AAA has been the major mediation and arbitration provider of services and education. By 1992, AAA handled one million cases nationwide with offices in every major city. Arbitration is now a fierce competitor of the courts. 90 percent of law schools now offer a course in alternative dispute resolution.

Backed by this long and experienced history, why is arbitration just now coming into favor? Because tradition crumbles very slowly, especially when it comes to the American court system. Although many large public and private organizations now accept alternative dispute resolution as preferable to the courts, many people hesitate to adopt new customs. We need to feel backed by tradition. We cling to ideals and standards. But now that our justice system recommends alternative dispute resolution, many American legal consumers are jumping on the bandwagon.

> The American Arbitration Association is the major mediation and arbitration provider. It's been in existence for 70 years.

| Discovery procedures that uncover facts of the case are depositions, document inspection demands, and interrogatories. |
| --- |

## DELAY MEANS EXPENSE

Costs generally get larger over time. That's just a fact of life. This is even more true in court litigation. Litigation carries with it adversarial conduct – the attitude of a fierce contest. Egos climb on board and everyone has something to prove. During the one to five years it takes to get to trial, the litigation contest is in full swing. Procedural guidelines are an arsenal of legal weapons. They mandate when steps are taken and how they should be answered. Attorneys are expected and encouraged to use them. In fact, if they don't, they may be sued for malpractice.

While litigants wait for their day in court, they take turns hurling threats from their legal arsenals. By the time the litigant gets to trial, he has depleted his arsenal at great expense. We find that delay alone is one reason why court cases cost so much more than arbitrations.

## DISCOVERY: THE REAL COST CULPRIT

Another cost culprit is discovery. Discovery is the set of legal procedures that uncover the facts of a case. These procedures are voluntary, equally available to all parties in a lawsuit, and governed by specific rules. Some of these discovery procedures are depositions, document inspection demands, and interrogatories. When you hear that someone outpapered their opponent, discovery is the cause.

Because the philosophy behind arbitration is economy, pre-hearing discovery is discouraged. The court system, on the other

hand, seems to encourage extensive and prolonged discovery. Court pre-trial discovery, in
the form of oral depositions before a court reporter and written questions to the parties, can
be horrendously expensive. The concept behind
arbitration is to streamline both cost and time.
When costs of arbitration are compared with
costs of court actions, the difference is glaring.

> **With court cases you want to know everybody's story before you get to trial, with no surprises.**

## DEPOSITIONS

The court system is built upon expensive
attorney-initiated practices. Typically, each
party taxes the deposition of the other parties.
A deposition usually takes one day and costs
about $700 in court reporter fees and $2,000
in attorney fees. That's just for one party. If
there are five parties, the parties collectively
spend about $12,000 in one day of deposition.
That's just for one deposition. The philosophy
behind court cases is that you want to know
everybody's story before you get to trial and
you never want to be surprised. As we all
know, everyone has a different story – and
usually, a pretty convincing one. Generally,
everyone's deposition is taken.

## INTERROGATORIES

Another favored practice is interrogatories, which are written questions to the parties.
Aware of the time-consuming abuses that can
occur, some courts limit the number of interrogatories that can be served without special
permission. But that does little to apply the
brakes. As though oral deposition questions
aren't enough, attorneys are trained to trip up
people. So, they elicit answers by two different
methods – depositions and interrogatories.

| You are the boss and you can limit your attorney's procedures. |
| :-- |

Usually one set of interrogatories is sent to each party for answering. Then, the attorneys compare their deposition answers with their interrogatory answers. This sets up an ideal drama at trial when the attorney gets one more chance to ask the same question. It's expensive, it's embarrassing for the person who answered differently, and it really doesn't make a whole lot of difference to anyone. Generally, people just explain they were confused. And they probably were. But it has cost a lot for the attorney to ask the same question three different times.

These attempts to confuse the opponent are encouraged by the litigation process. Attorneys are expected to follow the routine established long ago, but following that routine is not required. *You* are the boss, and you can limit your attorney's procedures. Likewise, your attorney should be able to tell you the consequences and financial savings of curtailing these procedures. Chapter 13 on *How to Hire a Lawyer* gives insider tips on establishing a more rewarding and less expensive attorney-client relationship.

## DOCUMENT INSPECTION DEMANDS

Another means of discovery available to litigants is the Demand for Inspection of Documents. In this process, physical evidence is obtained. But it's not that simple. Such requests must be prepared, explained, served, answered in writing and by making the documents available for inspection and copying. Then the documents obtained must be studied, analyzed, and selectively chosen as exhibits for trial. Imagine the complexity of analyzing six or seven versions of the same document, each with a different date. It's obvious a lawyer's time for discovery can be astronomical.

## WHY DISCOVERY IS SO COSTLY

We call these processes discovery procedures, but they could just as well be called expensive fishing expeditions. The cost to undertake these procedures is great, but so is the cost to review and analyze the responses. These costs multiply at trial preparation, when the attorney is expected to know each witnesses' testimony and have the raw materials at his or her fingertips. This means preparing indexes to depositions and interrogatories. Often discovery must be done more than once as trial dates are often continued for extended periods. Then, you finally get there and trial itself involves court delays, jury questioning, and other procedures which increase the expense substantially. There's just no getting around the fact that court litigation generally costs at least ten times what arbitration does.

Depositions and interrogatories are also used in arbitration, but their use is significantly limited. It all depends on the wording of your arbitration provision. If it states *no discovery*, then there is none. It can limit discovery and define those limits. Given the expense of depositions, they are generally not allowed as a matter of right. Often they are only permitted with the consent of the arbitrator. This is in line with arbitration's philosophy of keeping the cost down.

> **Court litigation generally costs at least ten times that of arbitration.**

## TRIAL BY JURY:
## A NOBLE (BUT EXPENSIVE) IDEAL

In arbitration
there is no jury.
It was created
to minimize the
expense, delay,
and formality
of court trials.

The court system was set up to be truly democratic. Its founders felt that the system of justice would only work if people were judged by their peers – and by a sufficient number of them. Thus, trial by jury is firmly etched in our justice system. Lawyers and litigants alike feel that trial by *a judge only* is a departure from the American way. All the while, trial by jury is far more expensive than a court trial.

The jury selection process takes a long time. In a jury trial, the rules of evidence are more strictly enforced. Procedural formalities are more closely followed. The judge, attorneys, parties, and witnesses all put on a show for the jurors. Dramas are created, issues are repeatedly driven home, and personal charisma is used to chalk up points. After evidence is presented, the jury's deliberation process can take as long as it wants. Through all this, the attorney fees skyrocket.

## ARBITRATION: A RELAXED MINI-TRIAL

In arbitration there is no jury – only the arbitrator. Arbitration was created to minimize the expense, delay, and formality of court trials. In fact, the arbitration atmosphere itself is quite informal. The arbitrator sits at an even level with the participants, not perched up behind a bench. He or she wears business attire, not a dark robe. Witnesses typically testify from their seats instead of taking the witness stand. People are able to present their evidence in a more straight-forward, relaxed way. Although arbitration is an adversary process, due to the relaxed proceedings, it appears much less so. The bottom line: the complexities and formalities of court trials are just simply out of date. Arbitration is truly a sign of modern times.

## WHY ARBITRATE? YOU'LL BUTTON DOWN YOUR HEARING DATE

Another significant advantage of binding arbitration is that you are assured of a date for your hearing. As soon as you submit your case to arbitration, you pick your hearing date. It can take place in as soon as a week. In the court system, you don't get a trial date for at least a year; then there's no guarantee you'll actually try your case once the year is up. In most instances you won't. Most often you receive a number of trial settings before you actually go to trial three to five years after your case began.

For each trial date you, your attorneys, and your witnesses prepare. It's expensive and it's emotional. All this, only to have the court tell you, "Sorry, we don't have a courtroom for you. We'll have to continue your trial another three months." Then, it happens again. A case I tried had *seven* continuances before it went to trial five years after it began. The trial preparation bill for all seven settings came to about $50,000. Over its five year course, plaintiff's attorney fees and costs were $198,000. The defendant's tab was $191,000.

> With arbitration you are set for a definite date, and on that date the proceedings begin.

If you already
filed a lawsuit,
your opponent
may be relieved
when you sug-
gest arbitra-
tion.

With arbitration you are set for a definite date, and on that date the proceedings begin. In court proceedings, once you finally are assigned a judge and courtroom for trial, your case must accommodate the court's other priorities. There are often days or part-days off for the court to conduct other matters. In arbitration, your case is the priority for its full duration – which is usually far less than a court trial.

There must be a better way, but the court system hasn't come up with it yet. By pointing people toward mediation and arbitration, the courts are taking a step in the right direction. Heed its advice. For all parties, arbitration is a winner, even if you're the loser. Even a loser in arbitration saves time, money, and energy that would be squandered in court.

### Your Best Opportunities to Propose Arbitration

It's wise to consider arbitrating your dispute at all stages. Whether you are a defendant or a plaintiff, cost-efficient arbitration makes good sense. In either role, you can propose binding arbitration to your opponent at any time. But some times are better than others. If you already filed a lawsuit, your opponent may be relieved when you suggest arbitration. Litigants who are unwilling to arbitrate before an action is filed sometimes get far more cooperative, once they are served with your legal papers. Service of legal process has a way of creating a whole new attitude. Once the legal loop takes hold, it's a real attention getter. The person served suddenly becomes a good listener. Now is the time to propose binding arbitration once again. The chances are far more likely at this stage that your defendant will be inclined to arbitrate your dispute. At this point, prepare a Binding Arbitration Agreement based on the forms in Chapter 12 and the Appendix.

Another ideal opportunity to propose binding arbitration occurs when your court case fails to go to trial. On your trial date, you and your witnesses are ready. You already spent all the money it took to prepare for trial. Your case comes up at last, then the court says, "Sorry, we just don't have enough courtrooms for you." This is the most frustrating moment in the entire legal process and this may be the single most important reason to suggest binding arbitration. Why does the court bounce you out when it's given you a trial date? Because there are too many criminal cases and criminal cases take priority over civil cases.

When you get bounced from trial, have your binding arbitration stipulation ready. The other party who spent so much time and energy to finally get this ordeal over is just as frustrated. This is an ideal time for all parties who are prepared and ready to go to submit their matter to binding arbitration. Typically, your arbitration will be heard in just a matter of days or weeks. If arbitration isn't selected at this point, your trial is postponed for three to six months and all the preparation time is wasted. You'll have to gear up all over again for the next trial date – preparing witnesses, re-checking the law as it changes daily, and submitting updated briefs. Trial continuances are one of the most costly nuisances of the court system that happen over and over again.

> **When you get bounced from trial, have your binding arbitration stipulation ready.**

> **If you want to have your dispute decided by binding arbitration, you must have a written binding arbitration agreement with all parties to the dispute.**

Other opportunities come up when arbitration appears to be a more attractive alternative to court. Early in your dispute, when attorneys send out notices of depositions, costs are about to skyrocket. The pre-deposition phase is an ideal time to propose arbitration. Not only can your arbitration proposal head off the delays and costs of trial; it can limit the number of depositions or exclude them entirely. You create your arbitration proposal so it's up to you.

### How Do You Arrive at the Arbitration Door?

If you want to have your dispute decided by binding arbitration, you must have a written Binding Arbitration Agreement with ALL parties to the dispute. Why? Everyone is entitled to have their dispute heard in the court system, and according to the rules of procedure, everyone who is a party to the dispute must participate in that system. Participation is a legal right and a legal obligation.

When parties agree to binding arbitration they are replacing the court system. The parties waive their right to have the dispute decided in court, and their right to appeal the dispute. In order to replace the court system as the forum for your dispute, you must have a written Binding Arbitration Agreement. If you don't have an arbitration agreement with the parties, an agreement signed now – by all parties to the dispute – will suffice. It doesn't matter when the agreement is signed; it just matters that you have one. If you don't have a Binding Arbitration Agreement with all parties to the dispute, you must take your dispute and all parties to the court system. There are some exceptions, but this is generally the rule.

## How Do You Choose an Arbitrator?

If you have an arbitration agreement with your opponent, it will specify where you will find your arbitrator. If it provides for arbitration under the rules of the American Arbitration Association, you will hire the American Arbitration Association to administer your arbitration. If it names Judicial Arbitration & Mediation Services – Endispute, that is your provider. If your agreement names another organization or individual, that is your forum. Some agreements do not specify an arbitrator choice. If you are left with this vague type of agreement, choose your arbitrator by mutual agreement with the opposing parties. If that is not possible, petition the court for its appointment. This is an expensive extra step that becomes necessary only because the agreement fails to nominate an arbitrator. Don't miss this important step in your agreement.

## What Is the Arbitration Process?

Chapter 11 entitled *The Arbitration Arena: Your Keys to Success* features this process in detail. But by way of introduction, here is a summary.

Binding arbitration is an adversarial process. It is best described as a mini-trial. Opening statements are given, witnesses are examined and cross-examined, and a judgment is rendered. Due to its adversarial nature, an arbitration proceeding is very similar to a trial, except the evidentiary rules strictly enforced at

> Binding arbitration is an adversarial process. It is best described as a mini-trial.

| Time consuming evidentiary objections and arguments are discouraged in arbitration. |
| --- |

trial are substantially relaxed. Often in arbitration, declarations take the place of live testimony. Time-consuming evidentiary objections and arguments are discouraged. The relaxation of these requirements cut down the time involved in preparing for the arbitration hearing and for the hearing itself. The aim of arbitration is served by making it expeditious and cost-effective.

## TAILORING YOUR ARBITRATION

What's so good about arbitration is that you can hand-tailor the process. If you already have a Binding Arbitration Agreement, your procedure will follow its terms. However, if you are creating your own agreement, you can contour the expense and procedures to fit the needs of your case and your budget. Your agreement can limit depositions to one for each party, or it can exclude depositions entirely. You can replace depositions with written questions that the parties answer under oath. You can nominate an arbitrator who is known for expertise in the area of law for your dispute. You can set the hearing date for an ideal time for all parties – a time they can count on.

This tailoring works both ways. Suppose you receive an arbitration proposal from your opponent. You can then counter-propose any terms you wish. Chapter 11 and Chapter 12 provide a wealth of information to use to tailor your arbitration agreement.

## THE VERDICT

In jury trials, winners and losers are announced while all parties are gathered and emotions are high. The announcement of the verdict is obviously marked by personal upheaval. In arbitration, you usually leave after a day or two of the hearing and receive the verdict in the mail within a few days to a month. By the time you receive it, you've had a chance to settle down and prepare for a range of results. Your verdict arrives by mail, so you may experience it in the privacy of your own home. The staging for receipt of the arbitration verdict is far less emotional, and more objective and businesslike, than the highly charged court trial announcement.

## WHAT AFTER ARBITRATION?

Generally, there is no appeal from an arbitration award. The decision of the arbitrator is final, and becomes a non-appealable judgment against the losing party. There are a few situations where *collusion* is present when the court will review such a verdict. But they are extremely limited grounds. The award of the arbitrator is final in every sense of the word. It is obvious that the key to a successful arbitration is to select the right arbitrator in the beginning. Arbitrator selection as a strategy is addressed in Chapter 11.

Legal consumers generally view this finality of verdict as a positive aspect. For most people, one trip through a legal dispute is enough. Often, it's more than enough. Appeal rights built into the court system are subject to abuse. A loser at trial can file an appeal,

> The decision of the arbitrator is final and becomes a non-appealable judgment against the losing party.

> **For most people, one trip through the legal system is enough.**

knowing the winner doesn't want to go through another few years of the dispute. Settlement then becomes the logical alternative. If settlement doesn't occur, it's a way of dragging on the inevitable, in yet another wave of expense.

With arbitration, there is no way to drag it on. Your dispute is heard and decided quickly. There's no door of second resort. It's a sign of the times when you can just finish it and move on. That's what arbitration does. It simplifies everything.

### WHICH SYSTEM DOES BETTER?

At times, arbitration has less than perfect results. It suffers with the same mission statement adopted by the court system – to achieve justice. But when comparing the two servers of justice, here's the bottom line. Would you rather get justice in a brief time with minimal expense? Or would you rather wait a few years and pay stiff attorney fees to get there? Do it swiftly and economically, before an arbitrator of your choice, and get it over with.

How about the level of justice achieved? Which system – arbitration or court trial – yields the best results? I believe arbitration does. Judges and juries are no less competent than arbitrators; it's just that arbitration affords you ample time to present your case. You have as much time as you want to pay for. Since the court system is severely understaffed and overbooked, it must limit the time available to trials. Recently I tried a case that waited five years to get to trial. It was a highly complex real estate case worth over a million dollars. The judge gave us three days to try it. Needless to say, the result we got was inadequate – directly proportional to the amount of time we had to present the case.

In arbitration, you can buy as much time as you want since arbitrators are paid by the hour. For this reason, your arbitrator has as much time to hear and consider your matter as you would like. Unlike the backlogged courts, arbitrators also have the luxury of performing legal research on your case, which can make all the difference.

\* \* \*

The case for arbitration is a winner. For time/cost efficiency, it triumphs hands down over the courts. But there's an even more powerful dispute resolution weapon in your arsenal: your own power of persuasion. Follow us into Chapter 5 for your lesson in how to enlist your opponent against the legal system, and become allies.

*— Chapter Five —*

# LAST CHANCE: SETTLE YOUR DISPUTE NOW

The last few chapters introduced you to alternative dispute resolution – and compared it with the court system. But before you contemplate court or ADR, you should first take a very important step— it's your Last Chance for settlement. This chapter shows you how to benefit from this fruitful process. Its psychology is interesting. With Last Chance, you convince your opponent that your mutual enemy is the legal system. We show you how to use three compelling persuaders: (1) the legal system's expense in dollars, (2) its cost in time, and (3) its emotional toll. The desired result: you and your foe will settle to avoid the laborious legal process.

| You are at a powerful crossroads. Now use your Last Chance to reach a solution by mutual agreement. |
| --- |

## HEADING OFF THE INEVITABLE

Are you ready to choose a method for resolving your dispute without attorneys, mediators, arbitrators, or the court system? If your response is "How can I do that? My opponent and I are at each other's throats. There's no way we can find resolution without outside help." Think again! There is a way.

A powerful crossroads now presents itself to you and your opponent. This is the point *before* you begin spending your bankroll and your valuable time and energy. This is your *last chance* to reach solution by mutual agreement, before committing your time and energy to hire lawyers, mediators, and arbitrators who will assist you – at varying prices.

If you are each wise enough to realize the expense of formal legal process is around the next bend, you *can* align against this mutual enemy, not against each other. It's your last chance to avoid the system and its burdening expense. Suddenly, you're not fighting against each other – you're solving a mutual problem.

Although the alternative dispute resolution system is far better than the court system, it carries with it an expense of its own. The ideal resolution for your dispute is mutual agreement. You may say, "That's why we're in conflict. If we were able to come to agreement, we would never be in this dispute." That's true. But circumstances are changing. Without settlement, your next step takes you either into mediation, or into adversarial litigation in arbitration or before the court. The timing is ideal to produce agreement between disagreeing parties – before they get swept up in the legal system.

## You're at a Crossroads

Before you use ADR methods or proceed up the courthouse steps, we strongly encourage you to see if you and your opponent can settle your problem by yourselves, using our Last Chance exercise. This is not a detour, nor is it a side step. Instead, this is a pivotal crossroads.

Why is this such a critical time, especially when neutral ADR may be your next step? When you enter formal dispute resolution, an element of war enters with you. In a far more formal way, you acknowledge that there is a dispute and you have hired an outside party as a referee. Though not as hostile as a lawsuit, formal ADR action still creates a cloud of threat.

Thus, this strategic juncture is especially effective in the early evolution of your legal dispute. It's your last chance – a crucial time out before making your choice between formal alternative dispute resolution or the court system. It's also your last chance before your dispute becomes another statistic in formal legal channels.

## This Is Your Turning Point

What makes this crossroads so important is its timing. Each of the processes, from mediation forward, are expensive and time-consuming. In proposing this settlement session, you create a window of opportunity – an ideal peacemaking time before the avalanche of hourly charges, administrative costs and filing fees.

> See if you can settle your legal problem using our Last Chance exercise.

An ideal peace-
making oppor-
tunity comes
about when
each party hits
bottom and it's
time to re-
group.

When you and your foe realize what lies ahead, reaching a settlement takes on new meaning. Your next step will commit you both to expense, time, and energy. Your potential savings – should you settle now – may be enormous, including legal fees, discovery costs, voluminous transcripts, and court costs. Money talks now, and it's saying, "Settle, if you can!"

## STOP THE TUG OF WAR

By the time you reach this point, you've probably had several discussions with your opponent about your dispute. Your prior exchanges probably consisted of accusations, denials and finger pointing. Typically, you fought for a certain position while your opponent pulled in the opposite direction. The conversation was: "You did that. No, I didn't. You're wrong. No, you're wrong." By each trying to advocate your point of view, you lose sight of compromise. It becomes an emotional tug of war. But this is also a pivotal point. This Last Chance session is marked by *neutrality*.

This is the moment where most parties give up and turn the matter over to counsel, or seek formal dispute resolution on their own. But this is an ideal peace-making opportunity – it comes about when each party hits bottom. This is the target time to regroup, enlist your opponent's help, and explore new ways of looking at the situation. You have a joint mission now – to avoid the legal system.

## THE LEGAL PROCESS BECOMES THE ENEMY

The fruits of this session come from viewing the situation as a mutual problem that, unless a solution is created, will demand a substantial commitment of time and money by both parties. Your common goal becomes: avoid time, turmoil, and expense. It's a no-fault scenario before the ruins of the legal battlefield take hold: paper wars, spent emotions, and depleted bank accounts.

> The decision to sue for war – or compromise for peace – irrevocably alters your life.

The decision to sue for war – or compromise for peace – irrevocably alters your life. If you don't look at compromise now, you and your dispute will be carried off on the great juggernaut of litigation, which is nearly impossible to stop. It invariably generates lots of paper, and its companion, exorbitant attorney fees. Even when alternative dispute resolution methods are implemented, the resolution tab begins to run. These alternative processes – from mediation forward – can also be expensive and time-consuming. Although they generate only a fraction of the litigation bill, ADR procedures involve their own level of time and expense.

## SETTING UP YOUR LAST CHANCE MEETING

How do you conduct this Last Chance strategy? What is involved? How can you persuade your opponent to do it with you? How do you turn finger-pointing into peaceful proceedings?

You are ready to propose a meeting where you and your foe will collaborate on your joint problem. But your foe probably feels pressured, angry, discouraged, or threatened. These emotions do not provide fertile ground for joint problem-solving or compromise. How do you defuse these emotions and set the stage for conciliation?

| Defuse your adversary's anger and threats and propose teamwork. |
| --- |

## THE INVITATION

Call your adversary. A suggested conversation would be: "We are clearly having a difference of opinion, to say the least. You feel I'm wrong and I feel you're wrong." Then surprise your foe: "But can we forget that for a minute and try to end this thing before we have to choose between formal dispute resolution or litigation? The legal system is very expensive. If there's any possible way we can head off this expense, this is the time to do it. Would you be willing to sit down with a single objective: to get past this dispute before its emotional and financial tolls take hold?"

You've acknowledged there is a problem; but you are attempting to set it aside temporarily. You want to defuse your adversary's anger and threats and propose teamwork. Your foe may be sufficiently surprised by your candor and willingness to talk – enough to momentarily set aside the conflict and listen. At this point, you may be well on your way to resolution.

## QUESTIONS ARE OPPORTUNITIES

Suppose they question your motives? What if you hear, "Why do you suddenly want a meeting?" or "What makes you think it will change anything?" This means they are genuinely interested and want to hear your proposal. *Seize your opportunity!*

Most likely, your foe wants to get past this conflict as much as you do. But they are suspicious and need good reasons for meeting. You'll give them those reasons. Consider the following proposal:

"These legal battles are financially draining. Consider the old adage: Only the attorneys win in litigation. It's true. We'll pay vast amounts of money to our lawyers and have to commit precious time and energy to our legal battle. So let's make one more attempt to resolve this before we take any further steps."

**Ask your opponent to come to the meeting you both agreed to without a need to blame or judge.**

## PROPOSE A MEETING

Your adversary will most likely respond to this about-face with a willingness to discuss. You should continue: "I've got some ideas to share with you. It can't hurt. How about lunch at . . ." Better yet, offer them the choice of lunch location. You want them to feel comfortable and if location choice will achieve that objective, let your adversary make the choice.

Ask your opponent to come to this session without a need to blame or judge, but with a single focus on what it will take to conclude the dispute now. This session requires the maturity of participants able to look dispassionately past the problem to the bigger picture. It encourages you to bring about compromise, simply because it will save the time, money, and emotion of legal procedures. Here, you meet in the middle, rather than bring in third parties who start the resolution tab running.

## YOU'RE SOLVING A COMMON PROBLEM

If you follow our Last Chance planning steps, your session can provide a level of comfort and purpose that you have not experienced around this dispute before. Why? For the first time you and your opponent will have joined to

> A peaceful, neutral atmosphere is mandatory for optimum success in reaching a settlement.

solve a mutual problem, instead of fighting against each other.

When your foe agrees to meet, you're ready to set the meeting stage for you and your foe to become a problem-solving team. Three key ingredients make up your stage setting process. First, relax and bring along your personality. Second, select an unhurried peaceful location for your meeting. Finally, create a no-fault truce environment.

### SETTING THE STAGE WITH PERSONAL TOUCH

A peaceful, neutral atmosphere is mandatory for optimum success. Typically, high anxiety accompanies the conflict resolution process. In fact, studies show that people in conflict are more uncomfortable and rigid than in any other interaction. When high anxiety hits, courtesy and finishing touches go out the window. We retreat into formality.

With this rigid mind-set, attempts at directing your Last Chance meeting toward solution dissolve into a rote, dry process too inflexible to work. Solution hides out in the midst of a rigid, stressful atmosphere. There's no motivation for conflict repair.

During times of conflict, creating a favorable atmosphere is the last thing on our minds. Yet, at these times personal touches need to be retained more than ever. When personal comfort is ignored, conflict is prone to recur or even escalate. This is the exact opposite of the condition you want in your session. After all, you're there to solve your problem – and theirs.

## CREATE A PEACEFUL ATMOSPHERE

Your stage must be set to encourage a relaxed, personable climate. In this neutral setting you and your foe will best be able to apply teamwork to solve your mutual problem – how to avoid the costs of the legal system. The key is to instill comfort and relaxation in the session. That's what setting the stage is all about. Don't let the nature of conflict resolution leave these characteristics in the dust – they may be just the thing to trigger a solution.

> In a neutral setting you and your foe will best be able to apply teamwork to solve your mutual problem.

## CREATING THE BEST AMBIENCE

You've now set in place the first of three keys to optimum Last Chance success. You've added the personal touches of courtesy and personality. Now your stage needs to be set with location ambience.

Ambience is atmosphere. A carefully selected location creates a conducive environment for effective resolution. What environment puts you most at ease? Choose an ideal location for the meeting. Take this step before you contact your foe to set up the meeting. This location should be a place that will be politically correct for you *and* your foe. Don't pick an environment suited to your foe unless it's also right for you and vice versa. When you contact your foe also be sure to offer the option of choosing the location.

I usually pick a restaurant that is light, airy, and spacious, providing the best forum for open discussion. Setting the Stage properly bestows your meeting table with all the ingredients for success. When my opponent and I meet on

> **Make a mutual problem the focus of attention and you will change the program to truce territory.**

the ideally set stage, we are more motivated to talk.

## TRUCE TERRITORY

You've set the stage with personal touch and ambience. Now, creating a truce territory makes the ideal setting for resolution. Make a mutual problem the focus of attention and you will change the program to truce territory. Within this neutral environment, your foe *can* become your ally. Consider the following scenario: Your mission is to turn your pre-litigation battleground into a bargaining table.

We think of the Last Chance stage as Truce Territory for a visual reason. The ego surrounding your dispute will want to rear its ugly head many times during this session. Stress and anxiety are high. Each person is inclined to throw up his hands and say, "I give up. Talk to my lawyer from now on." Don't give in to the ego. The ego loves litigation and spares no expense. The ego has no place in Truce Territory.

## BEWARE THE EGO

If ego takes hold, shift the focus back to solving your mutual problem. The legal process is the only enemy – expensive, emotionally draining, and time-consuming. You and your opponent are allied against it.

Each time the ego threatens to take over, remember you are in Truce Territory. You've probably discovered that ego doesn't solve problems – it fuels them. This is particularly true in the middle of conflict. Ego gets very energetic. It's hard to refocus the stubborn ego and it does take some trickery to do it.

The purpose of your meeting is to calmly create a settlement – not to argue positions. Each time your mind wanders back to the dispute and why you're right and he's wrong, breathe deeply and take a momentary time out. Realize that a truce has been called. It's different this time around and you realize that peace is the answer – and your cost effective solution.

> **The real enemy at this point is the legal process itself, and its cost in time, emotions, and money.**

## SUDDENLY, YOU'RE ALLIES!

With these three stage setting conditions in place, you have created your best chance for solution. You have a new objective at this meeting: to be allied against a mutual problem. It's a powerful change. The aim is not to place blame or adopt your old accusatory stances. The only agenda of this meeting must be to head off the debris of the legal battlefield – bank accounts assigned to attorneys and emotions as they run rampant – by settling the dispute now. The real enemy at this point is the legal process itself, and its cost in time, emotions, and money.

## BE CREATIVE WITH SETTLEMENT OPTIONS

Creative negotiations are always excellent tools to bring to your Last Chance session. You may have achieved the right state of mind, but without settlement options you may be out of luck.

When you've spent time in the dynamic arena of negotiation, you realize the answer is all in supply and demand. What is being demanded, and what can you supply to satisfy the demand?

> **To resolve your dispute, you or your adversary will want something of value from the other.**

To resolve your dispute, you or your adversary will want something of value from the other. Money is the standard way of compensating people. But compensation can come in many forms and many packages. It all depends on identifying a party's need. When you do so, you create a settlement option.

For instance, you bought a piano from Adam's Auction Company and you feel they misrepresented its features. They refuse to refund the purchase price and take back the piano. The next step is to sue them in court. At your Last Chance meeting with the company president, you discuss alternative proposals. An agreement is reached: you will give them three months to locate a piano with the features you were promised. As estate furniture auctioneers, they are best suited to find you exactly what you want. This arrangement will probably work out better than getting your cash back in the long run.

Another example: you're having a battle with your local computer vendor. He says your warranty for hardware doesn't cover your problem because it's a software problem. You say it's not. Instead of taking him to court, ask if he will fix the software problem. You'll pay him if he can. If he can't fix it, then it's a hardware problem and he'll honor the warranty.

### THE MAGIC WORD: BARTER

Whenever a dispute is in the brew, people are motivated – especially those under attack. If you are the responding party, identify your adversary's needs. If you are on the demanding side, find out what your opponent is best suited to supply, and see if you can find a match with your wish list. Do you need a new printer? Maybe your adversary has an extra one. Do you need a tenant for your rental property? Maybe your adversary has a tenant for you. See Chapter 10 on Mediation Mechanics for some good examples of creative settlement packages. The possibilities are endless.

> **Money is a standard form of compensation, but compensation can be part barter and part money.**

What if you can't pinpoint the ideal barter for you and your foe? Money is a standard form of compensation. However, money payment comes in many forms. You can agree to a payment schedule that will suit your opponent's needs. You can offer a discount for early pay off as an incentive. Compensation can be part barter and part money.

You can accept an assignment of rights. For instance, if your opponent holds a promissory note due to be paid, he or she can sign that over to you. They can stipulate to a judgment recorded on their property and you can agree to refrain from collection for a certain period of time to give them a chance to pay. See Chapter 9 for this option and more.

There are more ways than you could dream of to come up with a settlement and to structure it. Allow your imagination to work with you on this. You can create your own solution to your problem if you're innovative. If you need help coming up with more, consult with an attorney. Well intentioned attorneys enjoy nothing more than creating settlement options!

| Settlement is always your best option and should be explored many times over! |
| --- |

## SETTLEMENT IS NOT A ONE TIME PROPOSITION

If you've set your stage well and kept your focus firmly on reaching a solution to your mutual problem – avoiding expensive litigation – you should walk away from your Last Chance session with a settlement. There's no doubt that you can find solutions you never thought possible, especially with two motivated participants.

Throughout this book, settlement is continually explored. It's not something you do once. It's no coincidence that our dispute resolution techniques begin with it. Settlement is always your best option. And best options should be explored many times over!

## THE LITIGATION ROLLER COASTER

The litigation game is an emotional and financial roller coaster ride. The case and each party's attitude fluctuate as their dispute travels through the various stages of negotiation or litigation. Each new fact discovered alters the parties' posture in a court fight. Like a recipe, each new ingredient changes the taste. As you ride out your legal dispute, one day you feel like the winner; the very next you won't have a faint memory of success.

Watch carefully for these pivotal dips. They can be filled with opportunity. These are ideal times for settlement discussion. It's a time when people feel more vulnerable because their case takes on yet another complexion. Usually, the party in the lead has previously been in caboose position, and realizes that the lead position is short-lived indeed.

## PINPOINT SETTLEMENT OPPORTUNITIES

As your case evolves along litigation pathways through the court system or arbitration, continually evaluate whether your opponent is particularly vulnerable. Remember, whenever a new element is added, your case takes on a new dimension – and yields new reasons to settle. For instance, when attorneys are hired hearty retainers must be scraped together. People begin to realize the magnitude of how much this is going to cost. This is an ideal time to propose another settlement session.

> **Any change of circumstance that affects the dispute or the players provides fertile soil for settlement.**

Each juncture where the dispute receives attention provides a fruitful time to consider settlement. Has the complexion of your dispute changed? Has one party made a demand? Is someone about to hire a lawyer? Has a mediation hearing been set up? Have you filed a lawsuit? Any change of circumstance that affects the dispute or players provides fertile soil for settlement.

## IS SOMEONE ELSE ABOUT TO CONTROL YOUR DISPUTE?

Another ideal time to explore settlement is immediately after you take the first formal step – whether by submitting the case to mediation or arbitration, or by filing a lawsuit. Your opponent always takes you more seriously after you bring the case before a tribunal. Loss of control is an excellent motivator. When a third party – the court or dispute resolution system – threatens to take part in your dispute, your opponent takes a more serious look at settlement.

So keep in mind that settlement is not something you explore only at the beginning of

**Use the Last Chance settlement with your attorney by instructing him to write a persuasive settlement letter.**

your dispute. Propose settlement often. It can't hurt – and it can help immensely. It can end the dispute.

## PERSUADING WITH FACTS

The Last Chance settlement can also be accomplished by your attorney, if you wish. If you're hiring an attorney, instruct the attorney to begin the job by writing a legally and factually persuasive settlement letter. Just the fact that you bring in an attorney will cause your opponent to scrutinize settlement with a more serious eye.

When I represent a party I always start by writing a compelling case analysis letter to the opposing party. Usually it is highly persuasive, emphasizing the strengths of my client's case, the weaknesses of the opponent's case, and the general pitfalls of prolonged litigation. I even project each party's attorney fee tab. It rings true. People know that litigation is a costly and draining experience that often fails to create a true winner or a loser. My initial case analysis letter often leads to settlement of the dispute.

\*\*\*

If you have reached settlement, this book served its purpose – set it down and let us know of your progress. We'd love to hear. If you're not among those satisfied negotiators, fear not. Take a trip through The Pocket Lawyer Analyzer in Chapter 6 and evaluate your dispute. You'll find out how good or bad your case is and where to take it. Should you drop it off at the bone yard and chalk it up to another valuable learning experience? Or perhaps you will take it further: to mediation, arbitration or court.

# — Chapter Six —

# THE POCKET LAWYER ANALYZER: IDENTIFY YOUR CASE FEASIBILITY

Alternative dispute resolution is a huge step in the right direction. It creates a system for lay people to take charge of their disputes and resolve them. But a very important element is missing from the equation – the tools of legal analysis. Without effective legal analysis, alternative dispute resolution will not succeed. The Pocket Lawyer Analyzer was invented to bridge the gap – to provide you with legal analysis of your dispute. This chapter features The Pocket Lawyer Analyzer, available for use on your computer through the Order Form. Now, for the first time, you can deal with your legal dilemma yourself, and with confidence.

## THE POCKET LAWYER ANALYZER: YOUR TOOL FOR LEGAL ANALYSIS

Historically, case evaluation has been the exclusive province of lawyers. But now that the legal system is giving way to alternative dispute resolution, you, the consumer, can handle your dispute yourself. That is – if you can evaluate your case.

### THIS IS A FIRST!

Here, we present you with your own pocket lawyer, an evaluation system that allows you to evaluate your own legal case. Previously, lawyers weren't willing to hand over their jobs. Nor did they feel a program could provide legal analysis.

Understanding that concern, we offer this program with a preface: *The Pocket Lawyer Analyzer* is merely a tool to guide you through legal analysis. It's better than no tool at all, and probably less effective than hiring a lawyer. But it will assist you in taking your next step when you face a legal dispute.

### ITS FUNCTION

Although *The Pocket Lawyer Analyzer* simulates the legal analysis a lawyer undertakes, nothing can take the place of a good legal education and legal expertise. *The Pocket Lawyer Analyzer* certainly does not intend to do so. We present this system not as a substitute for lawyers or for common sense, but as a tool for you to evaluate your case. You may amplify it by hiring a lawyer, as well. You may substitute it for a lawyer, if you so choose. *The*

*Pocket Lawyer Analyzer* applies all of the important tests to a legal dispute to determine whether it should be pursued – or just forgotten. The potential savings from this exercise is abundantly clear.

## ITS RESULTS

Legal case evaluation is only one of *The Pocket Lawyer Analyzer* tests. But often, this was the *only* analysis performed by your lawyer. You, the person faced with the legal problem, are more motivated than anyone to look at *all* facets of your dispute. You need to look at the whole picture. Does it make economic and emotional sense to go ahead? And if so, how vigorously? This is the feasibility analysis you obtain from *The Pocket Lawyer Analyzer*. It looks at all facets of your dispute.

## CHAPTER 7: YOUR HELP MENU

*The Pocket Lawyer Analyzer* is a series of questions you answer, receiving a point score as you go along. Chapter 7 is your reference chapter: a step-by-step guide to answer each question. If you are using the software, your Help icon will pull up ongoing help. Chapter 7 is not just for reference, however. It is a lively discussion of basic legal principles we invite you to peruse even after completing *The Pocket Lawyer Analyzer.*

## CAN YOU FIND YOURSELF IN CHAPTER 8?

Chapter 8 is another reference chapter. It was created to work through four disputes using *The Pocket Lawyer Analyzer.* There, you will see how each case is treated, how the questions are answered in each sample, and the valuable results for each. Refer to Chapter 8 if you have questions after referring to Chapter 7. If you have no questions, feel free to read Chapter 8 for its interesting scenarios and solutions.

## HOW THE POCKET LAWYER ANALYZER WORKS

In a stroke of simplification, *The Pocket Lawyer Analyzer* is the *first ever* case evaluation system that uses a *point method*. What's more, this system includes the essential components of legal evaluation and feasibility analysis.

In order to determine feasibility, many factors beyond legal case evaluation must be considered. Take your contract, if you have one. Does it contain an attorney fee provision that will entitle you to collect your attorney fees if you win? Does it include a binding arbitration provision that will allow you to bypass the expensive, grueling court system? What about collectability? Will you be able to collect on your judgment – or will you be left with an expensive piece of paper for framing? (You can look at it every day, but beyond that it's useless!) *The Pocket Lawyer Analyzer* considers these essential factors and many more in providing you with your feasibility analysis.

## WHAT IS FEASIBILITY?

*The Pocket Lawyer Analyzer* bottom line analysis is in terms of feasibility. It takes its four evaluations and determines how reasonable and practical it is for you to pursue your dispute. That's what we're speaking of when we speak of feasibility.

## TYPES OF DISPUTES THE POCKET LAWYER ANALYZER ADDRESSES

*The Pocket Lawyer Analyzer* addresses legally solvable conflicts – with the exception of family law and criminal law. *The Pocket Lawyer Analyzer* doesn't reach marital problems, which have a different set of rules. Neither does it address criminal wrongs. The big question, then, is: What is a *legally solvable conflict*? Any conflict that can be solved within the legal system is considered legally solvable. It is difficult to know when, or if, your conflict may be a candidate for the legal system. Potentially, legal solutions may be applied to most problems. Thus, we suggest that you always work through *The Pocket Lawyer Analyzer* regardless of the type of dispute. If your dispute is one that is not solvable through the legal system, that will come clear to you in working with *The Pocket Lawyer Analyzer*.

## WHAT IS THE POCKET LAWYER ANALYZER

*The Pocket Lawyer Analyzer* is a powerful application that helps you assess – and direct – *your own* potential legal problems. Its purpose is to take your legal issue, demystify it and turn it into a *manageable* legal matter you can direct through the legal system, resolve through alternative dispute resolution (ADR), or forget.

We call this system *The Pocket Lawyer Analyzer* because it gives you a handy reference to consider and assess the legal options available to you and your foe in this dispute. Packaged by practicing attorneys, *The Pocket Lawyer Analyzer* is a streamlined course in *legal charting*. We call this legal charting because you use its checklist of questions to define your case in legal terms, and identify the legal options available to you.

What's more, *The Pocket Lawyer Analyzer* gives you an easy way to *control the predictable elements of your dispute*. How? By analyzing your dispute from many different vantage points:

- What are the issues?
- Whose fault is it?
- What is your case worth?
- Will you be able to collect on your judgment?
- Will you be able to get your attorney fees back?
- Will you have to travel the court system, or can you go to arbitration?

These many vantage points cause you to reflect on your dispute and tailor a plan to *control* the consequences that may result.

## THE STEPS OF THE POCKET LAWYER ANALYZER

*The Pocket Lawyer Analyzer* performs a critical seven-phase analysis:

**LEGAL EVALUATION:** Phase 1, Case Evaluation, assesses your likelihood of winning based on the legal issues.

**CASE VALUE ASSESSMENT:** Phase 2 assesses the value of your case and your realistic recovery.

**LEGAL OPTIONS ASSESSMENT:** Phase 3 evaluates your case based on the legal options available for your dispute.

**COLLECTABILITY ASSESSMENT:** Phase 4 analyzes your chance of collecting on any judgment you receive.

**COMPREHENSIVE CASE ANALYSIS:** Phase 5 concludes with a comprehensive analysis of the value of your case for settlement purposes and a *case feasibility rating.*

**FEASIBILITY ASSESSMENT:** The case feasibility chart is Phase 6. It takes your feasibility rating from the comprehensive case analysis and tells you whether you should pursue your case.

**CHOOSING YOUR FORUM:** Phase 7 only comes into play if your feasibility assessment indicates that you should pursue your dispute. If so, this phase assigns the forum you will enter – mediation, arbitration, small claims, or the higher courts.

## A CHART FOR YOUR LEGAL COURSE

*The Pocket Lawyer Analyzer* provides you with guidelines to chart your own legal course without consulting with an expensive lawyer. It puts legal answers within your reach in a simple, handy way. You may still choose to consult with an attorney after you've charted your way through *The Pocket Lawyer Analyzer,* but your consultation will be far more meaningful after you've completed your own charting.

To simplify *The Pocket Lawyer Analyzer*, we included just enough information for you to realistically evaluate your case's feasibility and navigate it through the legal system. That direction may be through ADR or through the courts. With *The Pocket Lawyer Analyzer*, you will gain the confidence that once came only through hiring an attorney. It's like having a lawyer in your pocket.

## DEFINE THE ISSUES AND SAVE MORE MONEY

*The Pocket Lawyer Analyzer* serves another mindful purpose: *preparation.* In your trip through the system, you'll spend time defining the issues surrounding your dispute. This is especially valuable if you ultimately hire a mediator, an arbitrator, or an attorney. Time is money, and you will be prepared to describe the important issues of your dispute briefly and accurately. You will also be able to make informed decisions on how your valuable time and money is spent.

## PUT A DOLLAR VALUE ON YOUR CASE

*The Pocket Lawyer Analyzer* serves another valuable function. It values your case in terms of *dollars.* People are often way out of the realistic ballpark when it comes to case value. They remember Perry Mason's courtroom dramatics which made anything possible. That was high drama, not high court. Unless your opponent's conduct was close to criminal, all you *really* get is what you've lost. It's as easy as that. *The Pocket Lawyer Analyzer* guides you to a realistic valuation of your case in dollars, and how much you will net after trial or arbitration – after deducting all the costs it took to get there. You'll also determine a *settlement value* for your case, and a sense of the headaches you'll forego if you can settle. Values are important, but often they are very difficult for feuding parties to establish. *The Pocket Lawyer Analyzer* helps to calculate these elusive values.

## COLLECTABILITY: A KEY TO YOUR CASE

What value is a judgment to you if you have little chance of collecting on it? None. Why pour your precious time and money into obtaining a judgment when you may never receive the money it orders? This important step is often skipped when an attorney analyzes the legal components of your case. This analysis may be the most important of all. Your case may be a real winner, but you'll be a loser if you can't collect on your judgment.

*The Pocket Lawyer Analyzer* assesses your chances of collecting to determine whether you should pursue your dispute. This is another valuable feasibility component you get from *The Pocket Lawyer Analyzer*.

## ATTORNEY FEES: HOW MUCH WILL YOU SPEND?

How much will you spend in attorney fees and how much you will you get back? *The Pocket Lawyer Analyzer* estimates how much of your judgment you'll give up to attorney fees. This, too, is an important factor which should be considered *before* you commit to your case. Can you afford these fees? Will your judgment warrant this expenditure?

## YOUR CONTRACT OPTIONS

Another essential feature *of The Pocket Lawyer Analyzer* is an assessment of your legal options. Do you have a mediation agreement, binding arbitration agreement, or attorney fees clause? One of these provisions gives your case better feasibility; all three make your case *far* more feasible. Why does it matter? If you don't have a binding arbitration provision, you have to travel the court maze to get your dispute resolved. If you pursue your case in court, any return dwindles as legal fees increase. If you're hiring an attorney to represent you and you are not entitled to receive reimbursement of your attorney fees, your case feasibility is reduced, along with your net case valuation. Clearly, these factors all affect the feasibility of your case.

Thus, *The Pocket Lawyer Analyzer* evaluates important options available in your case that directly affect your potential net recovery, and whether it makes sense to pursue your dispute at all.

## IT'S AN ECONOMIC ANSWER

Why, you might ask, could I possibly need *The Pocket Lawyer Analyzer*, when my own attorney is just a phone call away? The answer is simple. It might save you hundreds, or even *thousands* of dollars in legal fees.

### IT'S WISE STRATEGY

How many of us bolt to a lawyer at the first hint of a legal problem? Wait a minute! Before hiring an attorney, there are steps you can take. The court system is lawyer territory, and rightly so. But the steps *you* choose to take may sometimes lead you *away* from the court system toward mediation and arbitration – territory now available to you, the consumer. How do you choose these steps? By working through *The Pocket Lawyer Analyzer.*

### IT'S YOUR CHANCE TO SOLVE YOUR PROBLEM

Consider these questions: Who best knows the circumstances of your problem? What caused it? Who are the parties? What dynamics are in play? And what will it take to solve it? Indeed, you know the answers. But there is another set of answers to some of these questions. These are the expensive legal answers an attorney gives you – many of which you can now obtain with *The Pocket Lawyer Analyzer.* If you obtain these answers with *The Pocket Lawyer Analyzer,* the expensive, time-consuming set of lawyer's answers may not be necessary.

At any point, you can recite your entire problem to an attorney, for billable time. But first, give yourself the opportunity to create a solution that avoids or at least cuts down on costly lawyers and lawsuits. Take *The Pocket Lawyer Analyzer* in hand, follow the steps suggested, define your problem, project its outcome, and then direct it through the many available legal processes. Or, resolve it right now.

## Avoiding Negative Results

Over the course of long careers, we have watched clients achieve a wide spectrum of results from the conventional legal system. By use of *The Pocket Lawyer Analyzer,* we are hopeful that you will avoid these adverse results we've observed too often:

• Many spent vast amounts of time and money chasing after a righteous justice only to find out that justice is never clear cut – it's undefined and elusive.

• Some discovered that their reasoning was correct but the court or jury did not see it the way they did.

• Others found they were correct, but it just didn't pay emotionally or financially to prove their point within the legal system.

• Some got a judgment but there were no assets to collect upon.

• Still others collected on a judgment, but they were out-of-pocket for their attorney fees and case costs.

• Others collected and financially gained, but the emotional drain was not replenished.

• Embroiled in the adversity of the court system for too long, some completely lost track of what their dispute was all about.

Most of these results can be foreseen and avoided by adequately and realistically analyzing your case to begin with. The purpose of *The Pocket Lawyer Analyzer* is to provide you with a way to control the predictable elements of your dispute, and to make sound case decisions based on legal analysis and feasibility.

## THE BOTTOM LINE RESULTS OF THE POCKET LAWYER ANALYZER

So you can make these very important determinations now, before spending your bankroll or dedicating vast chunks of your valuable time, *The Pocket Lawyer Analyzer* targets a variety of elements surrounding your dispute. To provide you with the criteria you need to make these very important decisions, *The Pocket Lawyer Analyzer* yields the following results:

1. Your likelihood of prevailing in your dispute.

2. The value of your case.

3. The value of your case after you've considered possible defenses that may be posed by your opponent.

4. The value of your case after you've paid attorney fees and invested your valuable time.

5. The *settlement* value of your case.

6. The feasibility of your case based on whether you are likely to collect on your judgment.

7. Whether you will get back your attorney fees if you win.

8. How your choice of forum affects your decision to pursue the case or drop it.

9. Whether you should pursue the dispute, or chalk it up to a learning experience.

10. Whether you will want to represent yourself or hire an attorney.

11. Whether you should proceed to mediation or begin at the court house steps.

12. Whether arbitration will be your forum instead of the court system.

### IF YOU ARE A DEFENDANT

If a claim has been filed against you, or threatens to be filed, turn to Chapter 9 for *your* version of *The Pocket Lawyer Analyzer.*

### WHICH VERSION OF THE POCKET LAWYER ANALYZER DO YOU CHOOSE?

*The Pocket Lawyer Analyzer* is available in both software and the written version, which follows here. Those of you who have the software program will access it now, in place of the written program. If you want the computer version, complete the Order Form at the end of the book. The computer version prompts you to respond to the questions asked and instantly tabulates your results for you.

### GETTING HELP

• The software version of *The Pocket Lawyer Analyzer* provides Help icons throughout.

• Chapter 7 is your Instruction Manual. It answers any questions you have about responding to the questions of *The Pocket Lawyer Analyzer.* Just flip to the corresponding question and its instructions.

• Chapter 8 is your Illustrative Guide. It gives four real life examples worked through on *The Pocket Lawyer Analyzer.* These illustrative cases are fascinating samples of how *The Pocket Lawyer Analyzer* comes up with its case results. It's invaluable if you need help answering a question.

### GETTING READY FOR YOUR POCKET LAWYER SESSION

Your Pocket Lawyer session is best conducted in a quiet and secluded place. If you have a written contract, have it at your side. If your contract is oral, write down what you recall as your agreement. If you have no contract, you will be prompted to a response that fits your situation. If your dispute is against more than one person, complete *The Pocket Lawyer Analyzer* separately for each person you feel caused your damage.

Without further ado, we proudly present *The Pocket Lawyer Analyzer* in its workbook format on the following pages.

## The Pocket Lawyer Analyzer

### Phase 1: Legal Evaluation
**What is your likelihood of prevailing?**

**1.   What obligations did your adversary owe you?**

_____

_____

**2.   Did your adversary perform these obligations in a satisfactory manner?**

☐  Yes: Enter 0 and go to Line 6
☐  No: Enter 350                                    _____

**3.   Have you sustained legally recognized damages as a direct result of your adversary's conduct?**

☐  Yes:  Enter value of Line 2
☐  No:  Enter 0 and go to Line 6                    _____

**4.   Did you have a prior obligation to your adversary?**

☐  Yes: **(Note here)**

_____

_____

☐  No: Go to Line 6

**5. Did you perform your obligation in a satisfactory manner?**

☐ Yes: Enter score of Line 3
☐ No: Enter 0 here and on Line 6                    _____

**6. This is Your Legal Evaluation. Enter last value here, not to exceed 350.**                    _____
**If total is 0 do not proceed. Your case is not feasible.**

---

**Phase 2: Case Value Assessment**
**How much are you likely to recover?**

**7. Is there a damage defining provision in a written contract that pertains to this dispute?**

☐ Yes: ☐ A. Enter *liquidated* damages amount , or   A. $_____
         ☐ B. Enter damages *limit*                       B. $_____
☐ No: Enter 0                                              _____

**8. What is the amount of your damages?**

Select <u>one</u> option:

If 7A checked, enter that amount                    $_____

If 7B checked, enter your damages – 7B as maximum    $_____

Otherwise, enter your actual damages                $_____

**9.  Were you a cause of the situation that caused your damages? (Do not include conduct addressed above.)**

☐ Yes:  Reduce Line 8 by $ amount or percentage your conduct contributed to your damages (use 50% if unsure) and enter here

☐ No:  Enter value from Line 8                                    $_____

**10.  Did you receive a substantial benefit from the situation?**

☐ Yes:  Reduce Line 9 by $ amount or percentage to reflect value to you (use 50% if unsure) and enter here

☐ No:  Enter value from Line 9                                    $_____

**11.  Enter Line 10 here.**                                      $_____

**12.  Will you be represented by counsel?**

☐ Yes: Go to Line 13
☐ No: Go to Line 14

**13.  If you will be represented by counsel, select only <u>one</u> of the following options.**

☐ A.  A contract signed by you and your adversary contains both an attorney fee and binding arbitration provision. Enter the amount from Line 11 here.        $_____

☐ B.  A contract signed by you and your adversary contains an attorney fee provision, but no binding arbitration provision. Enter  80% of Line 11 here.                 $_____

☐ C.  A contract signed by you and your adversary contains a binding arbitration provision, but no attorney fee provision.  Enter 85% of Line 11 here.                 $_____

☐ D.  There is no attorney fee or binding arbitration provision in a written contract between you and your adversary. Enter 65% of Line 11 here.                 $_____

☐ E.  There is no written contract between you and your adversary. Enter 65% of Line 11 here.                 $_____

## 14.   Will you be representing yourself *or* otherwise putting substantial time into your case?

☐ Yes:  What is the approximate value of the time you will put in?   $_____.Divide this amount by 2 and enter here: $_____.Deduct this amount from last value above (Line 11 or Line 13) and enter here.

☐ No:  Enter last value above  here                 $_____

## 15.   This is your Case Value Assessment. Enter Line 14 here.                 $_____

## Phase 3: Legal Options Assessment:
**What are your legal options?**

**16.   Is Line 11 within Small Claims limit or are you willing to reduce your claim to fit that limit?**

☐  Yes: Select one option:
    ☐ If you have a binding arbitration provision in a written contract with your adversary:
        ☐ that excludes Small Claims cases, enter 125
        ☐ that does not exclude Small Claims cases, enter 0
    ☐ Enter 125 if above options don't apply
☐  No: Enter 0                                    _____

**17.   Do you have a written agreement signed by your adversary that contains an attorney fee provision?**

☐  Yes: Will you be hiring an attorney?
    ☐ Yes: Enter 50
    ☐ No: Enter 25
☐  No: Will you be hiring an attorney?
    ☐ Yes: Enter 0
    ☐ No: Enter 25                                _____

**18.   Do you have a contract signed by you and your adversary that requires binding arbitration?**

☐  Yes: Enter 85
☐  No: Enter 0                                    _____

**19.   Do you have a contract signed by you and your adversary that requires mediation?**

☐  Yes: Enter 15
☐  No:  Enter 0

_____

**20.   This is your Legal Options Assessment.**
**Add 16 through 19, enter here**

_____

---

## Phase 4: Collectability Assessment:
**What are your chances of collecting on your judgment?**

**21.   Select the <u>first</u> option that relates to your adversary:**

☐  is a corporation, enter **150**
☐  will be represented by insurance company, enter **150**
☐  is an operating business other than a corporation,
        enter **140**
☐  is a person who owns real property, enter **130**
☐  is a person who has assets _and_ is salaried, enter **120**
☐  is a person who has assets _and_ works for self as sole
        proprietor, enter **110**
☐  is a person with assets _and_ none of above apply,
        enter **90**
☐  if none of above or below apply, enter **75**
☐  has other judgments against them, enter **50**
☐  has no assets or means of support, enter **40**
☐  has bankruptcy proceedings pending, enter  **20**

_____

**22.   This is your Collectability Assessment.**
**Enter score from 21 here**

_____

## Phase 5: Comprehensive Case Analysis

23.   Enter your Case Value Assessment from Line 15   $_____

24.   Check the box below that relates to the value of Line 23:

☐   if within Small Claims limit, enter **50**
☐   if above $50,000, enter **50**
☐   if between $45,001 and $50,000, enter **45**
☐   if between $40,001 and $45,000, enter **40**
☐   if between $35,001 and $40,000, enter **35**
☐   if between $30,001 and $35,000, enter **30**
☐   if between $25,001 and $30,000, enter **25**
☐   if between $20,001 and $25,000, enter **20**
☐   if between $15,001 and $20,000, enter **15**
☐   if between $10,001 and $15,000, enter **10**
☐   if above Small Claims limit but less than
      $10,001, enter **5**                                       _____

25.   Enter Your Legal Evaluation from Line 6                    _____

26.   Enter Your Legal Options Assessment from Line 20 _____

27.   Enter your Collectability Assessment  from Line 22   _____

28.   Add Lines 24, 25, 26, and 27                               _____

29.   Divide Line 28 by 7 and enter here               _____%

30.   Enter amount from Line 11 here               $_____

31.   Your Settlement Amount:
Multiply Line 30 by Line 29 or 92%, whichever is <u>less</u>   $_____

32.   Enter percentage from Line 29: Your feasibility
assessment [See Phase 6 for rating]      _____%

## Phase 6:   Case Feasibility Assessment Chart

**Note:** Always remember to exhaust all settlement possibilities before pursuing your case through legal channels. Remember also, the case value we're talking about is the one at Line 23.

**91% and above:**   Case feasibility is very good. You should proceed forward with your case.

**81% to 90%:**   Case feasibility is good. You should proceed forward with your case, but make best attempts to resolve your dispute through Last Chance Exercise and mediation first.

**71% to 80%:**   Case feasibility is reasonably good. If binding arbitration is your route, move forward – but if there is an attorney fees provision, be aware that if you lose, you must pay your opponent's attorney fees. If binding arbitration is not your route, you should proceed forward with your case only after proposing a Multi-Step ADR Agreement or Binding Arbitration Agreement to your adversary [See Appendix]. If consent is not obtained, pursue your case only after you have repeatedly attempted settlement. And remember: you may be in this category with a winning case and the best chances of collection, but since you have to travel the court maze, your feasibility is reduced.

**61% to 70%:**   Your case feasibility is mid-range.

   • If you have a Binding Arbitration Agreement but no attorney fee provision, proceed forward. The dispute will be determined soon and you won't be paying your opponent's attorney fees if you lose. But first, attempt settlement and mediation.

• If you have a binding arbitration provision and an attorney fees provision:

1. If you are at the high end of this category, you should proceed forward with the reminder that if you lose you will pay your adversary's attorney fees.

2. If you are at the low end of this category, you should carefully consider your risk of losing and being hit with your opponent's attorney fee tab. Do everything you can to settle your case. Proceed cautiously if you must thereafter.

• If there is an attorney fee provision and no binding arbitration provision, you should lean more in favor of pursuing your dispute only by settlement. It may not be worthwhile to take this case into the expensive court forum, especially considering your exposure with an attorney fee provision. Proceed cautiously if you must.

• If there is no attorney fee provision or binding arbitration provision, proceed only if you are at the high end of this category. Otherwise, it may not be worthwhile to take this case into the expensive court forum. Proceed cautiously if you must.

**51% to 60%:** Make every attempt to settle your dispute at the suggested settlement figure. Carefully review all phases *of The Pocket Lawyer Analyzer* before you proceed. Always remember: if there's an attorney fee provision and you lose, you'll have to pay your adversary's attorney fees. If you have slim chances of collecting on a judgment, perhaps it doesn't make sense to proceed. If your case value is low and you have to travel the demanding court system, you may very well not want to go the long haul. If you are on the low side of this range, your feasibility indicates you should not pursue your case. Otherwise, proceed very cautiously if you must.

**50% and below:** You are discouraged from pursuing your case to judgment, but don't let your opponent know that or you'll never reach settlement. Encourage settlement again and again. After that, one mediation session is warranted. In view of mediation's 85% success rate and your realistic attitude (given your low feasibility rating), the chances of success at mediated settlement are very high.

**CONTINUE IF YOU HAVE DECIDED TO
MOVE FORWARD WITH YOUR DISPUTE**

## Phase 7: Forum Assessment.
## Where will you pursue your dispute?

33.  If yes to 18,  skip to Line  38 and enter binding arbitration

34.  If yes to 19, you must complete mediation before choosing a forum.  Check the box at Line 38.  But proceed, to see what is around the mediation corner

35.  Enter damages from Line 8 here                    $_____

36.  Enter Small Claims limit here                    _____

37.  Check option:
☐ If 35 is the same as or less than 36, enter Small Claims on Line 38
☐ If you are willing to limit your claim to Small Claims limit, enter Small Claims on Line 38
☐ If 35 is more than 36, enter "general civil court system" on Line 38

## 38.  Enter Your Forum Here:            _____

☐ **If mediation first, check here.**

Chapters 7 and 8 are companions to this chapter. Chapter 7 is your Instruction Manual. It answers any question you may have when working though The Pocket Lawyer Analyzer. Chapter 8 shows The Pocket Lawyer Analyzer in action, as it works through four dynamic legal disputes for you. If you've successfully worked through the Pocket Lawyer and require no instruction, Chapter 7 will educate you with its discussion of legal principles. Chapter 8 will interest you with its four dispute scenarios and their solutions. Enjoy!

# — *Chapter Seven* —

# USING THE POCKET LAWYER ANALYZER

---

This is a reference chapter. It can be read on its own, but has special value when you need help responding to a question in The Pocket Lawyer Analyzer. This chapter explains the reasoning behind each question and guides you through the program step by step to assure your best response. If you have The Pocket Lawyer Analyzer software, this chapter is at our Help menu. There's more help in Chapter 8, where you'll get a chance to see The Pocket Lawyer Analyzer in action. Chapter 8's four sample cases are worked through in detail on The Pocket Lawyer Analyzer. There's nothing like a good example to shine the guiding light.

---

## USING THE POCKET LAWYER ANALYZER

NOTE: THIS IS A REFERENCE CHAPTER. BUT IT IS ALSO A BRIEF DISCUSSION OF SOME BASIC LEGAL PRINCIPLES. YOU MAY READ THROUGH IT FOR ITS GENERAL VALUE, BUT WHEN YOU WORK THROUGH THE POCKET LAWYER ANALYZER, THIS CHAPTER IS AN INDISPENSABLE STEP-BY-STEP INSTRUCTION MANUAL. FOR MORE HELP, CHAPTER 8 ILLUSTRATES FOUR DISPUTES WORKED THROUGH THE POCKET LAWYER ANALYZER.

FOR SOFTWARE USERS: If you have *The Pocket Lawyer Analyzer* computer program, you will access this chapter through your computer Help menu. If you still have a question about how to respond after you refer to the software Help menu or this chapter, refer to Chapter 8.

### PHASE 1:   LEGAL EVALUATION

Whose fault is your dispute? You might think this answer is a foregone conclusion – that you are blameless and another person is at fault. But this is not always as clear cut as people think it should be, as you will see.

Liability, or responsibility for damages, is the first important determination of *The Pocket Lawyer Analyzer.* It's the basis for determining your likelihood of prevailing in your dispute. With Phase 1, you will perform a legal evaluation. *The Pocket Lawyer Analyzer* will determine responsibility for damages in your dispute by analyzing the duties and performance from which your dispute arose.

What obligations (duties) do you and your adversary owe to each other? In Phase 1 you define these obligations. All obligations are treated alike, whether they arise out of a written or oral agreement or out of an obligation imposed by law (for example, your obligation not to be careless while driving). *The Pocket Lawyer Analyzer* handles disputes that arise from agreements or from law. It covers the entire range, except marital disputes and criminal wrongs (anything you can be arrested for).

After defining the obligations, you determine whether those obligations were fulfilled. Phase 1 yields your likelihood of prevailing in the dispute.

## QUESTION 1: WHAT OBLIGATIONS DID YOUR ADVERSARY OWE YOU?

Defining your legal obligations is of great consequence – it determines your likelihood of prevailing. All legal disputes are based upon someone's failure to fulfill an obligation to another. Lawyers call this breach (violation) of duty. Legal disputes arise from a wide range of breaches. Such breaches include failure to provide a product that lives up to its warranty, failure to provide an apartment with adequate heating, or failure of a courier service to deliver a package on time. In Chapter 8, there are more examples. Breaches like these violate no criminal law. In other words, someone does not go to jail for breaching a duty. However, damages caused by that person's breach of duty may have to be paid.

### GUIDES TO DEFINING YOUR DUTIES

If you have a contract with your adversary, use it for reference as you answer the questions. Although a written contract is stronger evidence than an oral one, don't forget that an oral contract is still a contract. List exactly what you and your opponent agreed to do. If you do not have a contract, either written or oral, an obligation may be imposed by law. The primary obligations imposed by law are discussed below.

### DUTY OF GOOD FAITH

Parties dealing with each other have a duty to act in good faith. If you act in good faith, it means you have been honest in your dealings and have not taken unfair advantage. This duty keeps us all on a level playing field. If someone breaches this duty of honesty and causes another to be damaged as a result, they will be liable.

### AN EXAMPLE OF LESS THAN GOOD FAITH

A seller of a car tells the buyer that the transmission was replaced, but it was not, and two weeks later the buyer has a blown transmission. Here, the seller has breached his duty of honesty and good faith in his dealings with others.

### DUTY TO ACT REASONABLY

We all have a duty to behave reasonably and prudently toward one another. This is another basic duty imposed by law. When we act unreasonably toward others and cause them damage, legal responsibility follows. For example, all motorists have a duty to drive reasonably. When they do not, we describe their conduct as *negligent* and they are responsible to whomever they damage by their negligent conduct.

## EXAMPLES

The Case of the Daredevil Skier in Chapter 8 depicts one's duty to act reasonably and prudently. Like the prudent motorist, those skiing at the same location have a duty to act prudently and reasonably. In that case, an out of control skier careened into another. He was not acting reasonably and will be liable for resulting injuries.

A parking garage has a duty to keep the garage safe for its users. If a user is injured because of the garage owner's failure to reasonably carry out these duties, the owner has breached his duty and is responsible for the injuries caused by that breach. Most businesses have this duty to their customers. They have a duty to provide a location in a safe and reasonable condition for people to patronize their businesses.

## CHAPTER 8'S SAMPLE CASE

In the sample cases in Chapter 8, you will see how important it is to correctly define duty. For instance, in Chapter 8's Case of the Shifty Seller, the buyer thought he had been cheated by the seller because the roof leaked shortly after escrow closed. Is it the duty of the seller to tell his buyer that the roof leaks? Yes, but only if the seller *knew* about the leak.

In that transaction, one of the questions on the seller-disclosure form addresses the condition of the roof. The seller did not disclose any roof problems because he did not know of any. Merely because the roof leaked in the first storm after close of escrow does not mean it leaked before. The seller did not *guarantee* the condition of the property. His duty was to provide his best information with respect to *known* conditions of the property. The Case of the Shifty Seller illustrates the importance of carefully defining the parties' duties.

### GETTING LIMITED HELP FROM A LAWYER

What are the duties in your dispute? You may very well want to call a local lawyer just to get the answer to this very important question. There are savvy new ways of enlisting a lawyer's help. You get wise advice for a very limited expense. Most County Bar Associations have lawyer referral services that will refer you to a lawyer practicing in the topic of your dispute. Some referrals are free for half an hour, others are paid.

Given the importance of responding to the *duties* question accurately, a paid consultation is worthwhile. Lawyers are more reachable than they were a decade or two ago. They are more responsive to the consumer. You'll find it's relatively easy to book a brief appointment with a lawyer, paying only for the amount of time used. Some even take credit cards over the phone and will phone consult with you. The formalities once in place are giving way to consumer convenience.

### YOUR LAW LIBRARY

Another resource is your local law library. It has a book on every aspect of the law, and now many of those books are written in understandable lay person's terms. Or call us at the number listed at the beginning of the book to schedule a telephone consultation.

## QUESTION 2: DID YOUR ADVERSARY PERFORM THESE OBLIGATIONS IN A SATISFACTORY MANNER?

There are two tests to determine if someone has performed an obligation. The first deals with the scope of performance. Did your adversary do what was promised? The second deals with the quality of the performance.

First, determine whether your adversary performed his or her duties *for the most part.* The standard for determining performance is this: You and your opponent agreed to something – or the law said your adversary had a duty to do something (i.e., driving prudently). Did he substantially do what he was supposed to do?

The second part of the test determines if your adversary did what he was supposed to do in a *satisfactory* way. If he did what he agreed to do, but did it in an unsatisfactory way, then he has not done what he agreed to do. Satisfactory performance is required by law. It requires each person to perform each duty in a satisfactory manner.

### THE REASONABLE STANDARD

What is considered satisfactory performance? It is what would be acceptable to a reasonable person under similar circumstances.

The law forgives tardiness unless time is absolutely critical. Under the reasonable person standard, insignificant departures from what was agreed to are reasonable. Perfect performance is not expected – only reasonable performance. If you lean toward perfectionism, be careful with this question. The law only expects a person to perform a *reasonable* job.

The circumstances surrounding your particular matter must also be considered. If you were able to get a highly discounted price for something, the standard would be a little lower. The result you should then get is a reasonable one based upon the discount you've been given. The law does not allow you to have your cake and eat it too. You can't discount the price and expect a premium product. That's not reasonable.

If your adversary has not performed his duty in a reasonable manner, then he is considered not to have performed his duty.

## QUESTION 3: HAVE YOU SUSTAINED LEGALLY RECOGNIZED DAMAGES AS A DIRECT RESULT OF YOUR ADVERSARY'S CONDUCT?

This question is in two parts. First, you must have sustained damages. Second, your damages must be a direct result of your adversary's conduct.

## NO DAMAGES = NO RESPONSIBILITY

In addition to showing that your adversary breached an obligation owed to you, you must prove that you have been damaged as a result. Frequently, people believe they can mount a legal action just because someone violates a duty to them. This belief is reasonable, particularly when the wrong is great, but it will not suffice without a showing of actual legal damages.

The rule: legal responsibility only comes about if you have been legally damaged – if you have lost something tangible as a result of the conduct. If someone breaches an obligation to you, but you are not legally damaged, there is no responsibility. In this instance, you would answer *No* to Question 3.

## ONLY ACTUAL DAMAGES COUNT

Your damages must be actual. This is nothing like the televised courtroom dramas you've seen – with high price tags for speculative damages. This is real life – not a television show.

Many people feel they have suffered huge, immeasurable damages, *i.e.*, pain and suffering or emotional distress. They feel that when someone does them harm, that person should pay a price equal to the wrong that was done. That is not the way damages are counted. Except for *punitive* damages, which are rarely awarded, the amount of damages has nothing to do with the *wrongfulness* of the conduct. It is measured by the amount of financial loss you have suffered directly from this incident.

So it is essential for you to have experienced clearly defined damages. If in doubt, exclude the item. Do not count any losses that were not caused directly by your adversary.

This is not the time to toss in all the claims for damages you feel you should receive. A good standard to follow is: include an item if you paid for it or lost it as a direct result of your adversary's action.

## An Example: No damages

A contractor tells his client that he has built many custom homes similar to the design his client wants. When the job nears completion, the client finds out that the contractor has not built any other custom homes. At that point, he stops paying his bill. But the contractor's construction is adequate and in line with industry standards for custom homes. Thus, although the contractor misrepresented his background, his misrepresentation did not cause the client any damage. Here, the client cannot justify his failure to pay the bill based on a misrepresentation by the contractor. The client cannot prove damage.

## Cause of Damages

A person is not *automatically* liable for failing to complete an obligation. He is liable only if his failure was the *cause* of your damages. If it was not, this question is answered *No*.

## An Example

Suppose a neighbor's fire damaged your stereo system. Your apartment lease lists 5 things your landlord agreed to do. He violates one of these 5 things – the provision stating that he will only rent the other units in the complex to families of four or less. He rents the apartment above you to a family of eight. Clearly, he violated a term of your lease.

But has this breach of lease caused the damages you've experienced? *No.* Your damages were caused when the *next door neighbor* had a fire and the fire melted your new state-of-the-art stereo system. Yes, the landlord's rental to the people upstairs is in violation of the lease occupancy terms, but this violation did *not* cause your damages. Your damages were caused by a fire that began in another neighbor's apartment.

### QUESTION 4:   DID YOU HAVE A PRIOR OBLIGATION TO YOUR ADVERSARY?

Were you to perform an obligation to your adversary *before* your adversary was to perform his obligation to you? This is the limited situation covered by this question. Here, before you can complain about your adversary's conduct, you have to show that you completed *your own* obligations.

Usually, this question comes into play if your adversary has agreed to compensate you for something *you* were to do. For instance, you agree to file a tax return for a client. Your duty to file the tax return comes before his duty to pay you. Before you are entitled to payment, you have to perform your obligation.

Refer to Question 1, in responding to this question. Remember, Question 4 applies only in those situations where you have clearly agreed to perform an obligation prior to, or in exchange for, your adversary's performance.

### EXAMPLE

The tardy author example in Chapter 8 depicts a situation where the complaining party has an obligation to his adversary. There, the tardy author had a duty to deliver a manuscript. So when he seeks his royalties from the publisher, he has to prove that he completed his *prior* obligation to submit a manuscript. The author's obligation to submit the manuscript must be completed before the publisher has a duty to pay him.

### QUESTION 5: DID YOU PERFORM YOUR OBLIGATION IN A SATISFACTORY MANNER?

This question should be answered *Yes* if your performance was clearly adequate.

### WAS YOUR PERFORMANCE SATISFACTORY?

To determine whether your performance is satisfactory use the same *reasonable person* criteria stated under Question 2. For instance, the case of the tardy author in Chapter 8 shows that the author delivered the manuscript. Thus, this obligation was performed in a satisfactory manner. However, in response to Question 9 he admits that his royalties should be reduced slightly because he delivered the manuscript late.

### QUESTION 6: WHAT IS YOUR LEGAL EVALUATION?

Question 6 is a total of your score. The highest score earned is 350 points. If your tally is zero, there is no reason to continue on with analysis of your case. You have failed the very important legal evaluation test. You should not pursue your case.

## PHASE 2: CASE VALUE ASSESSMENT

Phase 2 provides value analysis. What will a judge, jury, or arbitrator find to be your case value? In this step you'll begin with one number and generally end with something completely different. It makes you a realist, instead of a dreamer – an essential step in evaluating your case.

## QUESTION 7: IS THERE A DAMAGE DEFINING PROVISION IN YOUR CONTRACT THAT PERTAINS TO THIS DISPUTE?

There are two types of *damage defining provisions – liquidated damages* and *limitation on damages*. A liquidated damages provision is an agreement that specifies the amount of damages the innocent party will receive in the event of breach. A provision limiting damages is different. It does not *fix* damages – it *limits* them. You still have to prove your damages, but they cannot go above the limit set. These provisions are always in writing. Chapter 12, *Loss Prevention,* describes these damage definition provisions in more depth.

Review your written agreement to determine if one of these provisions exists. In some states, this type of provision must be separately initialed immediately below the provision and set forth in a clear and obvious format.

## Does Your Damage Specifying Provision Apply?

If your contract *does* contain such a provision, and it has been agreed to by the parties, you must determine if the provision relates to your dispute. For instance, in many real estate purchase agreements, the provision relates only to disputes in which the *buyer* breaches the contract. If the seller breaches, the provision does not apply. So, you must determine whether the provision applies to *your* dispute. Read the provision carefully – does it include the dispute you're having?

## Liquidated Damages

A sample liquidated damages provision may read:

"The parties to this contract are uncertain about the amount of damages that will occur if the contract is breached, and they fix reasonable damages to the non-breaching party at $\_\_\_ or \_\_\_% of the contract price."

If there is a liquidated damages provision, and it relates to your dispute, your recovery is the amount set forth in that provision. Your response to Question 8 would then be the liquidated damages amount specified in the contract.

In the Crafty Computer Consultant case in Chapter 8, the contract contained a liquidated damages provision, but the client did not initial it. Thus, the provision did not apply since the law in that state requires separate initialing.

## LIMITATION ON DAMAGES

A sample provision may read:

"THE PARTIES AGREE THAT LIABILITY FOR BREACH OF THIS AGREEMENT SHALL BE LIMITED TO THE CONTRACT PRICE STATED HEREIN. THE PARTIES AGREE THIS LIMITATION IS REASONABLE UNDER THE CIRCUMSTANCES THAT EXIST AT THE TIME OF MAKING THIS CONTRACT."

If there is a provision for *limitation on damages*, and it relates to your dispute, your recovery is the amount of your damages *limited to that amount*. If your damages are more, they will be limited as specified. If they are less, they will be the lesser amount. You will answer Question 8 accordingly.

See Chapter 12 on *Loss Prevention* for more on these damage defining provisions. If there is no such provision, or it does not relate to your dispute, you will answer *No* to Question 7, moving on to assessment of your damages, Question 8.

## QUESTION 8:   WHAT IS THE AMOUNT OF YOUR DAMAGES?

This is the figure that will be used to choose a forum in Phase 7 of *The Pocket Lawyer Analyzer*. It is also the figure that forms the basis of your case value and settlement value. So it is important to carefully calculate your damages.

## WHAT CAN YOU CLAIM AS DAMAGES?

Review Question 3 in this chapter, which describes legally recognized damages. Use the following standards to firm up your damages:

If your case is based on a contract you had with your foe (including an oral one), your damages will include *what you would have gained* if the contract had not been violated.

If your dispute is not based on a contract, your damages will be *the cost of what you paid or lost*. The law attempts to restore you to where you were before this incident occurred.

Here is a list of some common damages:

- Medical bills
- Loss of wages
- Repair bills
- Replacement costs
- Refund of price paid
- Difference in value between item purchased and price paid
- Lost profits (only if definite and your foe knew breach would cause it)
- Expenses of holding a property for defaulting buyer

## FIRMING UP YOUR DAMAGES

Defining damages involves precise calculation. Often, investigation is required to come up with the correct figures. Your investigation can lead you to obtain an estimate for a replacement item. The estimate should be for a comparable replacement item, not for the better quality product. For instance, your next door neighbor drives over your flower box and you have to replace it. You replace it with a designer brick garden box that costs you five times what the flower box would have cost. You can only recover the value of a comparable replacement flower box. The Crafty Computer Consultant example in Chapter 8 has a good illustration of damages calculation.

## PAIN AND SUFFERING

Generally, damages do not include intangibles such as pain and suffering unless other tangible damages are present. If you weren't physically injured, you have no claim for pain and suffering. If you do have this claim, valuing pain and suffering can be tricky. Some tie the valuation to the amount of your medical bills. Some say 2 to 3 times this amount is adequate compensation.

## FUTURE DAMAGES

Some damages may continue into the future. For instance, you may face future medical bills for a personal injury. Obtain your best estimate of how much these future bills will be. If you are claiming that an employee stole your clients, you will suffer loss of income for a period of time. This too will have to be projected out to encompass future loss.

Limit the future to a reasonable period of time. The law is only willing to compensate you for enough time to recover from your injury or loss. Add these amounts to your present damages. You don't need to be an economist, but you can come close by careful analysis and investigation.

## A RULE OF THUMB

There are many laws which define damages, all too numerous to include in this analysis. Thus, this assessment is intended to provide you with an educated approximation. You'll use it to make some educated choices. Generally, the rule of thumb is: if it's a concrete out-of-pocket expense or loss, you can recover it. If in doubt about an item, exclude it. This program is for the realist.

If you want to define your damages more precisely, a consultation with a local attorney or research at your local law library may be warranted.

## AN EXAMPLE

For instance, you are involved in a collision while driving. Because of the accident, you miss a meeting with a client. You lose your job four months later. You are out of work for four months before you get another job. Your loss of wages is considered remote and is not recoverable unless you can prove that the loss of your job occurred *primarily* because you missed the meeting with your client when you were involved in the accident. Your damages must be *fixed and certain* – and they must also be the *direct* result of the incident you are complaining about.

## QUESTION 9: WERE YOU A CAUSE OF THE SITUATION THAT CAUSED YOUR DAMAGES?

Do not consider here any of the situations you have included above. For instance, if you indicated that you had not performed your duties in Question 5, you would not repeat that situation here. This question covers situations *not* yet described.

## AN EXAMPLE

A good example of this is the Case of the Daredevil Skier in Chapter 8. There, a skier was injured when another skier ran into her. But the injured skier was listening to her walkman and did not hear the out-of-control skier's warning to "Watch out." Had she not been listing to her walkman she probably would have avoided the collision. In that situation, Question 9 is answered *Yes* – the skier contributed to her own damages by failing to be alert to clear warnings. She wasn't the sole cause, but she did contribute. For this reason her damages have been reduced by 20 percent to reflect her partial responsibility for the collision.

## APPORTIONING FAULT

In your matter, you will have to specify the extent to which you were responsible. That can be done by assigning a dollar value or a percentage of fault.

A dollar value will reduce your damages by that amount. In the tardy author example in Chapter 8 the author reduced his damages by $12,000. That's how much more the publisher paid because the author was late with his manuscript.

To come up with a percentage of fault, you compare your conduct with the result and assign a percentage by which you contributed to the situation. In the Daredevil Skier example in Chapter 8, the injured skier identified her level of fault as 20 percent. If you cannot achieve precise apportionment, use 50 percent. This is not the most precise calculation, but at least it will be mid-range.

You will never be entirely responsible for your injuries. If you were, you would have answered *No* to Question 3. In Question 3, your damages must be the direct *result* of your adversary's conduct. If your damages were not caused by your adversary at all, Question 3 should be answered *No*.

### QUESTION 10: DID YOU RECEIVE A SUBSTANTIAL BENEFIT FROM THE SITUATION?

Even though you were damaged, if you received a substantial benefit from this situation with your adversary, your damages should be reduced to reflect that benefit. For instance, in Chapter 8's Case of the Crafty Computer Consultant, the client obtained a state-of-the-art computer system. It cost her a lot more than she thought it would, but she will benefit from it significantly. The law attempts to achieve an equitable solution by reducing damages by the amount of benefit you receive from the situation. In the Crafty Computer Consultant example, we reduced the injured party's damages by $6,975, the value of the computer system's upgrades (in order to show the benefit she obtained).

When you have benefited from the conduct or situation you are complaining about, you will have to reduce the damage amount by a percentage or an amount to reflect the benefit you have received. If you received partial services that have value, then you need to reduce your damages by that value. The best way to obtain a realistic figure is to have a knowledgeable third party provide a value for you. If you just can't come up with a value, reduce your damages by 50 percent. Again, you have not achieved a precision calculation, but at least your guesstimate is mid-range.

**QUESTION 11:   ENTER LINE 10 HERE**

**QUESTION 12:   WILL YOU BE REPRESENTED BY COUNSEL?**

This is a question you must answer before you begin your case. Your answer will depend on several factors:

- First, call the Small Claims Court and find out if your damages at Line 11 are within the Small Claims Court limit. If yes, or if you are willing to reduce your claim to that limit, you will most likely not be hiring an attorney to represent you. You will answer this question *No.*

- Is there a written attorney fees provision in your contract which entitles you to reimbursement for your attorney fees? If so, you will be more inclined to hire an attorney.

- Do you have enough cash on hand to fund an attorney's services until you win a judgment from the arbitrator or the court, and collect on it?

- Does the amount of your damages justify spending the money to have an attorney represent you?

- Will you have to access the court system to recover your damages, or is there a binding arbitration provision? With the latter as your forum, your attorney fees should be far less than if you were embroiled in the court system for years.

Your answer will depend upon your response to each of these pivotal questions. Chapter 12 discusses attorney fees and how to decide.

### QUESTION 13: IF YOU WILL BE REPRESENTED BY COUNSEL, SELECT ONE OF THE FOLLOWING OPTIONS.

The choices offered estimate how much you will spend on attorney fees, given the options available for your dispute. Attorney fees spent determine your net result. When assessing your case, you need to look at your projected bottom line – your net result. Only an accurate net result will give you a realistic case feasibility and settlement value.

Attorney fees soak up a lot of your recovery. The presence or absence of an attorney fee provision and a binding arbitration provision are the two most important factors in deciding how much of your damages will go to pay attorney fees.

The standards we have applied are general and, of course, will vary with each case. These standards make it possible to project your end result – an essential step in your economic analysis.

## NET RECOVERY STANDARDS

Your net result will be determined by the following standards we have established:

- If you have an attorney fee provision and a binding arbitration provision, you will get back almost all of your attorney fees if you win.

- If you have an attorney fee provision but have to travel the expensive and winding court system, you pay 20 percent of your damages as unrecovered attorney fees.

- If you have a binding arbitration provision and no attorney fee provision, you pay 15 percent of your damages as attorney fees.

- If you have neither an attorney fee nor a binding arbitration provision, you will give up an average of 35 percent of your judgment to attorney fees.

## QUESTION 14: WILL YOU REPRESENT YOURSELF OR OTHERWISE PUT SUBSTANTIAL TIME INTO YOUR CASE?

Another factor which projects a net result is the value of your own time. This step takes into account the value of the time you will devote to pursuit of your case.

## WHAT IS YOUR TIME WORTH?

Convert your current earnings into an hourly rate. If you are not working, supply a realistic estimate of how much your time is worth based on your last job. If you have never worked outside your home, use the rate for a job you feel qualified to perform.

## CALCULATING YOUR TIME

Whether you are representing yourself or acting as a party to the dispute, your time will be devoted to your dispute – more than you ever thought possible. You will gather documents, investigate facts, participate in discovery and attend trial. Here are some rules of thumb to follow:

• If your case will travel through the court system and you are represented by a lawyer, you should count on investing at least 75 hours of your time – 15 hours for your deposition and attending the deposition of your opponent, 20 hours for responding to document demands and interrogatories, 10 hours for miscellaneous items, and 30 hours preparing for and attending trial.

• If your case route will be binding arbitration, your time estimate will not be this high. However, it should still be at least 20 hours.

• If you don't yet know which route your case will travel, estimate 40 hours.

• If you do not use these rules of thumb, we suggest you double your time estimate.

People are unrealistic when estimating their case time commitments.

• Increase these estimates by 40 percent if you will be representing yourself. In both mediation and arbitration, written statements of facts and law are required. If you are representing yourself, you must expect to spend time on preparation and written presentation.

### CUT YOUR VALUE IN HALF

You will calculate your time value by multiplying your hourly rate by the number of hours you will devote to your dispute. Then, cut your value in half for purposes of this question. Why do we only use half the value of your time? Because you are a motivated, willing participant and your cost is time, not cash, we discount the value of your time by 50 percent.

### QUESTION 15: THIS IS YOUR CASE VALUE ASSESSMENT.

The calculations you have made through Phase 2 now yield a case value. This is the projected net value you will receive at the end of your dispute. Look at this number carefully. Usually it doesn't resemble what you thought you would receive.

Case value begins with the amount you originally projected. Most people stop there, deciding to pursue their cases based on unrealistic case valuation. But *The Pocket Lawyer Analyzer* has applied several value-reducing factors, including your own responsibility for the situation, the unreimbursed attorney fees you'll pay to pursue your dispute, and any benefit you may have obtained from the situation. *The Pocket Lawyer Analyzer* whittles your case value down to an authentic level.

### PHASE 3:   LEGAL OPTIONS ASSESSMENT

Phase 3 answers the following question: Given the legal options you have available, is it time and cost effective to pursue your action?

### QUESTION 16:   IS NO. 11 WITHIN SMALL CLAIMS LIMIT OR ARE YOU WILLING TO REDUCE YOUR CLAIM TO FIT THAT LIMIT?

Presumably, in response to Question 12, you have already called your county or district courthouse to determine the Small Claims Court limit. If your case value (as determined by Line 11) is below the Small Claims limit, or if you are willing to reduce your case value to that amount, you earn the highest legal options assessment. Your best legal option, in terms of minimum time and expense, is the Small Claims Court.

#### DO YOU HAVE A BINDING ARBITRATION PROVISION THAT EXCLUDES SMALL CLAIMS CASES?

If you have a binding arbitration provision, you may only bring your case in Small Claims Court if your binding arbitration provision *excludes* Small Claims cases. If it doesn't, that means you'll have to pursue your dispute in binding arbitration.

## QUESTION 17: DO YOU HAVE A WRITTEN AGREEMENT WITH YOUR OPPONENT THAT CONTAINS AN ATTORNEY FEE PROVISION?

Typically, an attorney fee provision in a written agreement provides that if one of the parties files suit to enforce the contract's terms, the prevailing party's attorney fees will be paid by the losing party. In some states if the provision is one-sided, it is considered two-sided in the eyes of the law. In those states, if I agree to pay your attorney fees if you win, you are automatically bound to pay my attorney fees if I win. Your score on this question also depends on whether you will be hiring an attorney.

### UNDERSTANDING ATTORNEY FEE PROVISIONS

In Chapter 8 the service agreement between Computer consultant and client, signed by both parties, contains an attorney fee provision. The provision reads as follows:

> CLIENT AGREES THAT IF COMPUTER CONSULTANT HIRES AN ATTORNEY TO COLLECT FROM CLIENT UNDER THIS AGREEMENT, CLIENT WILL PAY CONSULTANT'S ATTORNEY FEES IF CONSULTANT WINS.

In many states this one-sided provision would be interpreted as binding on *both* parties, with attorney fees awarded to either prevailing party. Thus, this provision might just as well read:

THE PARTIES AGREE THAT IF EITHER OF THEM COMMENCES LEGAL PRO-CEEDINGS TO ENFORCE THE TERMS OF THIS CONTRACT, THE PREVAILING PARTY WILL BE ENTITLED TO COL-LECT REASONABLE ATTORNEY FEES FROM THE OTHER PARTY.

If there is no written agreement for the payment of attorney fees, the parties are not reimbursed for attorney fees paid, no matter who wins. There are a few exceptions to this long-standing rule, but they are too few to mention here.

## CONSIDER THE LIFE OF YOUR CASE

This question relates to the potential life of your case. You may be representing yourself at mediation, but planning to hire an attorney to handle the next step if mediation is unsuccessful. If this is the case, you should respond that you *will* be hiring an attorney. If you never intend to hire an attorney during this case, no matter which route it travels, your answer is *No.* For purposes of *The Pocket Lawyer Analyzer*, always plan on your case moving beyond mediation.

## QUESTION 18: DO YOU HAVE A CON-TRACT SIGNED BY YOU AND YOUR ADVER-SARY THAT REQUIRES BINDING ARBITRA-TION?

A binding arbitration agreement is signed by all parties to the dispute, or at the very least, by the party with whom you want to arbitrate. The provision should specify that arbitration is *binding, final, unappealable,* or some other terminology to indicate that it is intended to unequivocally replace the court system. Other types of arbitration are referred to as *judicial* or *advisory* arbitration. These forms of arbitration do not replace the court system, and are not considered binding. So you must ensure that your provision specifies *binding* arbitration. Chapter 12, entitled *Loss Prevention*, presents a sample binding arbitration provision.

Most arbitration provisions will be validated as long as they are clear and signed by the disputing parties. The law favors arbitration, and the courts now lean in favor of resolving disputes outside the court system.

An excellent legal options assessment comes from having a binding arbitration provision. This is because attorney fees are substantially reduced in binding arbitration. In fact, they're often cut by 80 percent!

## QUESTION 19: DO YOU HAVE A CONTRACT SIGNED BY YOU AND YOUR ADVERSARY THAT REQUIRES MEDIATION?

Unlike arbitration, mediation does not replace the court system. Therefore, mediation provisions do not require the level of formality of arbitration provisions. A mediation provision needs to be in a written agreement signed by the mediating parties – or at least by the party with whom you wish to mediate. Chapter 12, *Loss Prevention*, presents sample mediation provisions. Your legal options assessment is improved by a contract requiring mediation.

### QUESTION 20: THIS IS YOUR LEGAL OPTIONS ASSESSMENT.

The highest assessment comes from having all three contract provisions: attorney fees, mediation, and binding arbitration.

### PHASE 4: COLLECTABILITY ASSESSMENT

Case feasibility is enhanced by the cash supply available to pay any judgment you get. Can you collect? Does your foe have assets? Who is financially responsible? This step evaluates your foe's ability to pay your judgment – whether payment is voluntary or by collection procedures. This is an essential step in analyzing your case feasibility. A rocky road after judgment will devalue even your best case. A piece of paper is only as good as the funds behind it. If you'll never collect on it, what good does it do to obtain a judgment?

### QUESTION 21: WHAT ARE YOUR CHANCES OF COLLECTING ON YOUR JUDGMENT? SELECT ONE OPTION.

This question may take a little investigation. Is your adversary a corporation? Does he or she own real estate – if so, is there any value after the mortgages? Does your adversary own a business? Does your adversary have other outstanding judgments? It is imperative to determine the options listed in the key to this question. A trip to the courthouse in the district where your adversary resides will answer most of these questions.

The County Recorder will have an index where you can locate real estate owned by name. Past judgments are on file with the court. You can also find out if your adversary owns a business. There are many simple ways of finding out about a person or business. Review books in your law library for additional sources. If you don't feel like taking these steps yourself, hire an asset search firm. They perform these searches quite inexpensively.

Your choice of asset-worthiness category indicates your likelihood of collecting your judgment against your opponent. If your opponent is a corporation, your likelihood is very high. If you know your opponent has insurance to cover your claim, your chances of collecting are also high. The categories and ratings decrease from there.

### Assets to Collect Upon

Does your opponent own a business? If so, your chances of collection are very good. If the business is a sole proprietorship, you'll want to have the complaint and judgment in the name of the business too. Does your opponent work for someone else? If so, you can garnish wages. Does he or she own real estate? If so, any judgment you obtain can be recorded on the property's title. Only when your opponent sells the property – and generally not until then – will your judgment be paid off. You can also record your judgment in any district where your adversary attempts to buy or sell property. He will have to pay off your judgment before closing escrow.

Bank accounts can be scooped up to satisfy a judgment. Boats and vehicles may be towed away and sold. There are limitations, but these are generally the rules. If your opponent has no assets or apparent source of income, there will be little chance of collecting on any judgment you obtain now. However, in most states your judgment is good for a number of years. And it can continually be renewed thereafter, as long as renewal is completed before its term expires. So make sure you find out how long a judgment lasts in your state and renew it a few months before it expires.

## A Judgment As an Investment

Most states set a high interest rate that accrues on a judgment until it is paid. The high rate works as an inducement for the debtor to settle up sooner. So if you can wait, and if your adversary is likely at some point to have enough money to pay your judgment and its interest, your judgment becomes a good investment. Some states have set 10 percent as the annual interest rate. Where else can you earn interest that high? It can be an excellent investment – if you know you will be able to collect.

## Phase 5: Comprehensive Case Analysis

Your Comprehensive Case Analysis yields two of your most important results: your case feasibility assessment and your settlement valuation. The results of your Legal Evaluation, Case Value Assessment, Legal Options Assessment, and Collectability Assessment determine your case feasibility. Your case feasibility then defines settlement value based on your Case Value Assessment (before offset for attorney fees and personal time).

## YOUR FEASIBILITY RATING

Keep in mind that your Feasibility Assessment is *not* your likelihood of prevailing. That was determined in Phase 1: Legal Evaluation. Instead, your feasibility assessment gives you the overall *practicality* of pursuing your dispute. Low collectability and absence of an attorney fee clause or arbitration provision will greatly reduce your feasibility rating. So, although you may have a winning case, if you have to travel the long, laborious court system and have no attorney fee provision to get back the fees you spend, it may not make sense to pursue your case. On the other hand, if your case valuation is high, you receive a bonus that bumps up your case feasibility.

## YOUR CASE VALUE

Your case value from Phase 2 is carried forward with Comprehensive Case Analysis. Your case value is no longer that idealistic figure you held when you began working *The Pocket Lawyer Analyzer*. When you think of case feasibility, remember the case value we're talking about is the one assessed in Phase 2 – not the one you first brought to the table. You've got to be realistic for *The Pocket Lawyer Analyzer* to produce accurate results.

## YOUR SETTLEMENT VALUE

Another essential assessment you get is settlement value. Based on a critical combination of factors, your damages assessment is adjusted to provide you with a realistic settlement value. The most difficult thing for people to come up with is a settlement value effectively reduced by the downside factors of their case. *The Pocket Lawyer Analyzer* does it for you. At mediation or in your Last Chance session, this figure will be your target.

We say *target* because this value should not be your *bottom line.* Always keep in mind that the next step is to battle it out in court or arbitration. It's a big step – especially if you're off to court. A compromising state of mind is needed for settlement. Always consider an offer that is below your target. Avoiding expensive adversarial battles is often worth giving up a few thousand dollars to button up a settlement.

### PHASE 6:   CASE FEASIBILITY ASSESSMENT

In this bottom line phase, the feasibility assessment you obtain in Phase 5 is analyzed to determine the ultimate question: Should you pursue your case or not? If you are prompted to move forward with your dispute, move on to Phase 7 which directs you to the appropriate door you'll enter to pursue your dispute.

### PHASE 7:   FORUM ASSESSMENT

After your feasibility assessment is complete and you've decided to move forward with your dispute, your Forum Indicator directs you to the appropriate dispute resolution forum. There are some matters, too few to include in this analysis, that can only be brought in federal court. But the vast majority fit into one of the categories listed in the Forum Indicator, generally depending upon value.

You may be entitled to proceed before a mediator, an arbitrator, the Small Claims Court or a general trial court, depending on the legal options in your agreement, the nature of your dispute, and the amount of your claim.

## CONCLUSION

You can see how *The Pocket Lawyer Analyzer* scrutinizes each component of your case and performs a precision combination of its assessments. No matter what course of action you take after completing *The Pocket Lawyer Analyzer*, you will be far more informed about your legal choices and the consequences of each.

* * *

There's nothing like a good example to make things perfectly clear. If you need some help responding to a question in The Pocket Lawyer Analyzer read on to Chapter 8, where four disputes are worked through on The Pocket Lawyer Analyzer. When you bring the program together with a real life situation, you see how very well it works.

*— Chapter Eight —*

# THE POCKET LAWYER
# ANALYZER IN ACTION

---

This chapter illustrates The Pocket Lawyer Analyzer in action. It steps you through The Pocket Lawyer Analyzer with four real life disputes. If you have any question about how to use The Pocket Lawyer Analyzer, this chapter will button it up for you. If you don't, you can glide past this chapter without skipping a beat. But if you read it, you'll find four eye-opening scenarios about people like you dealing responsibly with legal disputes. That's what this book is all about!

---

## REFERENCE TOOL

This chapter completes your reference manual for *The Pocket Lawyer Analyzer*. It illustrates four disputes worked through step-by-step. Feel free to skip this chapter if you have no question about how to respond to *The Pocket Lawyer Analyzer's* questions. But we encourage you to read it for its illustrative value – these four people were able to successfully direct their disputes by working through the program.

## FOUR SAMPLE DISPUTES

Our four examples represent disputes that may be encountered in the average person's life.

- The first concerns a computer user and a consultant. Given the current high tech age, many of us find it necessary to hire a computer consultant. These fairly new relationships are fertile for dispute.

- The second involves personal injury – one skier injured by another.

- The third example concerns the purchase of a home.

- Our final illustration involves an author and his publisher.

It is worthwhile to review all four examples to see how *The Pocket Lawyer Analyzer* applies to different types of disputes. With our examples established and our mission in mind, let's analyze our first case.

## THE CASE OF THE CRAFTY COMPUTER CONSULTANT

**COMPLAINING PARTY:**  Betty, the Business Consultant.

**THE DISPUTE THAT AROSE:**  In these days of trying to keep pace with high technology, many of us have hired a computer consultant. Betty, a business consultant, did. The consultant told Betty that he'd upgrade her computer system to a high-technology, state-of-the-art system. All Betty had to do was buy the supplies, pay him for his time at his hourly rate of $65, and he'd make it all happen. Betty asked for an estimate, which consultant provided in the range of $5,000. The upgrade took a painful 4 months and it ended up costing $18,000: $7,200 for the consultant's hourly services, $8,200 to upgrade computer hardware and $2,620 for software.

Betty's new system (including e-mail, modem, internet access and other high-tech features) is now considered state-of-the-art – at a state-of-the-art price tag of $18,000. Betty has paid $5,000 of the consultant's bill along with $10,820 for new hardware and software. She owes the consultant $2,200 on his bill. This is where things were when their dispute hit its peak. The network suddenly stopped working and the consultant told Betty she would need a memory upgrade for three of the four computers, which would cost her another $1,100. It was at this point that Betty decided this guy didn't know what he was talking about and it was time to get a second opinion. Her second opinion confirmed her suspicions.

**POSITIONS OF THE PARTIES:** Betty and the consultant had a number of conversations about how to resolve this hopeless matter and were deadlocked. Betty's position was that the consultant had grossly underestimated how much this upgrade would cost, things were already coming undone, and he should reimburse her for a lot of the unnecessary hardware and software costs she paid. Consultant did not agree. He advised, as he had when Betty first complained that he had exceeded his estimate, that the estimate he'd given had been only for his time – and it was only an estimate anyway. He had not understood that the estimate requested was to *include* materials. Thus, the estimate he gave Betty only represented the intangible factor – his time. He'd felt that Betty understood that hardware and software upgrades would be required and would be substantial. He said it was all an understandable miscommunication and he should get paid for all work he did. Furthermore, all supplies were necessary to get the job done to the high technology level Betty desired.

**THE UNDERLYING AGREEMENT:** The obligations of the computer consultant and Betty are spelled out in the written service agreement, and in several oral agreements and statements made thereafter. The service agreement contains an attorney fee provision but no mediation or binding arbitration provision.

**THE DAMAGES:** Betty has hired another consultant to advise how much it will cost to get the system operating correctly and how much she should have paid to get the technology upgrades she requested. He states that it should have cost $6,975 - $2,275 for 35 hours of consultant time and $4,700 for the hardware and software costs to get this job done. She'll now have to pay approximately $875 to get it redone correctly.

## PHASE 1:   LEGAL EVALUATION

### 1.   WHAT OBLIGATIONS DID THE COMPUTER CONSULTANT OWE BETTY?

**ANSWER:**   Computer consultant agreed to upgrade Betty's present computer system and promised Betty she would have a high technology office – state of the art. He agreed to charge her $65 an hour for his time with an estimate of $5,000.

### 2.   DID THE COMPUTER CONSULTANT PERFORM THESE OBLIGATIONS IN A SATISFACTORY MANNER?

**ANSWER:**   *No.* Although the consultant for the most part has done what he promised, he did not perform his services in a satisfactory manner. It will cost $875 to have the system reprogrammed to operate satisfactorily. Further, Betty's new consultant reports that many upgrades were not required, especially many of the expensive hardware purchases. Thus, Betty earns 350 points.

### 3.   HAS BETTY SUSTAINED LEGALLY RECOGNIZED DAMAGES AS A DIRECT RESULT OF THE COMPUTER CONSULTANT'S CONDUCT?

**ANSWER:**   *Yes.* Betty has sustained legally recognized damages. Her new consultant advises that it should have cost $6,975 to complete this upgrade. She has paid far more than the computer upgrades should have cost. These are concrete out-of-pocket damages she has paid. They meet the test of legally recognized damages. These damages were also the *direct* result of computer consultant's inadequate services. Betty retains her 350 score.

**4. DID BETTY HAVE A PRIOR OBLIGATION TO THE COMPUTER CONSULTANT?**

**ANSWER:** *No.* Betty only agreed to pay the computer consultant. Score remains at 350.

**5. DID BETTY PERFORM HER OBLIGATION IN A SATISFACTORY MANNER?**

**ANSWER:** *Doesn't apply.* Betty had no other duties. Score of 350 is carried forward.

**6. THIS IS BETTY'S LEGAL EVALUATION. ENTER SCORE HERE.**

**ANSWER:** Betty has earned 350 points in her legal evaluation.

## PHASE 2: CASE VALUE ASSESSMENT

**7. IS THERE A DAMAGE DEFINING PROVISION IN BETTY'S CONTRACT THAT PERTAINS TO THIS DISPUTE?**

**ANSWER:** *No.* These parties' written agreement *did* contain a liquidated damages provision fixing damages at $500 if consultant failed to complete the services requested. But, being a savvy business woman, Betty elected not to initial that provision. It would have limited her to $500 in any breach of contract action against the consultant. She felt this amount was unrealistic. Thus, the parties are not subject to a liquidated damages provision.

**8. WHAT IS THE AMOUNT OF BETTY'S DAMAGES?**

**ANSWER:** Betty has paid $15,820: $5,000 to the computer consultant and $10,820 for hardware and software. She will have to pay another $875 to get the system to correctly operate. Thus, her damages are $16,695. She will receive a substantial benefit from the computer upgrades once it gets up and running correctly. But that will be addressed below and her damages figure will be adjusted accordingly.

**9.   WAS BETTY A CAUSE OF THE SITUATION THAT CAUSED HER DAMAGES? (DO NOT INCLUDE CONDUCT ABOVE.)**

**ANSWER:**   *No.* Betty did not contribute to her damages.

**10.   DID BETTY RECEIVE A SUBSTANTIAL BENEFIT FROM THE SITUATION?**

**ANSWER:**   *Yes.* Betty will receive a substantial benefit from the upgrades when they are completed for the additional $875 she'll pay. Her new consultant advises that it should have cost $6,975 to complete this upgrade for consulting time, hardware, and software. Thus, Betty's damages of $16,695 (including the $875.00 she'll have to pay) should be reduced by the sum of $6,975, the value of this system to her, leaving damages of $9,720.

**11.   ENTER LINE 10 HERE.**
**ANSWER:**   $9,720.

**12.   WILL BETTY BE REPRESENTED BY COUNSEL?**

**ANSWER:**   *Yes.* Betty will be hiring an attorney to represent her if she and Consultant can't work something out. Her contract includes an attorney fee provision which makes her decision to hire a lawyer more palatable.

**13. IF BETTY WILL BE REPRESENTED BY COUNSEL, SELECT ONE OF THE FOLLOWING OPTIONS.**

ANSWER: (b) applies to Betty's case. Her contract does contain an attorney fee provision. Thus, 80 percent of $9,720 leaves $7,776. In essence, our formula shows that Betty will not recover about $2,000 of the attorney fees she pays. This is because she has to travel the expensive court system to resolve her dispute, and in court cases, attorney fee provisions generally get you back only a portion of your attorney fees.

**14. WILL BETTY REPRESENT HERSELF OR OTHERWISE PUT SUBSTANTIAL TIME INTO HER CASE?**

ANSWER: Betty estimates she will put about 50 hours of her time into this case. As a well seasoned business consultant her hourly rate is $50. The value of the time she will contribute to her case is $2,500 divided by 2, or $1,250. This amount is deducted from her $7,776 case value leaving $6,526.

**15. THIS IS BETTY'S CASE VALUE ASSESSMENT. ENTER HERE.**

ANSWER: $6,526

## PHASE 3: LEGAL OPTIONS ASSESSMENT

**16. IS NO. 11 WITHIN SMALL CLAIMS LIMIT OR IS BETTY WILLING TO REDUCE HER CLAIM TO FIT THAT LIMIT?**

ANSWER: *No.* Her case value is $9,720. The Small Claims limit in her state is $3,500. Her claim exceeds that amount and she is not willing to reduce it.

**17. DOES BETTY HAVE A WRITTEN AGREEMENT SIGNED BY THE COMPUTER CONSULTANT THAT CONTAINS AN ATTORNEY FEE PROVISION?**

**ANSWER:** *Yes.* Betty earns 50 points since there is an attorney fee provision and she will be hiring an attorney.

**18. DOES BETTY HAVE A CONTRACT SIGNED BY HERSELF AND THE COMPUTER CONSULTANT THAT REQUIRES BINDING ARBITRATION?**

**ANSWER:** *No.* Zero points are earned.

**19. DOES BETTY HAVE A CONTRACT SIGNED BY HERSELF AND THE COMPUTER CONSULTANT THAT REQUIRES MEDIATION?**

**ANSWER:** *No.* Zero points are earned.

**20. THIS IS BETTY'S LEGAL OPTIONS ASSESSMENT. ENTER HERE.**

**ANSWER:** Betty's legal options assessment is 50, her total points for Phase 3.

## PHASE 4: COLLECTABILITY ASSESSMENT

**21. SELECT ONE OPTION THAT RELATES TO THE COMPUTER CONSULTANT:**

**ANSWER:** Betty does not believe there will be any problem collecting against computer consultant. He is in good standing in the community and has been in business for a long time. Her collectability rating is 140 because computer consultant is an operating business.

**22. THIS IS BETTY'S COLLECTABILITY ASSESSMENT. ENTER SCORE FROM 21 HERE.**

**ANSWER:** Betty's Collectability Assessment is 140.

### Comprehensive Case Analysis

23.  Betty's Case Value Assessment
(No. 15)                                          $6,526

24.  Enter score for value of Line 23            5

25.  Enter Betty's Legal Evaluation
(Line 6)                                         350

26.  Enter Betty's Legal Options Assessment
(Line 20)                                         50

27.  Enter Betty's Collectability Assessment
(Line 22)                                        140

28.  Add Nos. 24, 25, 26, and 27                 545

29.  Divide Betty's answer to No. 28 by 7
Enter here and on Line 32                        78%

30.  Enter Amount from No. 11 here    $9,720

31.  Betty's Settlement Amount: Multiply
No. 30 by No. 29 or 92%, whichever is
less.                                      $7,581.60

32.  Betty's Feasibility Assessment:
(No. 29)                                         78%

## Phase 6:   Case Feasibility Assessment

**Betty's case feasibility reads as follows:**

**71% to 80%:** "Case feasibility is reasonably good. If binding arbitration is your route, move forward – but if there is an attorney fees provision, be aware that if you lose, you must pay your opponent's attorney fees. If binding arbitration is not your route, you should proceed forward with your case only after proposing a Multi-Step ADR Agreement  or Binding Arbitration Agreement to your adversary [See Appendix]. If consent is not obtained, pursue your case only after you have repeatedly attempted settlement. And remember: you may be in this category with a winning case and the best chances of collection, but since you have to travel the court maze, your feasibility is reduced."

**PHASE 7:  FORUM ASSESSMENT.** Betty will bring her case in the general court system.

**CONCLUSION:** Betty is in this category primarily because she will have to travel the long expensive court system to resolve her dispute. Otherwise, she would have received a far higher rating. Betty will pursue her case only after she takes a more realistic approach to settlement. The lowest amount she would previously consider was $10,000. Now she realizes the settlement value should be considerably lower.

By working through *The Pocket Lawyer Analyzer*, Betty learned she had to deduct the value of the computer upgrade from her damages. In realizing that, she hired the second computer consultant to value her current system and advise her on what it would take to bring her computer upgrade to a close. She also came to realize that even though she has an attorney fee provision, she is not guaranteed to get back all of her attorney fees. Through working the program, she realizes a fair settlement would be substantially lower than the amount she was considering. Now Betty is ready to discuss much more realistic figures with the Computer consultant. She also has her Multi-Step ADR Agreement in hand as her next tool to resolution if settlement does not come about.

## THE CASE OF THE DAREDEVIL SKIER

**COMPLAINING PARTY:** Lois, the injured skier.

**THE DISPUTE THAT AROSE:** About 7 months ago, Lois was skiing down one of the expert slopes at Squaw Valley. It was a beautiful sunny day and conditions were good, except it was icy. Lois was really enjoying herself listening to a walkman when suddenly a daredevil skier about three times her weight plunged into her, forcing her off balance and into a tree. Lois broke her arm, which healed over a few months, but her back was injured and she was laid up and unable to work for three months. Lois has just completed a seven month course of back therapy. She is fully recovered after a seven month setback.

**POSITIONS OF THE PARTIES:** Now Lois is ready to evaluate her case for purposes of settling with the daredevil skier or pursuing her legal remedy against him. Lois has talked with the skier and his parents about this matter. They have no insurance to cover this incident.

**THE UNDERLYING AGREEMENT:** On the verge of filing a lawsuit, Lois proposed a comprehensive ADR agreement to them. They have now agreed to mediate this dispute. Pending mediation, they want to hold off on signing the binding arbitration and attorney fees provisions.

THE DAMAGES: The following figures relate to Lois' damages: Medical costs: $1,650; Physical therapy: $4,325; Lost wages while off work: $11,750, for a total out-of-pocket damages of $17,725.

## PHASE 1: LEGAL EVALUATION

### 1. WHAT OBLIGATIONS DID THE DAREDEVIL SKIER OWE LOIS?

ANSWER: The daredevil skier agreed with the rest of the world that he would act as a reasonably prudent person in relation to them. This is one duty we all take on at birth. Thus, when we engage in sports with others we impliedly agree to undertake the sport reasonably and to act prudently.

### 2. DID THE DAREDEVIL SKIER PERFORM THESE OBLIGATIONS IN A SATISFACTORY MANNER?

ANSWER: No, the daredevil skier did not substantially fulfill his obligation to treat others prudently and reasonably while he engaged in skiing. He was out of control and because of that he careened into Lois. Thus, 350 points have been earned.

### 3. HAS LOIS SUSTAINED LEGALLY RECOGNIZED DAMAGES AS A DIRECT RESULT OF DAREDEVIL'S CONDUCT?

ANSWER: *Yes.* Lois has out-of-pocket damages consisting of physical injuries as well as wage loss. Thus, the score remains at 350.

### 4. DID LOIS HAVE A PRIOR OBLIGATION TO THE DAREDEVIL SKIER?

ANSWER: *Yes.* Lois has the same implied agreement with her adversary, as well as the world at large, to act reasonably and prudently in her skiing activities.

### 5. DID LOIS PERFORM HER OBLIGATION IN A SATISFACTORY MANNER?

ANSWER:   *Yes.* Lois fulfilled her obligation to act prudently and reasonably toward her fellow skiers. She has always been a reasonably prudent skier and she was conforming to this standard on the day in question. Lois probably could have been more audio aware, but listening to the walkman didn't interfere with Lois' prudent skiing practices – it only interfered with her ability to avoid this accident. (More on this in Question 9). Thus, Lois' 350 score remains unaffected.

### 6. THIS IS LOIS' LEGAL EVALUATION. ENTER SCORE HERE.

ANSWER:   350.   The case evaluation analysis for Lois is 350. But, as you will see in Phase 3, Lois contributed to her own injuries through her inattentiveness.

## PHASE 2:   CASE VALUE ASSESSMENT

### 7. IS THERE A DAMAGE DEFINING PROVISION IN LOIS' CONTRACT THAT PERTAINS TO THIS DISPUTE?

ANSWER:   *No.* These two people who collided on a mountain in Tahoe have no damage defining agreement.

### 8. WHAT IS THE AMOUNT OF LOIS' DAMAGES?

ANSWER:   Lois' doctors have advised that she has healed and there is no real probability of any recurrence or residual discomfort from her injuries. So, future pain and suffering and other future damages will not be considered. Lois' past out-of-pocket costs must be tabulated as well as a reasonable figure for the pain and suffering she endured during the last seven months.

Lois' out-of-pocket damages are $17,725. Although no formula is appropriate for determining pain and suffering, the total of *medical expenses times 2.5* is a rough approximation. Lois' medical expenses, which do not include wage loss, total $5,975. Multiplied by 2.5, pain and suffering would be $14,937.50. Thus, Lois' damages including out-of-pocket medical bills, wage loss and pain and suffering are reasonably expected to be $32,662.50.

**9. WAS LOIS A CAUSE OF THE SITUATION THAT CAUSED HER DAMAGES? (DO NOT INCLUDE ANY CONDUCT ADDRESSED ABOVE.)**
**ANSWER:** *Yes.* Lois contributed to her injuries by failing to exercise reasonable care to avoid the accident. Although Lois did not *actively* participate in causing her damages, she did contribute by failing to be audio attentive to the skier's verbal warnings. The law assigns minimal responsibility to someone for failing to heed warnings. Thus, we will assess Lois' responsibility at 20%, reducing her damages by 20%, leaving a value assessment of $26,130.00.

**10. DID LOIS RECEIVE A SUBSTANTIAL BENEFIT FROM THE SITUATION?**
**ANSWER:** *No.*

**11. ENTER LINE 10 HERE.**
**ANSWER:** $26,130 is carried forward.

### 12. WILL LOIS BE REPRESENTED BY COUNSEL?

**ANSWER:** *Yes.* If this case doesn't settle at mediation, Lois will be hiring an attorney to represent her. She doesn't have an attorney fees reimbursement provision, but she realizes that she will need a lawyer to represent her in the complicated court system. If arbitration is agreed to, she'll represent herself in that forum. But not in the court system.

### 13. IF LOIS WILL BE REPRESENTED BY COUNSEL, SELECT ONE OF THE OPTIONS OFFERED.

**ANSWER:** These parties do not have a contract containing either of these provisions. Thus, option (d.) is selected requiring Lois' damages to be multiplied by 65% to reflect an offset for attorney fees she'll pay to obtain a judgment in the court system, leaving a calculation of $16,984.50. Lois is expected to spend about $9,000 on attorney fees to travel the court sysem through trial.

### 14. WILL LOIS REPRESENT HERSELF OR OTHERWISE PUT SUBSTANTIAL TIME INTO HER CASE?

**ANSWER:** *Yes.* Lois intends to represent herself at the mediation session. She allots 15 hours for preparation and attendance. If the case does not settle it will travel the court system. She estimates that she will spend 70 hours on her case in deposition, responding to written discovery and appearing at trial. Lois' hourly rate is about $26.35 for a total time value of $2,240.00. 50% of this amount is $1,120. Thus, Lois' net case value is reduced by $1,120 to $15,864.50.

**15.  This is Lois' Case Value Assessment. Enter here.**

**Answer:** $15,864.50. Lois' case value has dropped from over $32,000 to about $15,000 – a $17,000 drop – in the value assessment phase. Part of the difference was for her own failure to look out for herself with a substantial portion attributable to projected attorney fees.

## Phase 3: Legal Options Assessment

**16.  Is No. 11 within the Small Claims limit or is Lois willing to reduce her claim to fit that limit?**

**Answer:** *No.* Line 11 is $26,130, far above the Small Claims limit.

**17.  Does Lois have a written agreement signed by the daredevil skier that contains an attorney fee provision?**

**Answer:** *No.* there is no attorney fee provision. Thus, no score is earned.

**18.  Does Lois have a contract signed by herself and the daredevil skier that requires binding arbitration?**

**Answer:** *No.* The daredevil skier would not agree to binding arbitration. He says he may if mediation does not settle the case. Unless Lois has it in writing signed by the other party, it doesn't count. So, no score is tabulated for this item.

**19.  Does Lois have a contract signed by herself and the daredevil skier that requires mediation?**

**Answer:** *Yes.* These parties have now signed a mediation agreement. So 15 points are scored.

**20. THIS IS LOIS' LEGAL OPTIONS ASSESSMENT.**

**ANSWER:** Lois has earned 15 points for her Legal Options Assessment.

## PHASE 4: COLLECTABILITY ASSESSMENT

**21. SELECT ONE OPTION THAT RELATES TO THE DAREDEVIL SKIER.**

**ANSWER:** During those long months when Lois was recuperating from her injuries, she conducted a little research on her adversary. The daredevil skier is 22 years of age, a junior in college and has no job or assets. The collectability assessment in this situation is 75 because no other choices apply.

Thus, unless a voluntary settlement is reached, probably by contribution from his parents who are funding his schooling, there will be little chance of collecting on any judgment for the next few years while this young man completes his college education and begins his profession. Of course, most judgments can continually be renewed. As long as Lois can afford to wait a few years, she will probably be able to collect any unpaid judgment. If Lois can't wait to collect, she won't see any funds unless a voluntary settlement comes about.

**22. THIS IS LOIS' COLLECTABILITY ASSESSMENT. ENTER HERE.**

**ANSWER:** 75 is Lois' collectability assessment.

## PHASE 5: COMPREHENSIVE CASE ANALYSIS

23.  Lois' Case Value Assessment
(No. 15)                                        $15,864.50

24.  Enter score for value of Line 23            15

25.  Enter Lois' Legal Evaluation (Line 6)   350

26.  Enter Lois' Legal Options Assessment
(Line 20)                                         15


27.  Enter Lois' Collectability Assessment
(Line 22)                                          75

28.  Add Nos. 24, 25, 26 and 27                  455

29.  Divide Lois' answer to No. 28 by 7
Enter here and on Line 32                        65%
*(This is your Feasibility Assessment.)*

30.  Enter amount from No. 11          $26,130

31.  Lois' settlement amount: Multiply
No. 30 by No. 29 or 92%, whichever
is less.                                    $16,984.50

32.  Lois' Feasibility Assessment:
(No. 29)                                          65%

## PHASE 6:   CASE FEASIBILITY ASSESSMENT

**61% TO 70%:**   " If there is no attorney fee provision or binding arbitration provision, proceed
only if you are at the high end of this category.
Otherwise, it may not be worth your while to
take this case into the expensive court forum.
Proceed cautiously if you must."

**PHASE 7: FORUM ASSESSMENT:** Lois will first take her case to mediation. If settlement does not occur at mediation, she will most likely bring her case to the expensive court system. But she plans to work carefully with her attorney to keep costs down.

**CONCLUSION:** Lois' feasibility rating, 65%, is midrange in the sector she's ended up in. Thus, Lois should carefully analyze her options.

Through working *The Pocket Lawyer Analyzer*, Lois discovered that she contributed to her own injuries by failing to be more audio aware. Also, she realizes she will have to bring her dispute in the expensive court system if she can't settle it, and she will not be reimbursed for any attorney fees spent in the process. Her attorney fees bill is projected to be about $9,000, which will net her $15,864 after trial in the court system.

She has also performed a realistic collectability analysis and realizes that her chances of collecting against this young skier are risky. She has a mediation provision and would do well to do her best to obtain a voluntary settlement at mediation for the suggested settlement amount of $16,984.50.

Why is her mediation settlement figure higher than what she is projected to net at trial? Because each valuation is based on differing factors. While post-trial value offsets attorney fees, settlement value does not. However, settlement value is adjusted by feasibility rating while post-trial value is not. Don't compare these figures because they are not related.

Lois' strategy after working *The Pocket Lawyer Analyzer* is to submit a Binding Arbitration Agreement to the mediator to propose to her adversary if settlement does not occur at mediation. She will do everything she can to detour her route through the court system to binding arbitration. Conversations she's had with the parents of the daredevil skier indicate that they too understand the extreme expense of the court system.

## THE CASE OF MR. SHIFTY, THE SUSPECT SELLER.

**COMPLAINING PARTY:** Sam, the home buyer.

**THE DISPUTE THAT AROSE:** Sam bought a house from Mr. Shifty, who did not disclose that the roof leaks. Sam didn't have the roof inspected, relying on the seller's disclosures that he knew of no problems with the roof. Escrow closes, the roof leaks.

**POSITIONS OF THE PARTIES:** As you'll later see, the issue in this case is: Did the seller actually know about the leaking? Mr. Shifty says he did not. The seller does not have a duty to disclose a condition of which he has no knowledge. Otherwise, the seller would be unconditionally warranting the condition of his property. He is not. If Mr. Shifty did not experience leaking himself and this rainy season is the first evidence of leakage, then it's Sam's problem. Sam should have had a home inspector or roofer evaluate the roof before closing the deal.

**THE UNDERLYING AGREEMENT:** The purchase agreement contains a liquidated damages provision, an attorney fees provision, a mediation provision, and a binding arbitration provision. The binding arbitration provision excludes Small Claims cases.

**THE DAMAGES:** It will cost $3,500 for a new roof.

## PHASE 1: LEGAL EVALUATION

### 1. WHAT OBLIGATIONS DID MR. SHIFTY OWE SAM?

**ANSWER:** Mr. Shifty has an obligation to deliver a home in the condition he represented it to be in. His obligation was to disclose conditions he knew about. If there was a condition he did not know about, then he doesn't have to disclose it. Mr. Shifty has a duty to act in good faith since he is involved in a transaction with Sam. The good faith obligation requires people to deal honestly with one another.

### 2: DID MR. SHIFTY PERFORM THESE OBLIGATIONS IN A SATISFACTORY MANNER?

**ANSWER:** Sam has spoken with the seller about this matter. Mr. Shifty said he never had any leaking, but the roof was old and it was inevitable that leakage would occur someday. Thus, Mr. Shifty did perform his obligations. He provided a home in the condition he represented it to be in *or* with conditions he knew nothing about. Of course, if the buyer can prove that the seller himself did experience a leaky roof, then the answer to this question would be *No.* But in this case, Sam has no such information. He's had a roofer inspect it and there is no evidence that the roof previously leaked. (If there is more than one condition the buyer is complaining about, he should evaluate each condition separately, because one condition may qualify as a breach of the seller's duty and one may not.) Because this seller has performed according to his duty, the answer is *Yes* and the score is 0.

The program instructs Sam to move to Line 6 and enter zero there. Line 6 advises Sam that there is no reason to proceed further. If Mr. Shifty has no legal responsibility, there is no reason for Sam to proceed with his case against him.

## THE CASE OF THE TARDY AUTHOR

**COMPLAINING PARTY:**   The tardy author.

**THE DISPUTE THAT AROSE:**   A publisher contracted with an author to write a book on computer technology. They paid him a $50,000 advance in return for his agreement to write the book and have it completed for editing in one year. They'd pay him an additional 5 percent royalty on each book sold. They agreed to fully market and distribute it through the US, Canada, and Australia. The author wrote the book, but it took him 1 year and 1 month. They edited it and were able to make the publication date only by hiring two more editors and promotions people. The publisher did market the book as agreed but couldn't get Australian distribution until a few months after the book was released.

**POSITIONS OF THE PARTIES:**   The author wants his full royalties. The publisher made sales of 150,000 books but it won't give the author all the royalties they agreed to because he was late submitting his manuscript. They owe him about $115,000 more if the 5 percent royalty is paid. They say that they had to hire more editors and expedite promotions because of his tardiness; thus, they should not pay his full royalty.

**THE UNDERLYING AGREEMENT:** Their agreement had mediation and binding arbitration provisions but no attorney fee provision.

### PHASE 1: LEGAL EVALUATION

**1. WHAT OBLIGATIONS DID THE PUBLISHER OWE ITS AUTHOR?**

**ANSWER:** To complete marketing and distribution as agreed and pay the author a 5 percent royalty.

**2. DID THE PUBLISHER PERFORM THESE OBLIGATIONS IN A SATISFACTORY MANNER?**

**ANSWER:** *No.* The publisher failed to pay the author the full 5 percent royalty. This amounts to unsatisfactory performance. They also failed to obtain distribution for the book in Australia until 3 months after publication. Because distribution was obtained and the sales reports indicate that order taking was not affected in any significant way, this second failure to perform would not amount to unsatisfactory performance. Applying the reasonable person standard, the publisher did perform its distribution obligations satisfactorily – although it was not to the letter of the contract. Thus, unsatisfactory performance is related only to the royalties payment. 350 points have been earned.

**3. HAS THE AUTHOR SUSTAINED LEGALLY RECOGNIZED DAMAGES AS A DIRECT RESULT OF THE PUBLISHER'S CONDUCT?**

**ANSWER:** *Yes.* The author has lost $115,000 in royalties he was entitled to under their contract. His loss was directly caused by publisher's refusal to pay full royalties.

**4.  DID THE AUTHOR HAVE A PRIOR OBLIGATION TO PUBLISHER?**

**ANSWER:**  *Yes.* The author had a duty to produce his completed manuscript in a form acceptable to the publisher in one year.

**5.  DID THE AUTHOR PERFORM HIS OBLIGATIONS IN A SATISFACTORY MANNER?**

**ANSWER:**  *Yes.* The author performed his obligation in a satisfactory manner. He produced a manuscript acceptable to the publisher. He was a month late, but the publication date was still met. The law only requires reasonable performance. The author did produce the entire manuscript and the one month delay hasn't caused any damages other than the publisher's cost of hiring a few more editors and publicists for a month. Given the entire situation, the law would find that the author has satisfactorily performed. His performance was tardy, but it was satisfactory. Thus, the author's 350 point score remains unaffected. (You will note in Question 9 that the author is assessed for the publisher's cost of hiring these extra people.)

**6.  THIS IS AUTHOR'S LEGAL EVALUATION. ENTER SCORE HERE.**

**ANSWER:**  The case evaluation analysis for the author is 350.

## PHASE 2: CASE VALUE ASSESSMENT

**7. IS THERE A DAMAGE DEFINING PROVISION IN THE AUTHOR'S CONTRACT THAT PERTAINS TO THIS DISPUTE?**

**ANSWER:** *No.* There is none.

**8. WHAT IS THE AMOUNT OF THE AUTHOR'S DAMAGES?**

**ANSWER:** $115,000, which is the difference between 5 percent royalties and what he has been paid by the publisher.

**9. WAS THE AUTHOR A CAUSE OF THE SITUATION THAT CAUSED HIS DAMAGES? (DO NOT INCLUDE ANY CONDUCT ADDRESSED ABOVE.)**

**ANSWER:** *Yes.* The author contributed to his damages in part by submitting the manuscript a month late. Instead of apportioning a percentage of his conduct, a better method would be to determine how much more the publisher paid to compensate for the tardy manuscript. He's discovered that they paid $12,500 to hire the additional help. Thus, the author's damages of $115,000 are reduced by that amount, leaving damages of $102,500.

**10. DID THE AUTHOR RECEIVE A SUBSTANTIAL BENEFIT FROM THE SITUATION?**

**ANSWER:** *No.*

**11. ENTER LINE 10 HERE.**

**ANSWER:** $102,500 is carried forward.

**12. WILL THE AUTHOR BE REPRESENTED BY COUNSEL?**

**ANSWER:** *Yes.* The author will be hiring an attorney to represent him. His agreement has no attorney fees provision, but he knows the publisher will be represented by counsel and he wants to be on equal footing. He also feels his case value warrants this extra expense.

**13.   THE AUTHOR WILL BE REPRESENTED BY COUNSEL, SO HE WILL SELECT ONE OF THE OPTIONS OFFERED.**

**ANSWER:** These parties' contract contains a binding arbitration provision. Option (c) is selected requiring the author's damages of $102,500 to be multiplied by 85% to reflect an offset for attorney fees he'll pay to obtain a judgment through binding arbitration. Thus, the author's anticipated net recovery after paying attorney fees is reduced to $87,125.

**14.   WILL THE AUTHOR REPRESENT HIMSELF OR OTHERWISE PUT SUBSTANTIAL TIME INTO HIS CASE?**

**ANSWER:** *Yes.* The author expects to spend about 40 hours at his deposition and publisher's. Since his case has a high dollar value, the arbitrator will probably allow these depositions. He intends to spend 20 hours at the arbitration or preparing. His hourly rate is $135 for a value of $8,100. Half of this amount is $4,050, reducing his net case value by that amount to $83,075.

**15.   THIS IS THE AUTHOR'S CASE VALUE ASSESSMENT. ENTER HERE.**

**ANSWER:** $83,075. The author's case value has dropped over $30,000 from $115,000 in the value assessment phase. Part of the drop in value was for his contribution to his damages and the rest was for the projected attorney fees.

## Legal Options Assessment:

**16. Is No. 11 within the Small Claims limit or is the author willing to reduce his claim to fit that limit?**

Answer:  *No.*

**17. Does the author have a written agreement signed by the publisher that contains an attorney fees provision?**

Answer:  *No.* There is no attorney fees provision. Thus, no score is earned.

**18. Does the author have a contract signed by himself and publisher that requires binding arbitration?**

Answer:  *Yes.* Their contract does require binding arbitration. The author earns 85 points for this provision.

**19. Does the author have a contract signed by himself and the publisher that requires mediation?**

Answer:  *Yes.* These parties' contract contains a mediation provision. So 15 points are scored.

**20. This is the author's Legal Options Assessment. Enter here.**

Answer:  The author has earned 100 points for his Legal Options Assessment.

## Phase 4:   Collectability Assessment

**21. Select option that relates to the publisher:**

Answer:  The publisher is a corporation; thus, 150 points are earned.

**22. THIS IS THE AUTHOR'S COLLECTABILITY ASSESSMENT. ENTER HERE.**
**ANSWER:**   150 is the author's collectability assessment.

## PHASE 5: COMPREHENSIVE CASE ANALYSIS

23.   The author's Case Value Assessment
(No. 15)                                       $83,075

24.   Enter score for value of Line 23          50

25.   Enter Your Legal Evaluation (Line 6)   350

26.   Enter the author's Legal Options
Assessment (Line 20)                            100

27.   Enter the author's Collectability
Assessment (Line 22)                            150

28.   Add Nos. 24, 25, 26 and 27               650

29.   Divide author's answer to No. 28 by 7.
Enter here and on Line 32.                     93%

30.   Enter amount from No. 11        $102,500

31.   The author's Settlement Amount:
Multiply No. 30 by No. 29 or 92%, whichever is
less.                                         $94,300

32.   The author's Feasibility Assessment:
No. 29                                         93%

## PHASE 6: CASE FEASIBILITY ASSESSMENT

**91% AND ABOVE:** "Case feasibility is very good. You should proceed forward with your case."

**PHASE 7: FORUM ASSESSMENT:** The author will first take his case to mediation. If settlement does not occur at mediation, he should feel quite confident bringing his case in binding arbitration.

**CONCLUSION:** Through working *The Pocket Lawyer Analyzer*, the author has discovered that he has a very good case. In all phases, he has scored nearly the highest score. He has also received 50 bonus points because of his high case value. He feels more confident about proceeding with his case after working *The Pocket Lawyer Analyzer*. Before he proceeds to mediation, he will conduct a Last Chance session with the head of the publishing company using the information and values he has attained from working *The Pocket Lawyer Analyzer*.

## SUMMARY OF THE FOUR EXAMPLES

By using *The Pocket Lawyer Analyzer*, our four parties have each reached different results:

**THE BUSINESS CONSULTANT AND HER COMPUTER DISPUTE:** Because Betty received a substantial benefit from the situation, she realizes her damages are less than she thought. She will repeatedly attempt to settle, using the realistic damages calculated with *The Pocket Lawyer Analyzer*. But if these efforts don't succeed, without a binding arbitration provision she will take her case to court.

**THE SKIER AND HER INJURIES:** Lois found that she partly contributed to her damages, and that her case value decreased because of that. There is no attorney fees provision, and her probability of collecting on a court judgment are risky, as well. *The Pocket Lawyer Analyzer* determined that her best result would be obtained by reaching a mediated settlement. This will save her about $9,000 in attorney fees.

**THE SUSPECT SELLER:** Sam the home buyer has saved himself a huge amount in attorney fees. With *The Pocket Lawyer Analyzer* he has discovered that the seller is not responsible for the roof condition because he did not know about it. Sam should have had the roof inspected.

**THE TARDY AUTHOR:** When *The Pocket Lawyer Analyzer* sorted out this dispute, the results were surprising. The author has a very good case. With the values and information he has obtained from *The Pocket Lawyer Analyzer*, the author can set up a Last Chance session with the publisher and has excellent reasoning for his settlement proposal. If this session doesn't succeed, his chances of prevailing at binding arbitration are very good.

\* \* \*

Each of these samples generated valuable information and calculations that gave each person what they needed to go to their next step. As you can see, The Pocket Lawyer Analyzer comes through with results in a wide variety of disputes. Coming up next: How to evaluate your opponent's case against you in "Suddenly You're a Defendant."

## — *Chapter Nine* —

# SUDDENLY, YOU'RE A DEFENDANT

---

What if you suddenly become a defendant, or you expect soon to be sued? Keep a level head, and read on. This chapter and its Pocket Lawyer Analyzer for Defendants will assist you in evaluating your next step. People become frightened when they are sued or find out they're about to be sued. This chapter will put you in the driver's seat when you're faced with the label "defendant." It is just a label, after all.

---

> If you've been named as a defendant in a complaint or expect to be, deal with it in an intelligent, empowering way.

## A Defendant Need Not Be a Victim

This chapter is for you if you've been named as a defendant in a complaint or expect to be. When served with legal papers, most people feel anger, anxiety and fear to varying degrees. You may be crippled by your feelings or you may just feel you've missed a stride. Whatever your response, it's something you'd rather not have in your life. But you needn't be a victim. Indeed, you can deal with your new role in an intelligent, empowering way.

## The Two Major Forums

The two primary legal forums we address here are the court system and the arbitration system. In the court arena, you are identified as a *defendant*. In the arbitration forum, you are a *respondent*. Whichever label you receive, they are the same – except in the court system you'll wear your label a lot longer. In both forums, you are required to respond, or a judgment will be entered against you. Each of these forums are separately discussed.

## If You've Been Served

First, you must legally protect yourself against any judgment found against you. This means reading the instructions contained in the documents you were served. The service documents are intended to give you information about what you need to do and what the case is about. In court proceedings, these documents are usually served by a process server. In arbitration, you typically receive notice by mail.

In the service documents you are given a specified time frame within which to file a response to the complaint or claim. Make sure you carefully watch your timing. By the time the response period is up, you need to have one of the following on file with the court or administering agency: a written extension of time signed by the opposing party, or a legal written response. Thus, you need to act quickly. But not *too* quickly. First you should work through *The Pocket Lawyer Analyzer for Defendants* presented later in this chapter.

## THE POCKET LAWYER ANALYZER FOR DEFENDANTS

*The Pocket Lawyer Analyzer* presented in this chapter has been tailored for defendants so you can evaluate your opponent's case against you. Be sure to work *The Pocket Lawyer Analyzer for Defendants* before you take any strategic steps. Follow the step-by-step instructions in Chapter 7 and the samples in Chapter 8 if you need help to respond to a question in the analyzer.

Armed with your evaluation of your opponent's case against you, you will make informed choices as to how to proceed. In fact, you will be prepared to claim a lead position. Why be on the defensive when you can be on the offensive? Instead of feeling victimized, as defendants often do, you can rise to a position of responsible involvement.

*The Pocket Lawyer Analyzer* will reveal the weak and strong points of your adversary's case. You can use its results to your advantage. Your adversary's strong points will reveal

> **With your evaluation of your opponent's case against you, make informed choices as to how to proceed.**

| A walk through The Pocket Lawyer Analyzer will alert you to important facts to use to negotiate with your opponent. |

a realistic settlement amount closer to his actual case value. His weak points will give you ammunition for settlement at a lower figure. A walk through *The Pocket Lawyer Analyzer* will alert you to important facts to use to negotiate with your opponent. For the most part, your results will identify legal and practical issues your opponent has most likely not yet considered.

### NEGOTIATING POINTS

In working through *The Pocket Lawyer Analyzer*, you will determine which of the following negotiating points relate to the dispute at hand:

• Does your adversary realize he won't get back his attorney fees unless you have a written contract with an attorney fee provision? This fact alone ranks high on our list of settlement motivators.

• Even if there is an attorney fee provision, rarely are full fees reimbursed. Further, your adversary must pay his attorney's bills as he goes along – an extraordinary expense most people find difficult to meet.

• With even the best case, the unpredictable can happen.

• An attorney fee provision could backfire on your opponent with an unexpected cost: *your* attorney fees.

• If the court system is the route for this dispute, your adversary will give up a good part of any judgment to attorney fees, even if there is an attorney fee provision. Rarely do attorney fee awards return all attorneys fees paid – 65 percent is the norm.

## COLLECTION ISSUES

What about collection? Your opponent may get a judgment against you, but is he assured of collecting on it? If you cannot pay, this is the time to advise your foe. If necessary, show your adversary all the debts you have accumulated. You're just not a good collection risk. If your financial picture is truly bleak, you should probably consider bankruptcy anyway. The *bankruptcy* word is settlement motivation at its best. But don't try using this shield unless your debts really do back it up. Settlement negotiations should be undertaken in the utmost of good faith.

## BARGAINING WITH YOUR POCKET LAWYER ANALYZER RESULTS

Depending upon the results you obtain, you may or may not decide to present your *Pocket Lawyer Analyzer* results to your opponent. We find in appropriate instances it is excellent ammunition for a Last Chance settlement session (Chapter 5). Its results bring a lot of legal realities to light that are often neglected in the shuffle to file a claim. Or you may choose to keep the results to yourself, using the figures as confidential guides for a settlement or mediation session. The case and settlement values recommended by *The Pocket Lawyer Analyzer* will navigate your path to settlement with your opponent.

> **Bankruptcy is a settlement motivation, but don't try using this shield unless your debts really do back it up.**

## SMALL CLAIMS COURT

> Look in the yellow pages or call the Bar Association in your area for a mediation firm that handles Small Claims disputes.

If the dispute is in Small Claims Court, you will want to consider two options. First, see if the Small Claims Court in your area has a mediation section. If so, you may be able to have your case mediated there for a nominal fee. If not, look in the yellow pages or call the Bar Association in your area for referral to a mediation firm that handles Small Claims disputes. These firms will charge far less than the big time providers.

You may ask, why even look for these alternatives when you'll be in and out of Small Claims Court in no time flat? Because your dispute – and all sides of it – will receive only about 15 minutes of the court's attention. Do you want your dispute decided with such a time limitation?

## MEDIATION SERVICES

Some locales also have specialized mediation boards for disputes between landlord and tenant, contractor and customer, and a wide range of other categories. If your dispute involves a professional license, the relevant licensing board may have a mediation section to handle disputes between consumers and its licensees. The same goes for professional associations. For instance, local bar associations often offer mediation services for disputes involving their members. Statistics show that 85 percent of cases settle at mediation. Thus, it would be worth your while to spend a little time locating a mediation resource for your case.

Another option you should always explore is to invite your adversary into a Last Chance session (Chapter 5). If none of the above pans out, private mediation may or may not be economically viable, depending upon the value of the case. Private mediation will be more expensive than the specialized mediators described above. If the case value is $2,000, private mediation costs may not be practical because it will cost at least $500 for the mediator's time. We find that even Small Claims cases take a minimum of three hours to present. Thus, proposing private mediation will depend on case value.

> Small Claims litigants often find the confidence they need with just one lawyer consultation.

### Consulting with a Lawyer

If you are headed towards the Small Claims door, we suggest you consult with counsel along the lines we've described in Chapter 13, *How to Hire A Lawyer.* Small Claims litigants moving forward on their own often find the confidence they need with just one lawyer consultation. The lawyer can serve a variety of advisory functions for you, which will make you feel all the more prepared for Your Day in Court – or should we say 15 minutes in court. Of course, this time estimate doesn't include the extensive waiting time that typically accompanies Small Claims Court. You're generally there for a half day waiting to be heard.

### All Courts Other than Small Claims

If you find yourself heading for the general court system, now is the time to propose an ADR Agreement to your opponent. Samples of these agreements are included in Chapter

> Take the reins and set up the best possible forum to decide your dispute.

12 and in the Appendix. In your new role as a defendant or respondent, you may want to succumb to the urge to procrastinate - but don't. Take the reins and set up the best possible forum to decide this dispute. It won't go away, so do your best to get past it soon with a minimum of time and money expense.

## THE MULTI-STEP ADR METHOD

We always suggest you begin with the comprehensive Multi-Step ADR Agreement described in Chapter 12 and included in the Appendix. Its three steps occur in sequence, and an optional step intervenes when attorneys come on board. If your opponent prefers a conservative approach, agreeing to one step at a time, you can cross out the remainder of the provisions or submit individual provisions. (See the Appendix for many formats).

## STEP ONE: LAST CHANCE

The first step gives you and your opponent a Last Chance opportunity to settle. This step traces the steps outlined in Chapter 5, *Last Chance*. Even if your opponent has already hired counsel – and because legal process has been filed, it's quite likely – you and your opponent are still free to communicate with one another. Now's the time to wage a unified war against attorney fees – before you're both staring huge bills in the face. If your foe won't meet for a Last Chance settlement discussion, send a copy of this book, pointing out the most noteworthy chapters. The information in this book is equally valuable to plaintiffs and defendants. It affords disputing parties an opportunity to find a better way to resolve disputes. You want the best decisions in the least amount of time with the least expense. That's what this book is about.

## STEPS TWO AND THREE: MEDIATION AND ARBITRATION

If Step One, Last Chance, does not work, Step Two is mediation. Step Three is binding arbitration. You will want to review the binding arbitration provision samples in Chapter 12 and the Appendix to determine the scope of the binding arbitration provision you propose. It is essential for you to define the procedures and discovery that will pertain to your arbitration. You may decide to limit the number and length of depositions, or to omit depositions altogether.

## STEP FOUR: DEMAND LETTER, IF SOMEONE HIRES AN ATTORNEY

If your dispute starts out with attorney representation of at least one party, this step will never come into play. The fourth elective step only applies when disputing parties are unrepresented at first, and one party hires an attorney later. The hiring party then instructs his attorney to prepare a written presentation stating his legal and factual position along with a settlement demand or offer. The unrepresented parties then respond to the offer/demand in writing.

This full set of dispute resolving options sets the stage for your dispute to resolve with the least expense and at the earliest possible time.

> **It is essential for you to define the procedures and discovery that will pertain to your arbitration.**

> Alternative dispute resolution was created to address your needs.

## A Simpler Mediation and Binding Arbitration Agreement

If you or your adversary decide the Multi-Step Agreement is too complex, then propose individual mediation and arbitration provisions or the Joint Mediation-Binding Arbitration Agreement. Samples are found in the Appendix. The difference between these agreements is that the Multi-Step contains more steps and a highly defined arbitration process, whereas the mediation and arbitration agreements comes in simpler format. Always remember: you and your foe can tailor these agreements to your needs. They're not etched in stone. Alternative dispute resolution was created to address your needs. Spell out your needs so they will be met with the help of the mediator or arbitrator you select.

## An Attorney Fee Provision Gets Everyone's Attention

If you intend to hire an attorney and you feel you will win the dispute, you should include an attorney fee provision in your agreement. If this provision is agreed to, whoever wins the dispute is entitled to reimbursement for the attorney fees they've paid. If you win your case, you would be the *prevailing defendant*. A defendant who successfully defends a case is considered the prevailing party. An attorney fee provision can bite the hand that drafted it – if it's the losing hand. If you lose, you'll be on the hook for your opponent's attorneys fees. For the winning party, it's the only provision that makes hiring an attorney worthwhile. Always think carefully before you propose an attorney fee provision.

## DO YOU HAVE A CLAIM AGAINST YOUR ADVERSARY?

An action brought against you can be responded to with an action (usually called a counter-action) against your adversary. In fact, you are usually required to bring any claim you have against your foe in the same proceedings. So, if you have a claim against this person, now is the time to bring it. It will offset your adversary's claim against you.

For instance, your accountant has sued you because you didn't pay his bill for preparing your last tax return. The reason you didn't pay is because the return was prepared incorrectly and you've been called in for an audit. You have a claim against your accountant for the taxes and penalties you'll owe if the audit does not go in your favor. Any claim you have against your adversary needs to be brought now within his proceedings against you.

Turn to Chapter 6's *Pocket Lawyer Analyzer* to evaluate *your* case against your opponent.

## WHAT IF YOU FEEL RESPONSIBLE?

If you feel you are responsible financially for the claim being made, then you may propose a *stipulated judgment* or a settlement agreement. A consultation with an attorney in your area will assist you in proposing these dispute terminating vehicles. Conduct some legal research yourself on these issues, as well. If you do come to agreement and your foe is represented by counsel, have your foes' attorney prepare the paperwork.

> If you feel you are responsible financially for the claim, then propose a Stipulated Judgment or a settlement agreement.

## STIPULATED JUDGMENTS

> **Stipulated Judgments are generally coupled with stays of enforcement meaning collection will be delayed until a stated time.**

You may settle your dispute by entering into a Stipulated Judgment. This is a judgment against you which is filed with the court. With a Stipulated Judgment, the prevailing party can enforce collection without taking any more steps. It is a valid judgment, as if a court or jury had awarded it. But why would you want to make it so easy for your opponent? Because you receive something valuable in return: a delay in collection.

Stipulated Judgments are generally coupled with *stays of enforcement.* This means that collection will be delayed until a stated time. When a defendant admits to responsibility but does not have the money to pay right now, it's a mature way to handle the situation. Consider this option, especially if you and your foe have an attorney fee provision in your written agreement. You'll save yourself from a judgment that also includes your foe's attorney fees.

### AN EXAMPLE OF A STIPULATED JUDGMENT

Suppose you have been served with a lawsuit or an arbitration demand. You feel that you are responsible, and you'd rather own up to your responsibility before spending more time and money fighting. You agree to pay $8,000 within 7 months as long as your adversary will delay collection on the judgment until then. You will receive a $1,000 credit if you pay the judgment off in 45 days. These facts are stated in a Stipulated Judgment which is signed by you and your opponent. In 7 months, you pay the judgment or your adversary can enforce it against you. A sample Stipulated Judgment is included in the Appendix.

## The Settlement Agreement

The settlement agreement proposes a full resolution of the dispute. Usually, money is paid and in return, the complaining party agrees to dismiss the claim. The settlement agreement can also include creative terms other than immediate cash payment. If you're motivated, there's no end to the settlement packages you can create.

For example, you are a contractor and you owe a friend $5,000 on a promissory note that's overdue. Your friend needs a new carport. You can agree to build a carport for your foe. The settlement agreement would contain all details about when the carport is to be built, the size, and the materials. Another example of creative settlement strategies is to establish a barter exchange instead of cash exchange. For instance, you own a hardware store. You agree upon a settlement amount of $5,000. Instead of paying cash, you give your foe a credit at your store. You will provide supplies on an as needed basis up to the settlement value. All settlement terms should be spelled out as fully as possible, so the obligations are very clear to both parties.

If the terms are not met, the court must understand exactly what was agreed to. In most states, settlement agreements are enforced by bringing a simple motion before the court. If you settle a dispute and then your

> The settlement agreement can include creative terms other than immediate cash payment.

Opponents become far more flexible when they discover their opposing party has hired counsel to meet them in battle.

opponent violates the settlement agreement, the court will step in to enforce the settlement. With a clear settlement agreement, you and your opponent will keep the settlement on track. Your opponent will also be assured that if you don't keep your promise he will have the aid of the court's strong arm.

## Hiring an Attorney

If you have been unsuccessful in settling this case through the above methods, you may choose to hire an attorney to represent you. If so, please refer to Chapter 13, *How to Hire a Lawyer: Insider Tips*. You may also choose to hire counsel for a limited mission: to advocate settlement. Yes, you've done everything *you* could to bring about settlement. Then why would an attorney do any better? It's the intimidation factor. Often, unbending opponents become far more flexible when they discover their opposing party has hired counsel to meet them in battle.

No one needs to know that this attorney's sole mission is to achieve settlement. If the mission fails, you may choose to retain that attorney to represent you in court or arbitration, or you may not. You cross that bridge when and if you come to it. But for now, every effort should be made by your selected counsel to bring about settlement. We find that a vast majority of cases settle with this important attorney-initiated step.

## Representing Yourself

If you've decided to represent yourself with or without limited attorney involvement, you must first identify the ground rules. Always obtain a copy of the rules of procedure that apply. If the court system is your forum, ask the court clerk about how to obtain their procedural rules. Although the clerks may not give legal advice, they do their best to assist people representing themselves. You may find an informal advisor who is willing to guide you, all the while admonishing that they are not giving legal advice. These advisors can be helpful.

> **Consult with a lawyer on a limited basis. For many clients a little legal hand holding makes a difference.**

Locate the local law library. Law librarians often provide limited special assistance to people attempting to represent themselves. The law library has many books about how to represent yourself. Spend some time with these books and call upon the expertise and help of the law librarian.

Of course, *The Pocket Lawyer Analyzer* gives you the legal evaluation you need. Armed with the information in this chapter and *The Pocket Lawyer Analyzer for Defendants*, presented on the following pages, you will be prepared to take on the defendant label with ease and assurance.

If you have any doubt after using these tools, you may want to consult with a lawyer on a limited basis. We have often advised clients on how to represent themselves. It provides them with the confidence and assurance they need. They handle their own case, but confer with us whenever needed, or call us in on a limited basis to respond to legal procedures on an as needed basis. For many clients a little legal hand holding makes a difference.

It's an affordable way to represent themselves and have legal guidance at the same time.

## Getting Help Working Through The Pocket Lawyer Analyzer for Defendants

- Remember, Chapter 7 guides you through the questions one at a time.

- If you are using the software version, pull up Chapter 7 on your Help menu as needed.

- Chapter 8 presents four illustrative samples of disputes worked through on *The Pocket Lawyer Analyzer,* so you may see how the results are achieved.

    And now you can proceed. Best of luck!

## The Pocket Lawyer Analyzer for Defendants

### Phase 1:    Legal Evaluation
What is your adversary's likelihood of prevailing?

**1.    What obligations did you owe your adversary? (Note here.)**

_____

_____


**2.    Did you perform these obligations in a satisfactory manner?**

☐  Yes: Enter 0 and go to Line 6
☐  No: Enter 350                                             _____


**3.    Has your adversary sustained legally recognized damages as a direct result of your conduct?**

☐ Yes:  Enter value of Line 2
☐ No:  Enter 0 and go to Line 6                          _____

**4.    Did your adversary have a prior obligation to you?**

☐ Yes: **(Note here)**

_____

_____


☐ No: Go to Line 6

**5. Did your adversary perform the obligation in a satisfactory manner?**

☐ Yes: Enter score from Line 3
☐ No: Enter 0 here and on Line 6                     _____

**6. Your adversary's Legal Evaluation. Enter last value here, not to exceed 350.**
**If total is 0, do not proceed. Skip to Phase 6**         _____

---

**Phase 2:   Case Value Assessment**
**How much is your adversary likely to recover?**

**7. Is there a damage defining provision in a written contract that pertains to this dispute?**

☐ Yes:  ☐ A. Enter *liquidated damages amount*, or      A.$_____
        ☐ B. Enter damages *limit*                    B.$_____
☐ No:   Enter 0                                       _____

**8. What is the amount of your adversary's damages?**

Select <u>one</u> option:

If 7A checked, enter that amount                      $_____

If 7B checked, enter damages – 7B as maximum          $_____

Otherwise, enter your adversary's actual damages      $_____

**9.   Was your adversary a cause of the situation that caused these damages? (Do not include conduct addressed above.)**

☐ Yes:  Reduce Line 8 by $ amount or percentage your adversary's conduct contributed to their damages (use 50% if unsure) and enter here

☐ No:  Enter value from Line 8                                    $_____

**10.   Did your adversary receive a substantial benefit from the situation?**

☐ Yes:  Reduce Line 9 by $ amount or percentage to reflect value to your adversary (use 50% if unsure) and enter here

☐ No/Unknown:  Enter value from line 9                           $_____

**11.   Enter Line 10 here**                                       $_____

**12.   Will your adversary be represented by counsel?**

☐ Yes: Go to Line 13
☐ No/Unknown: Go to Line 14

**13.   If your adversary will be represented by counsel, select <u>one</u> of the following options.**

☐ A.  A contract signed by you and your adversary contains both an attorney fee and binding arbitration provision. Enter the amount from Line 11.                                $ _____

☐ B.  A contract signed by you and your adversary contains an attorney fee provision, but no binding arbitration provision.
Enter 80% of Line 11                                              $_____

☐ C.  A contract signed by you and your adversary contains a binding arbitration provision, but no attorney fee provision.
Enter 85% of Line 11                                              $_____

☐ D. There is no attorney fee or binding arbitration provision in a written contract between you and your adversary.
Enter 65% of Line 11                                              $_____

☐ E. There is no written contract between you and your adversary. Enter 65% of Line 11                          $_____

**14.   Will your adversary be representing himself *or* otherwise putting substantial time into this case?**

☐ Yes:  What is the approximate value of the time your adversary will put in? $_____. Divide this amount by 2 and enter here:  $_____.Deduct this amount from last value above (Line 11 or Line 13) and enter here

☐ No:  Enter last value here                                     $_____

**15.   Your adversary's Case Value Assessment.
Enter Line 14 here.**                                            $_____

## Phase 3:   Legal Options Assessment
### What are your adversary's legal options?

**16.   Is Line 11 within Small Claims limit or are you willing to reduce your claim to fit that limit?**

☐  Yes: Select one option
    ☐  If you have a binding arbitration provision in a written contract with your adversary:
        ☐  that excludes Small Claims cases, enter 125
        ☐  that does not exclude Small Claims cases, enter 0
    ☐  Enter 125 if above options don't apply
☐  No: Enter 0                 _____

**17.   Do you have a written agreement signed by you and your adversary that contains an attorney fee provision?**

☐ Yes: Will your adversary be hiring an attorney?
    ☐ Yes: Enter 50
    ☐ No: Enter 25
☐ No: Will your adversary be hiring an attorney?
    ☐ Yes: Enter 0
    ☐ No: Enter 25           _____

**18.   Do you have a contract signed by you and your adversary that requires binding arbitration?**

☐ Yes: Enter 85
☐ No: Enter 0                 _____

**19.  Do you have a contract signed by you and your adversary that requires mediation?**

☐Yes: Enter 15
☐ No:  Enter 0                                              _____

**20.  Your Adversary's Legal Options Assessment.
Add 16 through 19 above, enter here**                       _____

## Phase 4:   Collectability Assessment:
**What are your adversary's chances of collecting on a judgment?**

**21.   Select the <u>first</u> option that relates to you:**

☐   if you are a corporation, enter **150**
☐   if you will be represented by an insurance company, enter **150**
☐   if you are an operating business other than a corporation,
        enter **140**
☐   if you own real property, enter **130**
☐   if you have assets *and* are salaried, enter **120**
☐   if you have assets and work for self as a sole proprietor,
        enter **110**
☐   if you have assets and none of above apply, enter **90**
☐   if none of above or below apply, enter **75**
☐   if you have other judgments against you, enter **50**
☐   if you have no assets or means of support, enter **40**
☐   if you have bankruptcy proceedings pending, enter **20**   _____

**22.   Your Adversary's Collectability Assessment.
Enter score from 21 here**                                  _____

## Phase 5: Comprehensive Case Analysis

23. Enter your Adversary's Case Value Assessment
from Line 15                                              $_____

24. Check the box below that relates to the value of Line 23:

☐  if within Small Claims limit, enter **50**
☐  if above $50,000, enter **50**
☐  if between $45,001 and $50,000, enter **45**
☐  if between $40,001 and $45,000, enter **40**
☐  if between $35,001 and $40,000, enter **35**
☐  if between $30,001 and $35,000, enter **30**
☐  if between $25,001 and $30,000, enter **25**
☐  if between $20,001 and $25,000, enter **20**
☐  if between $15,001 and $20,000, enter **15**
☐  if between $10,001 and $15,000, enter **10**
☐  if above Small Claims limit but less than
    $10,001, enter **5**                                 _____

25. Enter Your Adversary's Legal Evaluation from
Line 6                                                   _____

26. Enter Your Adversary's Legal Options
Assessment from Line 20                                  _____

27. Enter your Adversary's Collectability
Assessment from Line 22                                  _____

28. Add Lines 24, 25, 26, and 27                         _____

29. Divide Line 28 by 7 and enter here                   _____%

30.   Enter amount from Line 11 here                          $_____

31.   Your Adversary's Settlement Amount:
Multiply Line 30 by Line 29 or 92%,
whichever is <u>less</u>                                        $_____

32.   Enter percentage from Line 29: Your Adversary's
Feasibility Assessment [See Phase 6 for rating]           _____%

## Phase 6:   Case Feasibility Assessment Chart

**_91% and above_:**  Your adversary's case feasibility is very good. They should proceed forward with their case.

**_81% to 90%_:**    Your adversary's case feasibility is good. They should proceed forward with their case, but it is in your adversary's best interest to make best attempts to resolve your dispute through Last Chance Exercise and mediation first.

**_71% to 80%_:**    Your adversary's case feasibility is reasonably good. If binding arbitration is their route, they should move forward – but if there is an attorney fees provision, your foe should be aware that if they lose, they must pay your attorney fees.  If binding arbitration is not your adversary's route, they should proceed forward with their case only after proposing a Multi-Step ADR Agreement or Binding Arbitration Agreement [See Appendix]. If your consent is not obtained, your foe should pursue their case only after repeated attempts at settlement. Your foe must remember: they may be in this category with a winning case and the best chances of collection, but since they must travel the court maze, their feasibility is reduced.

___*61% to 70%*___:   Your opponent's case feasibility is mid-range.

•If there is a Binding Arbitration Agreement but no attorney fee provision, your foe should proceed forward. The dispute will be determined soon and your adversary won't be paying your attorney fees if they lose. But first, attempt settlement and mediation.

•If there is a binding arbitration provision and an attorney fees provision:

1.   If your foe is at the high end of this category, they should proceed forward with the reminder that if they lose they will pay your attorney fees.

2.   If your opponent is at the low end of this category, they should carefully consider their risk of losing and being hit with your attorney fee tab. Your foe should do everything possible to settle this case and proceed cautiously thereafter.

• If there is an attorney fees provision and no binding arbitration provision, your opponent should lean more in favor of pursuing this dispute only insofar as settlement is concerned. It may not be worthwhile to take this case into the expensive court forum, especially considering their exposure with an attorney fees provision. If they must, your foe should proceed cautiously.

• If there is no attorney fee provision or binding arbitration provision, your adversary should proceed only if they are at the high end of this category.  Otherwise, it may not be worthwhile to take this case into the expensive court forum.  If they must, your foe should proceed cautiously.

___*51% to 60%*___:   Your foe should make every attempt to settle this dispute at the suggested settlement figure. Your opponent should remember: if there's an attorney fees provision and they lose, they will have to pay your attorney fees. If your foe will have a slim chance of collecting a judgment, perhaps it doesn't make sense to proceed. If your foe's case value is low and they must travel the demanding court system, they may very well not want to go the long haul. If your opponent is on the low side of this range, their feasibility indicates they should not pursue their case. Otherwise, they must proceed very cautiously.

*50% and below*: Your foe is discouraged from pursuing the case to judgment. Let your opponent know that, and it will help you reach settlement. Your adversary should encourage settlement again and again. After that, one mediation session is warranted. In view of mediation's 85% success rate, your realistic attitude and your opponent's low feasibility rating, the chances of success at mediated settlement are good.

*0 in Phase 1, Legal Evaluation:* Your adversary's case against you is not good. Although you still have to take legal steps to protect yourself, you should do so with assurance.

---

## Phase 7:   Forum Assessment.
## Where will your foe pursue this dispute?

33.    If yes to 18, skip to Line 38 and enter binding arbitration

34.    If yes to 19, mediation must be completed before choosing a forum.  Check the box at Line 38.  But proceed, to see what follows mediation.

35.    Enter damages from Line 8 here                                   $_____

36.    Enter Small Claims limit here:                                         _____

37.    Check option:

☐ If 35 is the same as or less than 36, enter "Small Claims" on Line 38

☐ If your adversary has already filed a claim or lawsuit, enter the forum indicated on Line 38

☐ If 35 is more than 36, enter "general civil court system" on Line 38

**38.   Enter Your Forum Here:**_____
☐ **If mediation first, check here.**

# — *Chapter Ten* —

# MEDIATION MECHANICS: YOUR KEYS TO SUCCESS

Chapter 3 introduced you to mediation. Now, this chapter takes you through its doors. How did you get here? What can you expect now? What is the mediator's role? And how can you best achieve settlement? Chock full of tools and tips, this chapter will ensure mediation success for you and your dispute.

| Access media-<br>tion by signing<br>an agreement<br>to mediate with<br>your opponent<br>before or after<br>your dispute<br>begins. |
| --- |

## YOUR MEDIATION: KEYS TO SUCCESS

With some wise planning, you can achieve optimum results at your mediation. Here are the primary keys to your success:

- Hold the mediation session early on before emotions and attorney fees are high.

- Choose the right mediator: an experienced professional qualified to serve as a mediator and skilled in the area of law of your dispute.

- Act on your conciliatory state of mind. As parties who agreed to mediate, you and your opponent have a new, conciliatory attitude. Your main goal now is to get past your dispute and move on. Keep this in mind throughout your mediation proceedings.

If you cover these steps, your chances of walking out of mediation with a signed settlement agreement are excellent.

## HOW DID YOU GET TO MEDIATION?

You access mediation one of two ways: by signing an agreement to mediate with your foe before your dispute began, or afterwards.

**PRIOR AGREEMENT TO MEDIATE:** You previously signed a contract with your opponent stating that any dispute arising later between you is to be mediated. Mediation provisions are becoming more and more common in contracts. In fact, as we bridge to the 21st century, mediation is becoming the first door entered by disputing parties. If you have a written agreement, review it to determine if there is such a provision.

> **The best time for mediation is when your dispute begins.**

**AGREEING TO MEDIATE AFTER YOUR DISPUTE BEGINS:** You can agree to mediation at any time after your dispute begins. You and your opponent simply sign a form submitting your dispute to mediation. See the forms provided in Chapter 12 and the Appendix.

## PROPOSING MEDIATION

The best time for mediation is when your dispute begins. If the parties are not yet represented by counsel, consider proposing an agreement to all parties to participate in the mediation process without lawyers. (See the Appendix for a sample form.) There are some powerful arguments for mediating without counsel. You can share these arguments with your opponents when you propose mediation:

- **NEEDLESS EXPENSE:** Why incur fees for more legal beagles when it isn't necessary?

- **FAIRNESS:** The mediator listens equally to all parties. Because mediation is a cooperative, conciliatory process, you don't need an attorney advocate at your side.

- **RELEVANT LAW:** You select the right mediator, you'll have the necessary legal whiz on board. (See "Where Do You Find a Mediator" later in this chapter). You will hire someone trained in the area of your dispute.

If you don't
have a good
grasp of your
legal position,
hire an attorney
to appear with
you.

## PREPARING YOURSELF

If you decide to attend without an attorney in tow, make sure you understand and can state the legal and factual issues of your case. Yes, the mediator you choose will have background in the relevant area of law. But you need to be informed. Mediation is a settlement process. Each party needs to understand their position, legally as well as factually, and be aware of possible outcomes. Why? Because meaningful solution comes from negotiations, and negotiations need persuasive elements – such as legal position and facts of the case.

## DO YOU NEED A BRIEF PRIMER SESSION WITH A LAWYER?

If you don't have a good grasp of your legal position, it may be a good idea to hire an attorney to appear with you – or at least to prime you in the legal issues before your mediation.

We often conduct primer sessions for clients. We provide a memorandum about the law as it relates to their matter, then we discuss the high and low points of their case. In most instances, clients come away from a mediation primer session feeling well prepared and confident about the upcoming mediation. Sometimes we also prepare mediation briefs for our clients. These briefs provide the mediator with advance knowledge of the case. The brief also serves as our client's legal guide to present the case at mediation and respond to the mediator's questions.

### Your Lawyer's Role

Must you have a lawyer for your mediation? *No.* The mediator, by definition, is an informed go-between whose objective is to guide you and your foe to settlement. Many people do hire a lawyer, but it is not required. If you've already hired an attorney and the adversarial process has begun, it is a good idea to include your lawyer. Just tell your lawyer of your decision to mediate.

### If the Lawyer Balks, You're the Boss

Suppose your lawyer feels mediation is a waste of time? You can insist on it, if you wish. You hired your attorney. You're the boss. Issue a directive. Tell your attorney the truth. Before you commit yourself to the expense and rigors of arbitration or litigation, you want to exhaust all settlement options. This includes mediation.

Some lawyers will respond negatively because they are threatened by alternative dispute resolution methods. Some feel your best result will not come through settlement. Others are intimidated because they have little experience with the new methods, and are not sure how they work. And a handful of lawyers see settlement procedures as a threat to fees they may earn. To them, apparently, your interests don't come first. But you will find that the majority of lawyers will agree it is best to attempt solution early on. Endorsement of mediation by the courts is a powerful factor in the changing attitudes of lawyers.

> **The mediator is an informed go-between whose objective is to guide you and your foe to settlement.**

## WHERE DO YOU FIND A MEDIATOR?

If you and your opponent agree to mediate, you both sign a form submitting your dispute to mediation. Send the agreement to the mediation firm specified in your contract, or if none, to a mediation firm you mutually select. Many agreements state that mediation is to be conducted under the rules of the American Arbitration Association (AAA). With this provision, you have choosen AAA as mediator.

If your signed agreement does not specify a mediation firm, select another mediation provider that both parties agree to.

## ELECTING ANOTHER MEDIATION PROVIDER

The parties can always select another mediation provider as long as all parties agree. If not, the forum is the one designated in the written agreement. If your contract does not specify the agency to preside over the mediation, you and your disputant are free to elect any mediation agency you choose. If you cannot agree on a single mediator, select some neutral way to have the selection made. Some clients toss a coin. Others agree upon a large mediation firm, but cannot agree on which mediator. Then they often ask the impartial administrator at the mediation agency to make a random choice for them. A ranking system, where you and your foe rank your choices among several mediators, is also an option.

## CONTACTING PROVIDERS

As ADR becomes more popular, mediation providers are increasing in number. They can be found in your yellow pages under Mediation or Mediation Law or as a specialty under Attorneys and by contacting the Lawyer Referral Service of your local bar association.

## THE AMERICAN ARBITRATION ASSOCIATION: THE QUALITY LOW COST PROVIDER

The American Arbitration Association (AAA) was one of the first providers of mediation services. As the largest provider in the nation and the world, AAA is the primary choice for a mediation provider. With 36 offices nationwide, the AAA sets the standard and rules for mediation. Their comprehensive mediator training program provides carefully screened qualified applicants with essential mediator tools. As a not-for-profit corporation, AAA strives to provide these essential services and qualified panel members at a very reasonable price.

> The American Arbitration Association (AAA) is the largest mediation provider in the nation and the world.

As a direct result of AAA's contributions to mediation and its success, a rising number of businesses across the United States are improving their profit margin by choosing to mediate their disputes. After I received my mediator training from AAA and submitted a number of mediations to their panel, I found their mediation services to be excellent.

## JUDICIAL ARBITRATION AND MEDIATION: THE JUDICIAL PANEL

When ADR began taking off nationwide, the judges who spent years sitting on the bench banded together and created Judicial Arbitration & Mediation Services – Endispute (JAMS). It is the second largest ADR provider with over 30 offices nationwide. Their cost is much higher than AAA, but their panel members are primarily retired judges with years of experience hearing cases just like yours. So, if you feel more comfortable with your dispute

| Your mediation's success or failure depends on your choice of mediator. |
| :--- |

decided by a retired judge and the extra expense of this luxury is worth it to you, you may want to select JAMS – Endispute as your provider.

## SELECTING THE RIGHT MEDIATOR

Your mediation's success or failure depends on your choice of mediator. Of course, willing participants are fundamentally important to a successful mediation. But without the skill and training of the mediator, emotionally distracted parties generally cannot bring about their own settlement. This is why you're here. You need every bit of skill and experience your mediator can offer. If you follow our recommendations, they will help assure your best chance for settlement.

## THE MEDIATOR SKILLS TO LOOK FOR

Your ideal mediator has the following attributes:

- Formal mediation training, including facilitation, negotiation, and psychology techniques. Mediators trained by AAA fit this category.

- Extensive mediation experience.

- Broad knowledge of the subject matter of your dispute.

- Settlement navigator: A good track record.

- Scholar: Experience in cases like yours and relevant law.

- Legal Therapist: Experience with angry disputants and assisting in the release of such emotions.

- Reframer: Experience in altering the attitudes of participants.

- Scribe: Offering on-the-spot generation of settlement agreements.

> Select a mediator with formal mediator-psychological training and who conducts a large number of mediations.

## BACKGROUND AND TRAINING

You want to select a mediator with formal mediator-psychological training, who conducts a large number of mediations, and has broad knowledge of the subject matter of your case. Ask for a biography addressing each of these issues. Ask for their training history, the number of cases they facilitated and a summary of their experience with the topic of your dispute. Because most mediators are practicing attorneys or retired judges, you want to know this mediator has experience handling cases similar to yours.

Some retired judges who provide ADR services, including our own consulting author, Judge McGuire, are particularly well suited to mediation. But many are not. Although such judges make excellent arbitrators because of their judicial experience, they sometimes make less than effective mediators. They are used to the battles of the courtroom and are unaccustomed to a conciliatory atmosphere. If you gather information on the backgrounds of your potential mediators and carefully review that information, you will find a skilled and highly competent mediator.

| When you select the right mediator, his credentials make him an expert with your dispute. |

## THE MEDIATOR'S EXPERTISE IN YOUR DISPUTE

Recall the settlement negotiator from our Chapter 5 *Last Chance*. The mediator now assumes that role. And rightly so. When you've selected the right mediator, his credentials make him an expert with your dispute.

Mediators typically charge a high hourly rate, but the reality check they provide is invaluable. The mediator can share war stories about litigation or arbitration – often the perfect motivation for wrapping up a settlement package. With the right mediator, you'll have even more factors in favor of settlement:

- Often, the mediator is an attorney or retired judge who handled many cases similar to yours.

- Your dispute is familiar – through the legal arena and all the way to its final conclusion.

- Your mediator can recite the price tag and time it took to get through trial.

- You'll learn the probable outcome of your case.

Of course, when you're in the middle of your dispute you think there's never been one like this before. Bank on it – in the eyes of the judge or the jury, they all come down to a simple set of facts. Your case is nothing special to anyone but you.

## THE MEDIATOR'S OTHER ROLES

What are the traits of your ideal mediator? You consider these in order to evaluate a nominee as mediator for your dispute. It's not just the mediator's expertise that is important. It's the ability to master many roles. Most mediator's have completed psychological training in how to facilitate negotiation. They are masters of psychological technique and intervention. They can orchestrate a full range of settlement postures. These traits qualify the mediator for his or her most important job – to whittle away the settlement gap between the parties.

These are only a few of the roles played by mediators. They are instrumental in bringing the mediation process to its present level of success. As you can see from this brief glimpse, the mediator's job is truly comprehensive. The roles played by a good mediator range from legal therapist to settlement navigator to jurisprudent scholar, reframer, and finally, legal secretary. If the mediation is successful, as it is 85 percent of the time, your dispute is concluded. For this reason, most feel the mediator is as valuable as gold. In one day, a mediator can turn a bloody and expensive battle into a one-page settlement agreement.

## THE MEDIATION IN PROGRESS:
## INITIAL PROCEDURES

The mediation begins with all participants in one room. The mediator is the conductor – the facilitator – for your mediation. The mediator first makes introductions and reviews procedure. The parties are asked to sign

> **When you're in the middle of your dispute you think there's never been one like this before.**

**The roles played by a good mediator range from legal therapist to settlement navigator to jurisprudent scholar, reframer, and legal secretary.**

a confidentiality agreement promising to hold discussions confidential. In other words, the parties are asked to commit to the confidentiality of the process. They are also advised that, under evidentiary procedures governing the mediation, they may not disclose facts or documents submitted by another party at the hearing. Of course, the submitting party can always present its own evidence again later, in arbitration or trial, if those procedures become necessary. This initial sequence reinforces the session as one of conciliation, encouraging open communication.

## JOINT OPEN DISCUSSION

The parties are then openly encouraged to share their version of the facts by making an opening statement. The claimant (plaintiff) will usually go first and present a factual description of how they see the case. The respondent (defendant) follows. Some mediators, depending upon their training, recite both sides back to the parties in a joint statement. This process is called mirroring. Although it sounds redundant, it is an excellent communication tool. It serves a dual purpose as you hear someone else objectively describe your case, and you can check that description for accuracy. You may hear your story in a whole different way – including its flaws. This initial joint session is vital for the following reasons:

- Each party is encouraged to hear the other point of view

- Each party has an opportunity to air its own position

- The mediator identifies the key issues of the dispute

Of course, the mediator will most often have a Mediation Brief or Position Paper in hand from each party before the mediation begins. But it is still important at this initial joint session to give the parties an opportunity to hear each case perspective described aloud. Some parties may choose to waive an opening statement, feeling they adequately expressed their position in their written statement. The Joint Open Session draws to a close after case descriptions, at which time the mediator begins separate caucusing sessions. This introductory phase is usually the only time the mediation is held in joint session – until its conclusion.

> In separate caucuses, the mediator discusses issues that may be barriers to settlement.

## SEPARATE CAUCUSING

In a typical sequence, the caucusing process now begins. Its goal is negotiation. The mediator meets privately and separately with participants. In this very interesting behavioral process, he or she groups and regroups most advantageously as situations realign. Caucusing may begin with the complaining party, with or without attorney, or with one of the responding parties. Selection of the first caucusing party is the mediator's choice, depending upon the circumstances. For best caucusing, the mediator may require the use of several rooms to separately caucus with each party, and provide a separate private room for a party to evaluate settlement, when the mediator moves on to negotiate with another party. The American Arbitration Association

> **Most settlement agreements arising from mediations are enforceable in court.**

typically provides the mediator and parties with several caucusing rooms.

In these separate caucuses, the mediator discusses issues that may be barriers to settlement, shares war stories regarding possible results in later arbitration or litigation, and elicits settlement offers and demands. A true go-between, the mediator shuttles back and forth making offers, advocating positions, registering demands, and answering questions. Information you provide may or may not be shared with other parties, depending upon your instruction. If you want something kept confidential, let the mediator know. He or she will follow your instruction.

### NEGOTIATION SESSIONS

The mediator continues to caucus separately with the parties, whittling down the settlement gap by eliciting demands and conveying offers. The process continues until agreement is reached, or until the mediator decides that negotiations have gone full circle and there is no agreement. If the gap is closed, the mediator brings the parties together and advises that a settlement is reached, reciting the settlement terms. If the mediator determines there will be no settlement, the parties reconvene and are advised that negotiations have reached a natural conclusion without settlement. The mediation hearing is concluded. The parties are invited to contact the mediator again if a position changes, or the parties feel a continued session may be beneficial.

## SETTLEMENT

After a long session climaxing with settlement, the parties need written confirmation of exactly what they agreed to. The mediator then performs the role of legal recorder and prepares the parties' agreement in a written document. The mediation is not adjourned until all the settling parties have signed. Only after the agreement is prepared and signed is the mediation process complete. For these housekeeping reasons, most traveling mediators "have computer and printer that will travel." Not all mediators provide this service. Ask in advance if your mediator does. If not, you must ensure that someone will be able to perform this important task.

> There is no limit to the solutions available in a mediation with a creative facilitator and willing parties.

### YOUR MEDIATION SETTLEMENT: AN END TO THE BATTLE

Most settlement agreements arising from mediations are enforceable in court. This means that such an agreement is truly an end to your dispute. If a party reneges on the agreement, you can take it to court for enforcement.

### SOME CREATIVE MEDIATION SETTLEMENT PACKAGES

In mediation, you can get very creative. Money is not the only form of compensation. Although money is clearly the traditional way of compensating people for legal wrong, mediation is not traditional. It's the cutting edge. As such, mediation invites new methods of addressing legal problems – and new solutions generate new bargaining chips.

Tailor a settle-
ment package
with non-cash
demands that
works for your
opponent by
finding out
what he wants.

Outside the rushed court system, mediation focuses time and attention on creative
means to settlement. There is no limit to the
solutions available in a mediation with a creative facilitator and willing parties. The parties
are willing to mediate because they can avert
the legal system. For example, a settlement
may involve cash, barter of services, materials,
or an agreement to refrain from doing something.

## CASE EXAMPLES:
## CREATIVE MEDIATED SETTLEMENTS

Here, we present some telling examples
of creative settlements coming out of mediations. They each illustrate one of mediation's
finest achievements – assisting the parties to
create their own settlement.

- Settlements for other than cash
- Cash now as a settlement persuader
- Identifying the real dispute
- You'll win but you'll never collect, so settle Now
- Disputants utilize their talents to achieve settlement

## THE CASE OF THE GUILTY PARTNER

Cash settlement isn't necessarily the
only alternative. In fact, admitting you are
wrong might completely take its place. Consider a mediation that arose from an investment transaction. The claimant had an excellent case for fraud. The parties were in partnership for a few years. The claimant's potential recovery was in excess of $235,000. Had

we stopped there, without exploring the injured investor's demand drawer, we would have fished for cash – a difficult means to settlement. But during our second separate caucus we discovered that the investor was willing to settle for a package deal. He did not have the package put together. But we were able to tailor a package that worked for him by finding out what he wanted.

> **Mediation proceedings are confidential. Any admissions made during the settlement process are not admissible later in court or arbitration.**

The package consisted of several non-cash demands:

1. An admission by respondent to the limited partners that several statements he made were incorrect.

2. Withdrawal of the partner from the partnership.

3. An agreement not to compete in a similar transaction for five years, backed by a $300,000 pledge if he did breach.

4. Amendment of his tax return to transfer tax benefits he claimed to the limited partners.

Because mediation proceedings are confidential and inadmissible in any later dispute between the parties, a party can feel free to make admissions as part of the settlement process. If settlement does not come about and the dispute later goes to trial or arbitration, any such admissions are inadmissible for any purpose. They are completely veiled from disclosure. Thus, the mediator and the parties are free to creatively tailor settlement discussion and their written agreement.

> **Some mediations have nothing at all to do with the underlying dispute.**

A mediator skilled in creative settlement was the key to resolution of this dispute. The parties signed a settlement agreement containing the terms described. Following the mediation, a more detailed long form agreement was prepared based on the terms agreed to at the mediation.

### INSTANT GRATIFICATION CUTS THE BILL IN HALF

In just about any purchase, a cash offer up front can yield a good discount. The same applies to mediation. Each participant is at a different crossroads in life. One party's most important need right now may be cash. This party may be willing to compromise as much as 60 percent for a cash settlement. In one recent mediation, it became apparent the complaining party felt this way. I structured the settlement amount to decrease if payment was made in a shorter window of time. Three schedules were agreed to, each with a different bottom line. The schedule with pay off in 30 days was $35,000 less than the one with pay off in one year. That was the perfect inducement for the responding party to obtain cash she just couldn't find before.

### THE GREAT WIDGET COMPROMISE

Incredible as it may seem, some mediations have nothing at all to do with the underlying dispute. Sometimes the claimant just won't leave the other party alone until he feels compensated. In these situations I've been known to spend most of my caucusing time finding out what the frustrated party needs in his life. In a separate caucus, I determine which needs the responding party can fill. It's purely the law of supply and demand. In one such matter, the complaining party needed a better priced source for a particular widget. The responding party had access to such a source. By the way, their dispute had nothing to do with commercial enterprise. Their dispute related to a vacation home investment. We recessed the mediation for a week to give the responding party a chance to put the widget contract together. A week later we reconvened, the widget contract was in place and acceptable, the parties signed a settlement agreement and dismissed the case, which was pending in the court system. They also released the services of their attorneys, which to date had collectively billed $17,879 in fees. These parties learned that the legal system is expensive, especially when it comes to a judgment regarding fraud in a real estate investment transaction. After all they had spent, widgets did the trick.

> Your court judgment is nothing more than a piece of paper unless the loser has the means to pay it.

## THE CASE OF THE GLUED GAS LINES

If you win in court, will you be able to collect? The answer to this question can bring you to mediation instead of going to court.

Some people who know about the legal system will forego their egos and demand to stay out of the court system. Mediations are running an 85 percent success rate. After an unsuccessful mediation, however, when the next step is the court system, we find the success rate soars to about 90 percent. These days, the terrors of the court system are well known. What's more, your court judgment is nothing more than a piece of paper unless the loser has the means to pay it.

**You may be certain to receive a substantial judgment for your case, but may have to pay more attorney fees to collect.**

In one mediation everyone, including the guilty contractor, agreed the work he did was hazardous, defective, and in multiple violation of the uniform building and plumbing codes. The most flagrant violation occurred when the contractor punctured the gas pipes he installed, and instead of replacing them, he made it worse by applying epoxy and tape to the pipes. Everyone, including the claimant-owner and the guilty contractor, agreed that his shoddy workmanship and his reckless disregard of building codes caused serious damage to claimant's project. Without punitive damages, just based on out-of-pocket reconstruction costs, the owner's actual damage exceeded $71,000. Nonetheless, at their mediation the claimant-owner let the contractor out of the case for only $12,000. Why?

At mediation, a lot of realistic thinking comes into play. Instead of focusing on the substantial award the owner could receive from the contractor at trial, the principal issue was how much the owner would actually *collect* from the contractor. The owner-builder contract did contain an attorney fee provision which entitled the prevailing party to reimbursement for attorney fees. And each party incurred substantial fees. The owner paid $19,000 to date. The contractor paid nearly $13,000.

No one doubted that the owner would receive a substantial judgment and a substantial attorney fees award. But could the owner collect on the judgment? The contractor claimed imminent bankruptcy. He produced several other judgments against him and a stack of outstanding bills. Sure, the owner would undoubtedly receive a big judgment, but would have to pay more attorney fees to get there.

These mediation discussions are confidential, and can't be used in court. The contractor nearly admits fault, but vows to claim innocence in the court action. He fought this case all the way and intends to continue. His contractor's license is at stake.

In a separate caucus with owner and her attorney we calculate it may take another $16,000 to get to trial and obtain a judgment. Given the probability that owner will never collect a cent on her judgment from the contractor, the owner quite realistically looks to saving the $16,000 in future attorney fees.

We recessed the mediation for three weeks for the owner to realistically consider dismissal. During this period she hired an investigator to confirm some of the financial information produced by the contractor at the mediation. She also confirmed that the contractor had his bankruptcy option available to him. She also met with her accountant to consider any tax advantages from this situation. On the other hand, the contractor set off to scrape $12,000 together.

When we reconvened three weeks later the owner dismissed her case against the contractor in return for $12,000. As part of the settlement, the contractor also agreed to give up his contractor's license for three months, complete a course of study focusing on safety in the contracting trade and submit to a reexamination by the licensing board. The

> A mediator's skillful application of supply and demand and the realistic projection of the post-trial result can make a settlement successful.

**Use your nego-
tiating skills to
remedy the
woes of the
disputant.**

contractor's licensing board was cooperative and agreed to oversee this process.

The mediator's skillful application of supply and demand and the realistic projection of the owner's post-trial result made this settlement successful. Had the mediator not explored the contractor's financial ability, his inability to pay would not have become known. It was this very assessment that motivated the claimant-owner to bring the attorney meter to a halt. In fact, compared with her best possible result after a prolonged trial, the owner decided she was in pretty good shape, cutting her losses now.

One impediment to settlement still existed. The owner didn't want this contractor to do the same thing to another innocent homeowner. Tailoring a license rehabilitation agreement was the mediator's answer. This mediation took only ten hours to complete, instead of a lengthy expense-ridden road to trial.

### REAL ESTATE AGENTS TO THE RESCUE

In another instance, the disputants were able to use their talents to settle their matter. In this mediated settlement, a real property transaction was cancelled. Usually, when a transaction is cancelled, a seller who defrauded a buyer takes back the property. But here, the parties' innocent real estate agents knew that this lawsuit was going to be too expensive for them. Even though they felt they would not be found liable, these agents knew the realities of real estate litigation. Being involved in real estate and exposed to the rigors of litigation for many years, they decided to do anything they could to keep this dispute from heading toward trial. The real estate market was their place to make deals happen. The agents used their negotiating skills to remedy the buyer's woes.

> It doesn't matter what the need for each party is or who meets it. What matters is the need is identified and filled.

The buyer no longer wanted the property he bought. The seller failed to disclose things about the property which made it undesirable. The buyer agreed to list the property for sale with these agents, as long as the agents found a comparable property for the buyer to purchase. Because of their contacts in the real estate field, the agents were able to find a comparable property. Then they listed the disputed property for sale, finding a buyer in two months. The agents waived their commissions on both transactions, but it was worth it. Settlement occurred and they got past the whole dispute.

The guilty seller ended up contributing very little to the settlement cancellation package, but the buyer was compensated by obtaining a new home at no additional cost. This case was pending in the court system for five months. Settlement concluded with a full dismissal. It took this mediator a day and one-half to put this settlement package together. The mediator's masterful facilitation and the real estate agents' realistic attitudes kept this case from running a lengthy and expensive route through the court system.

> **Binding arbitration is approached after the mediator determines that settlement is not possible.**

Both real estate agents did well in the real estate business over the years. They proscribed to the principle that these situations were a cost of doing business. They were willing to quickly and effectively do whatever they could to end this dispute without paying hard cash. Through their services, they were able to meet the needs of the complaining party. It doesn't matter what the need is or who meets it. The need was identified and filled.

## WHAT IF YOU DON'T SETTLE AT MEDIATION?

If you know you have done all you can to avert disaster, your conscience is clear. Parties interviewed after unsuccessful mediations are nevertheless pleased that they pursued all possible settlement processes before moving on to the battle. They realize that the next step, whether it be court litigation or arbitration, will be grueling and expensive. They feel that mediation was a wise detour before invoking the warrior tactics.

And what is their next step? If they have entered into a Binding Arbitration Agreement, arbitration is next. If they have not, the court system will be their forum. If they decide they prefer to expeditiously and economically resolve their dispute, they may now elect binding arbitration. In fact, many of our best mediators sign up the parties for binding arbitration if the mediation session fails to conclude in settlement.

Binding arbitration is approached after the mediator determines that settlement is not possible. If the parties do not already have a Binding Arbitration Agreement, they are asked for their interest in signing such an agreement. Often, although the mediating parties did not achieve settlement, they decide against the court system and on binding arbitration as their legal forum. This makes them feel the mediation session was well worth the time and expense.

## SHOULD YOU LET THE MEDIATOR SERVE AS ARBITRATOR?

Many confidential disclosures and positions taken at mediation would not be inappropriate at arbitration.

If you proceed into arbitration, you do not want to hire the mediator who just heard your dispute. Although it may seem more cost effective, many confidential disclosures and positions taken at mediation would be inappropriate at arbitration. Arbitration is an adversarial procedure, while mediation is purely conciliatory in nature. The two must be kept separate. While sitting as mediator, I have been asked by a number of disputants who just can't agree on a resolution to take off my mediator hat and become an arbitrator. They were so sick of their dispute they just wanted it over with, and further efforts to agree on resolution just weren't working. They asked that I take the information I have and make a binding decision in favor of one or the other. I have refused.

First, it gives the parties an easy way out and robs them of mediation's most satisfying opportunity: to find the solution themselves. Second, the mediator has a conflict of interest and is performing a disservice to the parties if he allows himself to serve in these dual roles. Although I often sit as mediator in some cases and arbitrator in others, the roles are very different and cannot be confused. So do not ask your mediator to arbitrate your dispute. Take these two steps separately.

*  *  *

There is no solution more satisfying and long lasting than the one you achieve yourself. 85 percent of mediating parties will emphatically agree. The other 15 percent, for whom settlement is elusive, would do well to choose arbitration as their next step. If they don't, they will have no choice but to spend years and hard earned bucks traveling the court maze. Hopefully, arbitration is your choice. If it is, Chapter 11 will escort you through the arbitration process for a quick and easy end to your battle. If arbitration is not your choice, Chapter 13 will guide you through your lawyer hiring process, while Chapter 14 will help you make the most out of the court system.

*— Chapter Eleven —*

# THE ARBITRATION ARENA: YOUR KEYS TO SUCCESS

We introduced you to arbitration in Chapter 4. Now, you've chosen arbitration and need to prepare for it. Here's your escort into the arbitration arena, from agreement to hearing. Armed with the fruits of this chapter, you'll be able to set up and streamline your arbitration for optimum results in a minimum of time. And because time is money, spending strategic time setting the stage before you get there can make all the difference. Your mini-trial is about to begin.

## YOUR ARBITRATION: KEYS TO SUCCESS

> You want a fair chance to have your dispute heard and decided by an arbitrator with skill, experience, and wisdom.

There are two basic keys to arbitration success. When we use the term *success* here, we don't mean only the best legal result. Time and cost savings are just as important. A successful arbitration controls both time and expense. Why? You're there because you don't want a long, drawn out, expensive, draining experience. You want a fair chance to have your dispute heard and decided by an arbitrator with skill, experience, and wisdom.

The two keys to get the job done are:

- Selecting the right arbitrator
- Controlling discovery

You can set up your arbitration for maximum success utilizing these two keys.

### KEY ONE: SELECT THE RIGHT ARBITRATOR

The first key is to select the right arbitrator. Later in this chapter, we discuss the selection process in detail. Select someone, preferably an attorney or retired judge, who has extensive experience in the subject matter of your dispute. After all, this individual will be judging your dispute and you want someone who has substantial experience in your dispute subject matter.

### KEY TWO: CONTROL DISCOVERY

The second key to your arbitration's success is to control discovery. Fact-finding discovery can be limited in your arbitration agreement for optimum benefit and least expense. You'll want to agree to a discovery package that meets the needs of your dispute. In some cases, that may take only one 4-hour deposition per disputant. In others, it may allow production of documents by each party. In still others, it may include written questions to one another. What are *you* going to need? Some parties choose to forego expensive discovery altogether and proceed directly to arbitration, discovering the other parties' positions for the first time in the arbitration proceedings. This latter group of disputants decide they want to put their cards on the table just once, do the best they can, get a judgment and move on from there.

> **Set up your arbitration with the right arbitrator and discovery plan, to be on your way to a judgment that makes sense.**

Once you set up your arbitration with the right arbitrator and the appropriate discovery plan, you'll be well on your way to receiving a judgment that makes sense. These key factors will be fully explored later on in this chapter. First, let's take a look at how you've reached the arbitration door.

## HOW DO YOU GET TO ARBITRATION?

You always come through the arbitration door with an agreement signed by you and your disputing parties. No one can be compelled to arbitrate unless they agree to do so. This is different from the court system. The court system is a legal right that comes along with living in the United States. Everyone can use it and everyone must respond to it – otherwise the court will automatically impose a judgment against the non-responsive party.

## WHY MUST YOU HAVE A WRITTEN AGREEMENT TO ARBITRATE?

> Once the Binding Arbitration Agreement is signed, each party gives up the right to use the court system.

Because arbitration is not an automatic legal right, you cannot *make* your opponent use it. Your opponent must voluntarily agree to it. The agreement must be in writing. It may be signed by the parties before the dispute arose, or it can be an agreement the parties are now signing amidst the dispute. See the Appendix and Chapter 12 on *Loss Prevention* for form agreements.

Why must the agreement be in writing? Because the disputants are giving up their legal right to have their dispute decided by the court system. Once they sign the arbitration agreement – as long as it is *binding* arbitration, as opposed to advisory arbitration – they have no right to use the court system to decide this dispute.

Because these important legal rights are affected by arbitration agreements, the legislature has created stringent rules for writing and wording these agreements. In some industries, a certain bold type and specific wording must be used. For this reason, in the next chapter we recommend use of the most detailed provision if you are preparing an arbitration agreement. In this way, although your provision may be overly detailed and specifically formatted, it should assure your goal – to enter the arbitration door and close the gates to the court system.

## HAS YOUR AGREEMENT ALREADY SPECIFIED YOUR ARBITRATOR?

Since arbitration is by written consent, you must follow the terms of your arbitration agreement. The arbitration provider listed in your arbitration agreement will be your arbitrator. Of course, you and your opponent may agree later to another provider. But without later consent by all, the arbitrator nominated in the written agreement rules.

Generally, the agreement names an arbitrator. If the provision states, "under the rules of the American Arbitration Association," the American Arbitration Association will serve as arbitrator. Sometimes the agreement states, "to be arbitrated by an arbitrator of the parties' choice." Leaving arbitrator choice to the disputing parties is not a good idea. Such an open agreement is strongly discouraged. Because disagreement is already in the air, and the party whose conduct generated the dispute is usually uncooperative, agreement is often impossible. In this situation, the party seeking arbitration must petition the court to appoint an arbitrator. It's a costly extra step that should not be necessary. So always make sure your arbitration provision clearly nominates a specific arbitrator to hear your dispute.

> **Leaving arbitrator choice to the disputing parties is not a good idea and is strongly discouraged.**

## HOW TO FIND AN ARBITRATOR

If you're drafting your own arbitration agreement or supplementing an agreement that fails to appoint an arbitrator, you'll want to know how to locate one. First, call the American Arbitration Association (AAA) and talk to them about their services. They have a

> **Retired judges can be ideal for arbitrations, because they have the relevant experience and background.**

toll free number (888-873-0000) which will guide you to their office closest to your location. Tell them the nature of your dispute. They have many different panels of arbitrators, each carefully selected for their expertise with certain types of disputes. Ask them to send you a copy of their rules relating to your matter. Or, visit their web site at http://www.adr.org.

You may also want to call Judicial Arbitration & Mediation Services (JAMS)— Endispute at 800-352-5267. If AAA or JAMS—Endispute is not your choice of forum, proceed to the trusty yellow pages. As ADR is becoming popular, more arbitration providers can be found in your yellow pages under Arbitration or as a specialty under Attorneys and by contacting the Lawyer Referral Service of your local bar association. Given the high acclaim ADR is receiving, new arbitration providers are popping up all over the country. But the two providers we've mentioned are the biggest and best.

### RETIRED JUDGES: A VALUABLE ARBITRATION RESOURCE

Many of these arbitration firms were created by retired judges who, depending upon their expertise on the bench, should have considerable experience with your type of dispute. We find retired judges to be ideal for arbitrations because they have the relevant experience and background. You might ask, then, "Why are they so good off the bench when their results in court were sometimes less than perfect?" Our response: the problems on the bench arose from complicated legal procedures and a serious lack of time to devote to cases.

These problems don't come up in arbitration. Formal legal procedures are relaxed. The parties can also schedule as much of the arbitrator's time as they choose. And for that time, they have the arbitrator's focused, dedicated attention. The only drawback to using the services of a retired judge is cost. They often charge twice the price of non-judicial arbitrators. How valuable is it to you to obtain the best arbitration decision? Only you know the answer.

> In arbitration, the parties can schedule as much of the arbitrator's time as they choose.

### SPECIALIZED ARBITRATORS

In the age of specialization, even arbitration providers are specializing. For instance, because I am a real estate broker and attorney, my alternative dispute resolution company hears primarily real estate, construction, and contract disputes. In this way, we can provide top-notch expertise to your dispute and cut down on the explanation and time needed to digest complicated, lengthy documents. For the most part, we know these documents by heart after seeing them over and over again.

Thus, if your dispute concerns employment law, it may be wise for you to locate a provider that hears only labor matters or lists arbitrators who specialize in labor law. The American Arbitration Association has several specialty panels for a wide variety of disputes.

### YOUR FIRST KEY TO SUCCESS: SELECTING THE RIGHT ARBITRATOR

Once you find out which firm will be your provider, there's an important step to take before you open the door to arbitration

> **It is in the best interest of all parties to hire an arbitrator with a high degree of authority, competence, and experience.**

success. You have to pick the correct arbitrator at the firm you've chosen. Most firms have a lengthy panel of arbitrators from whom to select.

All parties to the dispute should strive to work together on arbitrator selection. It is in the best interest of all parties to hire an arbitrator with a high degree of authority and competence, and a generous helping of experience in the subject of your dispute. Even if you don't have cooperation from your adversary, your efforts *alone* can ensure selection of the right arbitrator. The result of the arbitration depends largely upon the competence and expertise of your arbitrator. If the right steps are taken, your arbitration will be on the road to success.

### AAA's Arbitrator Selection Method

For instance, if you submit your dispute to the American Arbitration Association, they will give you a list of arbitrators from the specialized panel you select. Arbitrator resumes will help you evaluate the candidate's qualifications. Some resumes reference prior arbitrations they've heard. You are encouraged to call candidates with specific questions you may have. If references are not included, you may want to call attorneys in your area for their prior experiences with this candidate. Each party is entitled to confidentially select the top three arbitrators they feel would be best for their dispute. Each party is also entitled to strike out the candidates they feel are least suitable. AAA takes each partys' selections and attempts to select the arbitrator who received top positioning, making sure another party did not strike this candidate from their list.

If your choice was one of the firms providing retired judges, they too will have a list of candidates for you to choose from. First, ask the firm to provide you with biographies of judges who have experience handling the topic of your dispute. Review those biographies. Second, have other disputants praised the arbitrator candidate's work? Ask the firm to share those compliments with you. Otherwise, call the law librarian at your local law library and ask if they have a compendium of arbitrators which lists past arbitrations heard by each person. If so, review that arbitrator's past record. Check around with attorneys who practice in the area where the judge or attorney is located. By the time you complete your investigation, you will have enough information to make an informed arbitrator choice.

Sometimes parties have agreed upon an arbitration provider, but they cannot agree on which arbitrator to use. In these situations, it is a wise choice to ask the impartial administrator at the arbitration agency to make a random choice for you.

## YOUR SECOND KEY TO SUCCESS: CONTROLLING DISCOVERY

Your second key to arbitration success is to take control of discovery. You chose arbitration because it was inexpensive and fast. Discovery is the biggest gobbler of time and money in law. So, what is this thing we call discovery? It's a set of legal procedures to discover facts about the dispute. *Deposition* is the favorite of

> **Take control of discovery to limit expenses and your time commitment.**

> **Discovery is a set of legal procedures to discover facts about the dispute.**

these methods. A deposition is an oral question-answer process whereby one party is questioned by another. Either you or your attorney may ask the questions. This testimony is given under oath and is recorded by a court reporter.

## COSTS OF DISCOVERY

The process is expensive. Often a deposition of one person takes an entire day. Your attorney's time is close to $2,000 for the day. You've spent a day of your own valuable time either being questioned or observing the process as an *interested party*. The court reporter's services cost close to $1,000.

The philosophy behind arbitration is to save time and money. In that spirit, if discovery is not controlled, the goals of your arbitration are not being met. Some attorneys proceed into arbitration as they would in court – with a full arsenal of discovery techniques to launch at their opponent. If you're being represented, it's up to you to tell your attorney, early on, that this is not your intent. Your intent is to save time and money, while obtaining the fairest result possible – and discovery should be limited.

## DISCOVERY TOOLS AVAILABLE TO YOU

If your case is valuable and you feel it is important to discover facts before the arbitration hearing, there are several ways to accomplish your mission. Written questions, called *interrogatories,* can be sent to your opponent to be responded to in writing under penalty of perjury. Documents can be obtained from your

opponent by making a written demand speci-
fying which documents you want to review.
Depositions can and should be limited to a
certain time frame – such as 3 or 4 hours –
with the agreement of your opponent. It is in
both of your interests to save money. In many
cases, depositions just aren't necessary. The
expense outweighs their benefit.

## LIMITING DISCOVERY

> If you are
> drafting an
> arbitration
> agreement, this
> is the time to
> cover the
> scope of dis-
> covery for your
> arbitration.

If you are drafting an arbitration agreement, this is the time to cover the scope of discovery for your arbitration. If you've just submitted your dispute to arbitration, review your
arbitration agreement. It may already define
discovery rights. For example, in California, if
an agreement says the parties have the right to
discovery in accordance with California Code of
Civil Procedure §1283.05, that section defines
the scope of their discovery.

In other states, there are similar provisions. In each state you must review discovery
provisions to determine their scope. The California rule states that you can conduct any
discovery you could have conducted in the
court system, except depositions can be taken
only with the permission of the arbitrator. If
your agreement does not address discovery
rights, now is the time to draft an agreement
defining the discovery you want in your case. It
is clearly in the best interest of all disputing
parties to define discovery rights. So, seek your
opponents' cooperation in achieving this goal.
Chapter 12 and the Appendix contain examples of arbitration provisions that limit rights
to discovery.

| Arbitration is vastly different from mediation. Consider representation by counsel to protect your interests. |
|---|

## Your Lawyer's Role

Since arbitration is an adversarial process in which many of the formalities of court trials are adhered to, you should seriously consider representation by counsel. Remember, arbitration is vastly different from mediation. Your mediator's role was as a neutral evaluator and facilitator. As such, the mediator evaluated and balanced out the interests of you and your opponent. In arbitration, no one protects your interest or evaluates your case. All you've got is you. The arbitration process is almost identical to a court trial, except the rules of evidence and other procedural formalities are somewhat relaxed. Other than that, it's adversarial and confrontational. Due to these factors, in most instances it is worthwhile to hire counsel to represent you. See the guide for making that hiring decision, below.

## Hiring a Lawyer for Your Arbitration: How to Decide

Your decision to hire a lawyer will be based upon several factors:

- How much is the case worth?
- Is there a provision to recover your attorney fees in the underlying contract?
- What are your chances of winning?
- How confident do you feel representing yourself?

You discovered these answers by using *The Pocket Lawyer Analyzer*. Chapter 13 entitled *How to Hire a Lawyer: Insider Tips* covers the lawyer hiring process in more detail.

> **If the dispute amount does not justify hiring attorneys, move ahead without counsel.**

If there is no right to recover your attorney fees and you decide to represent yourself, you may want to obtain an agreement from your opponent that he will not be represented by counsel either. At least you and your opponent will be on even ground without attorneys. If your opponent goes back on his agreement and shows up at the arbitration with counsel, you will have good cause to ask the arbitrator for a *continuance* of the hearing so you can hire a lawyer. If the amount in dispute does not justify hiring attorneys, it is wise for all disputing parties to move ahead without counsel.

## PERHAPS A CONSULTATION IS ENOUGH

If you have decided to represent yourself, a brief attorney consultation is highly recommended. You can bet your opponent has done the same thing. We often sit down with clients who are pursuing Small Claims or arbitration cases and step through the facts, law, strong points, and weak points with them. More often than not, we prepared their Small Claims or Arbitration Brief for submission to the court or arbitrator. This document guides them through their presentations. Clients have found these aids give them the knowledge and confidence that makes all the difference.

| An arbitration is similar to trial, except it does not take place in a courtroom. |
| --- |

## THE ARBITRATION IN PROGRESS: PROCEDURES

An arbitration is similar to trial, except it does not take place in a courtroom. No judge sits in robes behind an elevated bench to preside over the hearing. There is no jury to weigh the evidence. Instead, there is an arbitrator – or a panel of several, if your agreement so specified – who sits at a conference room table with the parties and their counsel, if they are represented. Aside from these factors, the hearing itself is nearly identical to trial.

In advance of the hearing, each party submits a position paper to the arbitrator outlining the case's history, its status and their legal position. The hearing proceeds:

- Each party is invited to summarize or supplement the information they presented in their written statement. Often, in order to save time and money, parties forego this opportunity, standing on their written summary.

- Then, the complainant puts on its witnesses and each party is given an opportunity to cross-examine.

- Each respondent then puts on its witnesses and each party is given an opportunity to cross-examine.

- Each party then gives a closing summation.

- The arbitrator advises that the matter is taken under submission and a decision will be mailed to the parties. The decision is generally received within a month.

## DIFFERENCES FROM THE COURT TRIAL

**THE ARBITRATION HEARING ITSELF:** Yes, arbitration is similar to the court trial – in fact, it is appropriately referred to as a mini-trial. This is fitting, because an arbitration takes far less time, complicated evidence and procedure rules are discarded, and because there is no jury, points are driven home with far less repetition. Furthermore, arbitration comes about shortly after the dispute arose, when memories are fresh and issues targeted. In the court trial, the incident usually happened years before. The facts have become convoluted with the passage of time. Unfolding mounds of discovery make the issues much more complex. Due to these differences, the arbitration hearing itself typically takes only 20 percent of the time a jury trial would take.

**WHAT YOU'VE DONE TO GET THERE:** The other more notable difference is your journey along the road to arbitration. The court system is a forum where expensive paper wars take place. Depositions, motions, and other costly adversarial techniques are encouraged. And it's time consuming. Before you entered your trial courtroom you've spent several years battling your opponent. You are frustrated and at wits end. But when you convene your ideal arbitration hearing, it's early in your dispute. You've taken very few preliminary steps, and you're in a forward-moving rhythm toward resolution. Arbitration, then, is streamlined in every sense of the word.

> Arbitration comes about shortly after the dispute, when memories are fresh and issues targeted.

| From begin-<br>ning to end,<br>arbitration is a<br>swift, consis-<br>tent process. |
| --- |

**EMOTIONAL TOLL:** Litigation in the court system is an emotional experience. From beginning to end it is fraught with emotion. If you're the plaintiff, your case usually begins with a hefty deposit to your lawyer. If you're the defendant, it starts when a process server intrudes upon your privacy; then comes your hefty lawyer deposit. Over several years, you relive the experience that brought you here through emotional surges along the way: depositions, interrogatories, document productions, endless questions and answers. Then comes the dramatic trial, with one emotional day after the next. Finally, you experience the crescendo when the judge or jury renders the verdict. In one quick moment, the drama you've been living for years is decided.

Arbitration does not create an emotional roller coaster like the court system does. From beginning to end, arbitration is a swift, consistent process.

**A LESS ADVERSARIAL TONE:** If you're the complaining party, you file a submission form with the arbitration firm you and your foe have selected. It's not a lengthy complaint, using legal terminology as is required in the court system. It's a simple factual statement. As the responding party, you receive a notice in the mail that an arbitration proceeding is pending, and advising you of the responsive procedures. It's not adversarial in tone; it's more like a business arrangement. In the court system the parties are designated as John Doe *versus* Jane Doe. The process is confrontational in every sense. In arbitration, the designations are John Doe *and* Jane Doe. This designation carries with it a more professional air. It indicates a matter involving people, without designating one against the other.

**A DIRECT ROUTE TO YOUR JUDGMENT:** After you transmit your arbitration submission to your provider, an arbitrator is selected. Shortly thereafter, you're at the arbitration hearing presenting your case. The process is swift and to the point. When arbitration participants adhere to its philosophy of minimal time and expense, it is truly a forward-moving process. Unlike the court system, there are few discovery proceedings and legal maneuvers. It's a direct route from your dispute to its termination. In these times of high technology, we don't have time to wrestle with our disputes for years. Arbitration is clearly dispute resolution's cutting edge.

**RECEIVING THE RESULT IN PRIVATE:** Arbitration also concludes in a more professional, less emotional manner. Instead of being hit with the winner-loser report on the spot, in open court, you receive the arbitrator's decision in the mail. This gives you the comfort of receiving important news in the privacy of your home, instead of the tense litigation environment. For all of these reasons, arbitration is a more mature way of dealing with our legal differences.

## YOU CAN'T APPEAL THE ARBITRATOR'S DECISION

Generally, there is no appeal from an arbitration award. The decision of the arbitrator is final and becomes a non-appealable judgment against the losing party. There are a few situations where *collusion* is present. But these are extremely limited situations. Thus, the

> When arbitration participants adhere to its philosophy of minimal time and expense, it is a forward-moving process.

| Draft your arbitration agreement to refine the award making process. |

award of the arbitrator is considered final in every sense of the word.

There are ways to draft your arbitration agreement to refine the award making process. You can require the arbitrator to issue a tentative decision, thereafter reviewing each side's written objections thereto, before a final decision is made. A sample arbitration agreement including this stipulation can be found in Chapter 12 and the Appendix. This process allows the parties to point out any error in the arbitrator's decision before it becomes final, which is an important step that almost replaces the appellate process – but at a fraction of the cost. It gives you one more chance to state your case.

### NON-APPEALABILITY: WHAT ARE ITS ADVANTAGES?

Why is arbitration's non-appealability feature a good thing? In the court system, you finally get to trial after years of backlog, only to find that the losing party often files an appeal. Then you've got another few years to battle it out in the appellate court – using up the money, time, and emotional investment that comes with it – before you can be deemed the victor. After six or seven years warring over one dispute, you certainly don't feel like a winner. And your bank account is no longer your treasure.

In arbitration, when the arbitrator makes a ruling you're done. You've presented your case, you've had your best shot. You have no choice. It's over! Now it's time to move on with the rest of your life. In the long run – it's a much better choice than a lengthy, costly appeal.

As long as you've followed the steps we recommend, you have done the best job you can and received the best result. On those few occasions when you feel you haven't received your best outcome, you've only spent a few months getting there – not seven stressful, financially draining years of your life. Arbitration is the choice of forward-thinking people who just don't have years to surrender to a legal dispute.

\* \* \*

Chapters 10 and 11 escorted you through the mechanics of mediation and arbitration – the two alternative methods of dispute resolution that help you avoid the multiple costs of going to court. But you're about to acquire an even more powerful tool: how to head off legal losses in the first place. Read on for Chapter 12's primer, Loss Prevention: Heading Off Disputes.

# — Chapter Twelve —

# LOSS PREVENTION: HEADING OFF DISPUTES

Legal disputes may come about, but did you know you can protect yourself against them? How? By building loss prevention into every business relationship. After reading this chapter you will be aware of loss control provisions that should be written into every contract you sign. If there's no contract, create one. You'll now have the tools. You can set up your future so you will never again get into a lengthy court battle. With a full array of loss control provisions you will handle your future legal disputes with ease and confidence. Here follows your mini-course in loss prevention.

> **Include loss prevention provisions in a written agreement with any business transaction continuing in the future.**

**Disclaimer of Liability: Laws differ all over the country. Procedure in one state may be entirely different than in another. The provisions we suggest below are generally acceptable in most states, but you are cautioned to confirm validity in your particular locale.**

## HEADING OFF LOSSES

You can conduct loss prevention in advance when you enter into any business transaction that will continue into the future. You hire an employee, a computer consultant to set up and maintain your system, a contractor to renovate your downstairs bathroom. All of these relationships will continue. Therefore, they have potential for problems.

Include loss prevention provisions in a written agreement with each of these people, even if they are providing a service to you at home. Protecting yourself should always reach your home as well as business.

## THE LOSS PREVENTION TERMS YOU NEED

Along with the general terms of your arrangement, your written agreement should provide for three things – possibly four.

- First, the parties agree to mediate any dispute that later arises.

- Second, they agree to submit their dispute to binding arbitration if mediation does not succeed.

- Third, the arbitration winner is entitled to receive an award of the attorney fees they spent to get there.

- The fourth and optional provision is to liquidate (fix) or limit damages. Damage control will protect you when you agree in advance to specify or limit the damages due if someone fails to complete his obligation.

> **Make sure any contract you sign contains provisions for attorney fees, mediation and arbitration.**

These provisions are included in this chapter and the Appendix, and they are available through the Order Form at the back of this book.

## HOW TO INTRODUCE YOUR LOSS PROVISIONS INTO A CONTRACT

You are about to hire a contractor to install some skylights in your house. You interview three contractors, obtain estimates and hire one. Make sure the contract contains provisions for attorney fees, mediation and arbitration. Most contracts omit many of these provisions. And when they do appear, their terms are inadequate. Our Loss Prevention Agreement that follows, available through the Order Form, includes all of these provisions.

Before you sign any contract, cross out any of these provisions that appear in it, and present your own. It's simple. Attach the Loss Prevention Agreement we've provided and mark *"See Attached Loss Prevention Agreement"* prominently above your signature. Also sign the agreement attachment. Let the other party know what you're doing. If the drafting party objects, show them this chapter so they may understand that these provisions best protect *both* your interest and theirs. In essence, they are getting free legal advice in the form of sound legal provisions. These terms will ensure

> Loss provisions will ensure that any later dispute will go first to mediation, then to arbitration, if necessary.

that any later dispute will go first to mediation, then to arbitration, if necessary, and the winner will get their attorney fees back. That's what most informed people want.

## LOSS PREVENTION AGREEMENT

I. ANY AND ALL DISPUTES ARISING OUT OF OR RELATING TO THIS CONTRACT OR ITS SUBJECT MATTER SHALL PROCEED AS FOLLOWS:

STEP 1: THE PARTIES SHALL CONSULT AND NEGOTIATE WITH EACH OTHER, IN GOOD FAITH, AND ATTEMPT TO REACH A JUST AND EQUITABLE SOLUTION SATISFACTORY TO ALL PARTIES. IF THEY DO NOT REACH SUCH SOLUTION WITHIN 45 DAYS, THE NEXT STEP SHALL BE FOLLOWED.

STEP 2: ANY SUCH DISPUTE SHALL BE SETTLED BY BINDING ARBITRATION PRECEDED BY MEDIATION, BOTH ADMINISTERED BY THE AMERICAN ARBITRATION ASSOCIATION [OR ADR SERVICE OF YOUR CHOICE], AND JUDGMENT ON THE AWARD RENDERED MAY BE ENTERED IN ANY COURT HAVING JURISDICTION THEREOF. ANY CLAIM THAT MAY BE BROUGHT WITHIN THE SMALL CLAIMS COURT IS EXCLUDED FROM ARBITRATION. THE PREVAILING PARTY IN ARBITRATION SHALL BE AWARDED FEES PAID TO THE MEDIATOR AND ARBITRATOR AND THE MEDIATION-ARBITRATION ADMINISTRATOR.

THE INTENT OF ARBITRATION IS TO CUT COSTS, PARTICULARLY DISCOVERY COSTS. THUS, THE PARTIES SHALL HAVE ONLY THE FOLLOWING RIGHTS TO DISCOVERY:

(1) WRITTEN DISCOVERY: AS TO EACH ADVERSE PARTY, A PARTY MAY USE ANY COMBINATION OF 35 OF THE FOLLOWING:
   A. INTERROGATORIES WITH NO SUBPARTS.
   B. DEMANDS TO PRODUCE DOCUMENTS OR THINGS.

C.  REQUESTS FOR ADMISSIONS.

(2) DEPOSITIONS MAY BE TAKEN ONLY WITH THE CONSENT OF THE ARBITRATOR.

(3) ANY AND ALL OTHER DISCOVERY, EXAMINATIONS AND INSPECTIONS MAY BE CONDUCTED ONLY WITH THE CONSENT OF THE ARBITRATOR.

**BY INITIALLING IN THE SPACE BELOW YOU ARE AGREEING TO HAVE ANY DISPUTE ARISING OUT OF THE MATTERS INCLUDED IN THIS PROVISION DECIDED BY NEUTRAL BINDING ARBITRATION PRECEDED BY MEDIATION AND YOU ARE GIVING UP ANY RIGHTS YOU POSSESS TO HAVE THE DISPUTE LITIGATED IN COURT OR BY JURY TRIAL. YOU ARE GIVING UP YOUR RIGHTS TO DISCOVERY AND APPEAL EXCEPT AS PROVIDED HEREIN. IF YOU REFUSE TO SUBMIT TO MEDIATION OR ARBITRATION AFTER AGREEING TO THIS PROVISION, YOU MAY BE COMPELLED TO MEDIATE OR ARBITRATE. YOUR AGREEMENT TO THIS PROVISION IS VOLUNTARY. I HAVE READ AND UNDERSTAND THE FOREGOING. (/S/ INITIALS OF PARTIES.)"**

II.  IN ANY PROCEEDING INVOLVING ANY DISPUTE BETWEEN THE PARTIES TO THIS AGREEMENT RELATING TO MATTERS ARISING FROM THIS AGREEMENT OR ITS SUBJECT MATTER, WHETHER IN CONTRACT, TORT OR OTHERWISE, THE PREVAILING PARTY SHALL BE AWARDED ATTORNEY FEES BASED ON THE ACTUAL TIME INCURRED BY THE ATTORNEY FOR THE PREVAILING PARTY FOR THOSE SERVICES NECESSARY TO BRING THE DISPUTE TO JUDGMENT.

## Loss Prevention: Attorney Fees

> **Attorney fees generally cannot be recovered unless the contract signed by the parties provides for it.**

In most states, each party to litigation or arbitration pays their own attorney fees. As we're all aware, attorneys are very expensive. Generally, attorney fees can only be awarded in a dispute if a contract signed by the parties includes a term awarding attorney fees to the prevailing party. Without an attorney fees provision, the prevailing party frequently comes out a loser. This is especially true after lengthy involvement in the court process. Attorney fees can easily exceed your judgment amount.

Some one-sided contracts cover attorney fees by stating that only one party is required to pay them, and does not limit payment to the prevailing party. However, some states have laws that apply these one-sided provisions to both parties, requiring the losing party in litigation or arbitration to pay the other's attorney fees. The provision is thereby made *reciprocal*.

## Read a Contract Carefully Before Signing

Because attorney fees generally cannot be recovered unless the contract signed by the parties provides for it, look for such a provision before signing a contract. Does the contract provide for an award of attorney fees to the prevailing party? If it does, it strengthens the position of the party more likely to win, and weakens the position of the party more likely to lose. Why? Because the winning party is entitled to reimbursement of its attorney fees *in addition* to damages claimed in the lawsuit or arbitration.

## WITHOUT AN ATTORNEY FEE PROVISION THE WINNER CAN BE A LOSER

The expense of a lengthy court battle can only be justified when there is an attorney fee provision. Without one, even if you win, your recovery is diminished by the fees you have paid. And attorney fees can be a substantial chunk. In fact, sometimes the attorney fees spent getting through the court maze are higher than any recovery you achieve.

Thus, without an attorney fee provision you and your opponent would be wise to settle for less. Lack of an attorney fee provision is quite often the most powerful reason for settlement. Otherwise, all you'll do is make attorneys richer and prove the old adage: In legal battles, the attorneys are the only ones who come out ahead. But now you know better. As you evaluate your dispute with *The Pocket Lawyer Analyzer*, you know the significance of an attorney fee provision.

In too many situations, clients have found themselves winners at trial but losers when they tally the attorney fees they paid to get there. In one case where there was no attorney fee provision, a business owner sought recovery of $42,000 in lost profits. After 3 depositions, hiring an expert and a 4-day trial, the attorney fees had run up to $31,000. The business owner won. She recovered all $42,000. But her win was expensive. After paying $31,000 in attorney fees to get there, her net result was only $11,000. She didn't feel like a winner.

> **Lack of an attorney fee provision is quite often the most powerful reason for settlement.**

> An attorney fee provision generally entitles the winner to attorney fees, but only a portion of attorney fees are awarded.

## A Narrow Attorney Fee Provision

Armed with a sound attorney fee provision, you can head off inadequate fee awards caused by vague attorney fee terms. A typical attorney fee provision reads as follows:

> IN ANY DISPUTE RELATING TO THIS CONTRACT, THE PREVAILING PARTY WILL BE ENTITLED TO REASONABLE ATTORNEY FEES TO BE DETERMINED BY THE COURT OR ARBITRATOR.

This provision is *inadequate* to best protect your interests if you win.

An attorney fee provision generally *entitles* the winner to attorney fees. Note the word *entitles*. There may be entitlement, but in the real world, only a *portion* of attorney fees are actually awarded. To establish an award of *reasonable* attorney fees, often the court or arbitrator uses a schedule or other system. Such a system has little relationship to actual fees paid. Sometimes the fee award is related to the amount recovered. Some awards are calculated on what *reasonable* attorney fees *should* be in a perfect world. Since there is no perfect world in litigation, fee awards based on these unrealistic principles are also unrealistic.

For the most part, attorney fee awards are disproportionate to actual fees paid. The award is sometimes only one-half of the fees you paid. If your matter is decided by an arbitrator, and not the court, you have a far better chance to be awarded an amount closer to your actual fees paid. Why? The arbitrator is often a practicing attorney who realizes your attorney's time was necessary to represent you adequately.

More often than not, however, valuation results in reimbursement of 65 percent of a party's out-of-pocket attorney fees. Even the winner of an award feels like a loser. For this reason, we suggest the use of the broader provision that follows, which directs the court or arbitrator to make an award based on *actual* time spent. It doesn't guarantee you'll get full fees, but at least it does issue the instruction.

> Attorney fee awards are disproportionate to actual fees paid, and are sometimes only half of the fees paid.

## THE ATTORNEY FEE PROVISION MAY NOT APPLY TO YOUR DISPUTE

Sometimes the *typical* attorney fee provision does not apply to your case. The court may find that the dispute does not involve the contract; thus, your attorney fee provision is useless.

## AN EXAMPLE

For instance, you buy a home and bring an action against your seller because the seller misrepresented the condition of the property. The court finds that the seller was less than candid and awards you all the damages you seek – except your attorney fees. The court states, "This was not an action under the contract." Your action was for misrepresentation; so the attorney fee provision doesn't apply. What a shock to the defrauded buyer who spent $17,000 in fees, banking on his attorney fee provision! To avoid this appalling problem, your provision should be broadened to include *any* type of dispute. See the broadened attorney fee provision that follows.

> When considering your attorney fees provision, remember that it can work against you as well as in your favor.

## A Word of Caution

When considering your attorney fee provision, remember that it can work against you as well as in your favor. It all depends upon whether you win or lose. With a narrow fee provision, the blow may not be so bad if you're the loser. If you win, though, you may not feel like you've taken the cat bird seat. Evaluate the win/lose scenarios when you're proposing fee provisions in any of your transactions. Each transaction and each dispute scenario is different.

## A Broader Attorney Fee Provision

There's no guarantee that the court or arbitrator will find that the broadened provision relates to your dispute, or that they will award your full attorney fees, but your chances are better with a broader, more specific provision.

The following provision extends an attorney fee award to *any* dispute, and specifies *actual* fees paid. You will have a better chance of the court or arbitrator finding that the attorney fee provision extends to *any* dispute arising from the agreement or relating to its subject matter. It also instructs the judge or arbitrator to use the prevailing party's actual fees as the measure for the attorney fee evaluation:

IN ANY PROCEEDING INVOLVING ANY DISPUTE BETWEEN THE PARTIES TO THIS AGREEMENT RELATING TO MATTERS ARISING FROM THIS AGREEMENT OR ITS SUBJECT MATTER, WHETHER IN CONTRACT, TORT, OR OTHERWISE, THE PREVAILING PARTY SHALL BE AWARDED

ATTORNEY FEES BASED ON THE AC-
TUAL TIME INCURRED BY THE ATTOR-
NEY FOR THE PREVAILING PARTY FOR
THOSE SERVICES NECESSARY TO BRING
THE DISPUTE TO JUDGMENT.

## LOSS PREVENTION:
## ARBITRATION PROVISIONS

> A Binding Arbitration Agreement results in a waiver of legal rights to be heard in court and to appeal a ruling.

If you don't have a written arbitration provision with your opponent, your route to resolution will be the court system. It's as simple as that. Everyone has a legal right to have their dispute heard in court. But, there is no legal right to have your dispute decided by binding arbitration – unless there's a signed arbitration agreement with your adversary.

A binding arbitration agreement results in a waiver of legal rights to be heard in court and to appeal a ruling. Because important legal rights are given up, some laws contain special requirements for binding arbitration agreements. We have written our suggested arbitration provision in order to meet stringent requirements.

### DISCOVERY IN ARBITRATION

You and your opponent have a legal right to conduct discovery within your legal proceeding. Discovery is an inherent part of the court process – and it just so happens to be the biggest money drain of all, except for trial itself. Depositions – oral questions and answers taken down by a court reporter – are the most expensive of all discovery techniques.

> Limit all discovery methods with the intention to keep arbitration swift, effective, and affordable.

Arbitration attempts to limit discovery. Typically, in an arbitration, depositions are only allowed with the permission of the arbitrator. The arbitrator is aware that the goal of arbitration is to cut costs and speedily decide disputes. Depositions are contrary to these goals. The arbitrator you select is best able to judge whether depositions are warranted, and to what extent.

You can cut your losses by limiting discovery at the beginning – in the arbitration provision you add to your contract. You want to limit written discovery, as well. This includes Interrogatories, Requests for Admission, and Demands for Production of Documents. These written discovery methods eat up your time and money. Our suggested provision limits discovery. Again, the intention is to keep arbitration swift, effective, and affordable.

## A SAMPLE ARBITRATION PROVISION

The following is one sample provision you may want to use. Although it meets stringent requirements, you are cautioned to check with the applicable laws in your area to ensure that our model provisions conform.

ANY AND ALL DISPUTES ARISING OUT OF OR RELATING TO THIS CONTRACT OR ITS SUBJECT MATTER SHALL BE SETTLED BY BINDING ARBITRATION ADMINISTERED BY THE AMERICAN ARBITRATION ASSOCIATION (AAA) [OR ADR SERVICE OF YOUR CHOICE], AND JUDGMENT ON THE AWARD RENDERED MAY BE ENTERED IN ANY COURT HAVING JURISDICTION THEREOF. ANY CLAIM THAT MAY BE BROUGHT WITHIN THE SMALL CLAIMS COURT IS EXCLUDED FROM ARBITRATION. THE PREVAILING PARTY SHALL BE AWARDED FEES PAID TO THE

ARBITRATOR AND THE ARBITRATION ADMINISTRATOR.

THE INTENT OF ARBITRATION IS TO CUT COSTS, PARTICULARLY DISCOVERY COSTS. THUS, THE PARTIES SHALL HAVE ONLY THE FOLLOWING RIGHTS TO DISCOVERY:

1. WRITTEN DISCOVERY. AS TO EACH ADVERSE PARTY, A PARTY MAY USE ANY COMBINATION OF 35 OF THE FOLLOWING:

    A. INTERROGATORIES WITH NO SUB-PARTS.
    B. DEMANDS TO PRODUCE DOCUMENTS OR THINGS.
    C. REQUESTS FOR ADMISSIONS.

2. DEPOSITIONS MAY BE TAKEN ONLY WITH THE CONSENT OF THE ARBITRATOR.

3. ANY AND ALL OTHER DISCOVERY, EXAMINATIONS AND INSPECTIONS MAY BE CONDUCTED ONLY WITH THE CONSENT OF THE ARBITRATOR.

THE ARBITRATOR SHALL OBSERVE THE FOLLOWING PROCEDURE IN RENDERING THE AWARD: (A) WITHIN 30 DAYS OF SUBMISSION A TENTATIVE AWARD EXPLAINING THE FACTUAL AND LEGAL BASIS FOR THE DECISION WILL BE MADE BY THE ARBITRATOR. (B) WITHIN 15 DAYS AFTER MAILING OF THE TENTATIVE AWARD ANY PARTY MAY SERVE WRITTEN OBJECTIONS THERETO. THE ARBITRATOR MAY THEN CALL FOR ADDITIONAL EVIDENCE. (C) IF NO OBJECTIONS ARE SERVED, THE TENTATIVE AWARD BECOMES FINAL AND BINDING. (D) IF OBJECTIONS ARE SERVED, WITHIN 30 DAYS AFTER RECEIPT, THE ARBITRATOR WILL EITHER MODIFY OR CONFIRM THE TENTATIVE AWARD, WHICH AWARD WILL THEN BE FINAL AND BINDING.

> With an 85
> percent chance
> of settling your
> case by
> mediation, it
> makes good
> sense to
> include a
> mediation
> provision.

NOTICE: BY SIGNING THIS AGREEMENT YOU ARE AGREEING TO HAVE ANY DISPUTE ARISING OUT OF THE MATTERS INCLUDED IN THIS PROVISION DECIDED BY NEUTRAL BINDING ARBITRATION AND YOU ARE GIVING UP ANY RIGHTS YOU POSSESS TO HAVE THE DISPUTE LITIGATED IN COURT OR BY JURY TRIAL. YOU ARE GIVING UP YOUR JUDICIAL RIGHTS TO DISCOVERY AND APPEAL EXCEPT AS PROVIDED HEREIN. IF YOU REFUSE TO SUBMIT TO ARBITRATION AFTER AGREEING TO THIS PROVISION, YOU MAY BE COMPELLED TO ARBITRATE. YOUR AGREEMENT TO THIS PROVISION IS VOLUNTARY. I HAVE READ AND UNDERSTAND THE FOREGOING. (/S/ INITIALS OF PARTIES.)"

## LOSS PREVENTION: MEDIATION PROVISIONS

A mediation provision is the perfect partner to an arbitration provision. Why chalk up the costs of arbitration – hiring an arbitrator and at least two attorneys – when you have an 85 percent chance of settling your case by mediation? It makes good sense to include a mediation provision. Some people do not believe in the conciliatory process and feel that mediation is an unnecessary expense. Some non-believers in the arbitration process nevertheless want mediation to precede their court battle. Thus, we present you with a standalone mediation provision to include in any contract.

## A SAMPLE MEDIATION PROVISION

ANY AND ALL DISPUTES ARISING OUT OF OR RELATING TO THIS CONTRACT OR ITS SUBJECT MATTER SHALL BE SUBMITTED TO MEDIATION ADMINISTERED BY THE AMERICAN ARBITRATION ASSOCIATION (AAA) [OR *ADR PROVIDER OF YOUR CHOICE*].

### MEDIATION IN REAL LIFE

Since mediation is an entirely cooperative process, it really doesn't work to *drag* someone through the mediation door. If your opponent signed a mediation provision but refuses to mediate, just move on to your next step.

Your goal at mediation is to bring about a cooperative settlement. You'll never reach this goal with an uncooperative party. You're better off if you skip this step and its expense when encountering an uncooperative party – even if the party signed the mediation provision. But do be sure to get your opponent's refusal in writing if you have an attorney fee provision. The court or arbitrator may consider mediation refusal in making its attorney fee award.

You ask: "If you're not going to enforce a provision, why put it in an agreement?" Because people generally abide by their agreements – even disputing parties. Most people also recognize mediation's value and the savings they will achieve if their dispute settles at mediation. Thus, we do find that most people who have agreed to mediate do so. And only 15 percent of these people move on to litigation afterwards.

The following provision combines mediation and arbitration in one concise term.

> **Most people recognize mediation's value and the savings they will achieve if their dispute settles.**

## LOSS PREVENTION:
## A JOINT MEDIATION-ARBITRATION PROVISION

ANY AND ALL DISPUTES ARISING OUT OF OR RELATING TO THIS CONTRACT OR ITS SUBJECT MATTER SHALL BE SETTLED BY BINDING ARBITRATION PRECEDED BY MEDIATION, BOTH ADMINISTERED BY THE AMERICAN ARBITRATION ASSOCIATION (AAA) [*OR ADR PROVIDER OF YOUR CHOICE*] AND JUDGMENT ON THE AWARD RENDERED MAY BE ENTERED IN ANY COURT HAVING JURISDICTION THEREOF. ANY CLAIM THAT MAY BE BROUGHT WITHIN THE SMALL CLAIMS COURT IS EXCLUDED FROM ARBITRATION. THE PREVAILING PARTY IN ARBITRATION SHALL BE AWARDED FEES PAID TO THE MEDIATOR AND ARBITRATOR AND THE MEDIATION-ARBITRATION ADMINISTRATOR.

THE INTENT OF ARBITRATION IS TO CUT COSTS, PARTICULARLY DISCOVERY COSTS. THUS, THE PARTIES SHALL HAVE ONLY THE FOLLOWING RIGHTS TO DISCOVERY:

1.  WRITTEN DISCOVERY. AS TO EACH ADVERSE PARTY, A PARTY MAY USE ANY COMBINATION OF 35 OF THE FOLLOWING:

    A.  INTERROGATORIES WITH NO SUB-PARTS.
    B.  DEMANDS TO PRODUCE DOCUMENTS OR THINGS.
    C.  REQUESTS FOR ADMISSIONS.

2.  DEPOSITIONS MAY BE TAKEN ONLY WITH THE CONSENT OF THE ARBITRATOR.

3.  ANY AND ALL OTHER DISCOVERY, EXAMINATIONS AND INSPECTIONS MAY BE CONDUCTED ONLY WITH THE CONSENT OF THE ARBITRATOR.

THE ARBITRATOR SHALL OBSERVE THE FOLLOWING PROCEDURE IN RENDERING THE AWARD: (A) WITHIN 30 DAYS OF SUBMISSION A TENTATIVE AWARD EXPLAINING THE FACTUAL AND

LEGAL BASIS FOR THE DECISION WILL BE MADE BY THE ARBITRATOR (B) WITHIN 15 DAYS AFTER MAILING OF THE TENTATIVE AWARD ANY PARTY MAY SERVE WRITTEN OBJECTIONS THERETO. THE ARBITRATOR MAY THEN CALL FOR ADDITIONAL EVIDENCE. (C) IF NO OBJECTIONS ARE SERVED, THE TENTATIVE AWARD BECOMES FINAL AND BINDING. (D) IF OBJECTIONS ARE SERVED, WITHIN 30 DAYS AFTER RECEIPT, THE ARBITRATOR WILL EITHER MODIFY OR CONFIRM THE TENTATIVE AWARD, WHICH AWARD WILL THEN BE FINAL AND BINDING.

NOTICE: BY SIGNING BELOW YOU ARE AGREEING TO HAVE ANY DISPUTE ARISING OUT OF THE MATTERS INCLUDED IN THIS PROVISION DECIDED BY NEUTRAL BINDING ARBITRATION PRECEDED BY MEDIATION AND YOU ARE GIVING UP ANY RIGHTS YOU POSSESS TO HAVE THE DISPUTE LITIGATED IN COURT OR BY JURY TRIAL. YOU ARE GIVING UP YOUR RIGHTS TO DISCOVERY AND APPEAL, EXCEPT AS PROVIDED HEREIN. IF YOU REFUSE TO SUBMIT TO MEDIATION OR ARBITRATION AFTER AGREEING TO THIS PROVISION, YOU MAY BE COMPELLED TO MEDIATE OR ARBITRATE. YOUR AGREEMENT TO THIS PROVISION IS VOLUNTARY. I HAVE READ AND UNDERSTAND THE FOREGOING. (/S/ INITIALS OF PARTIES.)"

| Enter in to a Multi-Step ADR agreement at the first sign of a difference of opinion. |
|---|

## Loss Prevention: A Multi-Step ADR Agreement

A Multi-Step ADR Agreement is included in the Appendix and available through the Order Form at the end of this book. This is a truly comprehensive alternative dispute resolution agreement. We encourage disputing parties to enter into this agreement at the first sign of a difference of opinion. It sets up four steps for resolving your conflict, the last of which is binding arbitration. Each step provides a 30 to 90-day window within which to complete that step. The fewer steps taken, the sooner you have reached resolution. Each step is summarized below.

### 1. In Person Meeting

The first step gives you and your opponents a 30-day period to explore settlement options in person. This is the time to implement your Last Chance strategies from Chapter 5 to head off your dispute at this ideal early juncture.

### 2. Hire a Mediator

The second step gives you and your opponents 30 days to hire a mediator to facilitate a mediation session. Review Chapters 3 and 10 on mediation.

### 3. (optional) Written Demand by Attorney

This optional 30-day step automatically comes into play if a party hires an attorney. If none of the parties are represented by counsel, skip this step. This step requires the attorney retained to state the client's legal position and submit a proposal for resolution of the matter. That settlement proposal is sent to the opposing parties or their attorneys, if they are also represented. The opposing parties or attorneys have 10 days to respond.

#### 4. BINDING ARBITRATION

The final step, with a 90-day window of time, is binding arbitration. This step states all parameters of the arbitration process. It limits any pre-arbitration discovery the parties may undertake. It nominates the arbitrator who will preside over and decide the arbitration. It estimates the length of the arbitration hearing. Basically, it defines the variables in advance so the parties may plan ahead for scheduling and cost. It halts all prolonged discovery tactics and tailors an arbitration process to fit these parties' needs. Review Chapters 4 and 11 on arbitration.

## LOSS PREVENTION:
## LIQUIDATED DAMAGES PROVISIONS

Another way to accomplish loss prevention is to include a *liquidated damages* provision in your contract. Provisions for liquidated damages are agreements by the parties to *fix* the damages available in the event that one of the parties violates the contract. It's a fixed penalty for default. That party will be liable to the other for that amount, regardless of the actual damages. These provisions are always in writing.

> **Binding Arbitration Agreements should define the variables of the case in advance to plan ahead for scheduling and cost.**

| **Accomplish loss prevention by including a liquidated damages provision in your contract.** |

Because these parties give up their rights to other damages resulting from violation of the contract, there are often stringent requirements for these provisions. Always check the laws of your locality to confirm compliance before using our model provisions.

There are advantages and disadvantages to liquidated damages provisions. One advantage is that you are not required to prove damages in a later dispute. This can save significant time and expense in both the court system and arbitration. One disadvantage is that the amount you've selected in advance may end up much higher or lower than the actual damages that have resulted. So always think twice before using provisions that fix damages. They can be a blessing or a burden.

### ADVANTAGES OF LIQUIDATED DAMAGES: A DETERRENT TO DEFAULT

Liquidating (fixing) damages in the event of violation can be an excellent way of preventing loss. It can also be the fairest road to justice – because you and your potential opponent decide what would be fair if one of you defaults. Contracting parties are clearly the best evaluators of potential damage if there is a default. And the best time to assess damages is when these parties are making a contract and carefully analyzing their duties and positions.

For this reason, we encourage contracting parties to extend their contracts to liquidate damages on default. What's more, knowing the penalty for default is a great deterrent. Lack of clarity causes most disputes to arise. When people fix their own damages, they are far less likely to quarrel over the consequences of default. You can't argue with a clear contract, especially one you created.

> **The best time to assess damages is when making a contract and carefully analyzing duties and positions.**

## REQUIREMENTS OF LIQUIDATED DAMAGES PROVISIONS

Generally, the language and circumstances must show that the parties are fixing damages in advance because it would be extremely difficult to do so after a dispute arises. The amount of liquidated damages must be reasonable under the circumstances. The parties must be aware that they are giving up their legal right to prove damages. If your contract contains a provision that liquidates damages, the party violating the contract will be liable to the other in the amount fixed, regardless of their actual damages.

Some industries and localities require these provisions to be set forth in a certain bold type size and initialed by the parties directly below the provision. For this reason, our sample provisions meet these requirements.

## THE EFFECTS OF A LIQUIDATED DAMAGES PROVISION

Liquidated damages provisions streamline legal damages assessment by fixing an amount for damages. At arbitration or trial, the parties do not have to prove up damages. They must only prove that the other party violated the contract. On the other hand, liquidated damages provisions can work a grave injustice if the fixed amount isn't enough to cover the damages a party may suffer when the contract is violated. Thus, it is very important to arrive

| **Liquidated damages provisions streamline legal damages assessment by fixing an amount for damages.** |
| --- |

at a liquidated damages value that comes close to the damage a party may suffer from the other's default.

For instance, many residential real estate purchase agreements contain liquidated damages provisions which may be selected by the buyer and seller. These provisions limit damages to 3 percent of the purchase price. They limit the liquidated damages provision to contract violations by the *buyer*. If the seller violates the contract, it does not apply.

## A SAMPLE LIQUIDATED DAMAGES PROVISION

IN THE EVENT THAT EITHER PARTY TO THIS CONTRACT DEFAULTS IN THE PERFORMANCE OF THIS AGREEMENT, THE AMOUNT OF $15,000 IS FIXED AS LIQUIDATED DAMAGES. ALL PARTIES AGREE THAT SAID AMOUNT IS DETERMINED TO BE REASONABLE IN THE EVENT OF DEFAULT IN VIEW OF ALL CIRCUMSTANCES EXISTING ON THE DATE OF THIS AGREEMENT. **THE PARTIES ACKNOWLEDGE THAT BY SIGNING THIS PROVISION THEY ARE GIVING UP THE RIGHT TO PROVE AND/OR RECOVER ACTUAL DAMAGES.** (/S/ INITIALS OF PARTIES.)"

## PROVISIONS LIMITING LIABILITY

You may also want to consider a provision *limiting* liability to a certain amount in the event of violation of the contract. The difference between a provision limiting liability and one liquidating liability is the one limiting liability does not *fix* the amount of damages – it *limits* the damages. The damages paid by the defaulting party can be any amount *up to* the amount designated. When damages are *fixed,* there's no range. The amount specified is the amount recovered – no more and no less.

For instance, a roofer's contract reads: "damages caused by violation of this agreement are limited to the amount paid under this agreement." Some laws prohibit limitations on liability, especially where a public interest is involved. For instance, a passenger airline carrier involves the public interest and cannot limit their liability to passengers. So be sure to determine that any limitation on damages you propose is not prohibited under the laws of your jurisdiction. Generally, these limitations are valid as long as the parties to the contract have equal bargaining power.

> **Consider a provision limiting liability to a certain amount in the event of violation of the contract.**

## A SAMPLE LIMITATION ON DAMAGES PROVISION

IN THE EVENT ROOFER DEFAULTS IN THE PERFORMANCE OF THIS AGREEMENT, OWNER'S DAMAGES SHALL BE LIMITED TO THE AMOUNT OF THIS CONTRACT. THE PARTIES HAVE CAREFULLY CONSIDERED THE AMOUNT OF DAMAGES THAT WILL RESULT BECAUSE OF BREACH AND FIND THIS LIMITATION TO BE REASONABLE UNDER ALL CIRCUMSTANCES NOW EXISTING. THIS PROVISION FORMS PART OF OWNER'S VALUABLE CONSIDERATION PAID FOR THE SERVICES TO BE RENDERED AND THE PRICE OFFERED BY ROOFER IS DISCOUNTED DUE TO THIS PROVISION. **BY SIGNING THIS PROVISION THE PARTIES GIVE UP THEIR LEGAL RIGHTS TO RECOVER DAMAGES IN EXCESS OF THE CONTRACT PRICE. (/S/ INITIALS OF PARTIES.)"**

## Loss Prevention Provisions Provide Certainty

> Contract provisions provide a way of taking charge of your dispute – before it takes charge of you.

The value of these loss control provisions is abundantly clear. They bless the parties' contract with clarity and certainty and state the default cost . With a degree of certainty, disputing parties can become very responsible to one another. If responsibility is clear, there's little reason to ask the court or an arbitrator for a judgment as parties know what it will be.

These provisions can make your life easier if a dispute arises. With a broad attorney fee provision, the defaulting party should be obligated to reimburse you for the actual attorney fees you pay. With a liquidated damages provision, he'll pay the amount agreed to in the provision. With a limit of liability provision, he'll pay no more than the damage limit. Mediation and arbitration provisions render the court system off limits. The detailed arbitration provision controls the procedures and costs of your arbitration proceedings. These provisions provide a way of taking charge of your dispute – before it takes charge of you.

***

Now that you have controlled your losses by creating the appropriate terms of your contract, you're about to utilize another, more subtle type of loss prevention. For those times when you require lawyer representation, you'll learn insider tips on how to best interview and hire one. In Chapter 13, you will learn savvy strategies to bring a lawyer on board and prevent losses at the same time.

# Chapter Thirteen

# HOW TO HIRE A LAWYER: INSIDER TIPS

---

Should you hire a lawyer to represent you in your dispute? If the answer is yes, we present you with an Insider Checklist to interview your lawyer candidates. Is it important to like your lawyer? How can you best control the costs of your case, including your lawyer's fees? What different types of fee arrangements can you propose to your lawyer? This chapter puts you in the driver's seat when hiring an attorney. You're paying, and you should be the boss.

---

## WHEN SHOULD YOU HIRE A LAWYER?

> There are four situations that warrant representation by an attorney.

Although this book empowers you to handle your legal dispute on your own, there may be some situations where you will want representation by an attorney:

- When your dispute will have to be resolved in the court system.

- When you do not feel sufficiently competent to represent yourself.

- When an attorney fee provision entitles you to reimbursement of your attorney fees if you prevail.

- When your case value warrants legal representation.

## YOU'RE IN THE COURT SYSTEM

Given the complexities of the court system, you will most likely choose to be represented by counsel when entering its arches – whether you are a plaintiff or a defendant. Of course, this doesn't include Small Claims Court – where lawyer representation is prohibited in some states and discouraged in all.

Small Claims Court is the ideal forum for people to handle their own disputes. Rules are few and procedures are simple. The process is streamlined, so your dispute is heard within weeks of filing your claim. Learn more about the ideal Small Claims Court forum in Chapter 14, entitled *If You Must: How to Make the Most of the Court System.*

## THE JUGGERNAUT OF COURT RULES

Whether you are the initiating or responding party, the court system mandates legal rules and formalities that only a lawyer can tackle. Both a complaint and an answer to a complaint must conform to a full array of legal checklists. These requirements are so complex that even the trained lawyer is challenged by them. Some states have adopted form complaints and answers that can be used for filing and responding to a complaint. Knowing which form to use and whether that form covers all facets of your dispute is something only a lawyer can know. Although the court system is trying to be accessible to the consumer, it is not yet *user friendly*. When you're entering the court system, except for Small Claims, you will most likely find you need to retain an attorney.

## A LAWYER'S ROLE FOR YOUR SMALL CLAIMS CASE

Always consider hiring an attorney when you don't feel comfortable representing yourself. In Small Claims Court, you'll want to do the leg work at the hearing, but you can certainly consult with an attorney to get you there in style. Check your budget. Your attorney can guide you through the process with as much or as little participation as you need. A lawyer can evaluate your case, provide you with applicable law, and put a Small Claims Position Statement together for you to summarize the facts and law, identifying exhibits that support each. This document is signed by you and submitted to the court at your Small Claims hearing. When we prepare a Position Statement for our clients, it provides them with the confidence

> If you're entering the court system, other than Small Claims Court, you will most likely need to retain an attorney.

Hire a lawyer for mediation if you are not comfortable representing yourself.

they need to present their cases clearly and briefly. We also often coach clients on case presentation. These Small Claims preparation sessions are quite valuable to clients, and their results in Small Claims Court clearly justify the expense.

## HELP AT MEDIATION

If you're headed toward mediation and don't feel comfortable representing yourself, you will want to hire counsel. Counsel's role can range from evaluation to consultation to full representation. It all depends on how much or how little you need from your chosen attorney. You can limit your attorney's task to working through *The Pocket Lawyer Analyzer* with you to evaluate the feasibility of your case. They can participate by preparing your Mediation Position Paper and reviewing mediation procedure with you. Or you can invite counsel on board to represent you at the mediation hearing. It will all depend upon your comfort level with self-representation, the value of your case and your feasibility rating from *The Pocket Lawyer Analyzer.*

## HELP FOR BINDING ARBITRATION

Another situation when you may want to be represented by counsel is when you enter binding arbitration. If your opposing party has a lawyer, you should, too. Even if your opponent is not represented, you may still want to hire counsel. The arbitration arena is adversarial territory, with most legal procedures and theories intact. So if neither of you are represented by counsel, you may feel comfortable in the arbitration arena. Otherwise, you will probably want to hire a lawyer.

If your case value is sufficiently high you should also seriously consider hiring an attorney. Although the expense of retaining counsel will cut into your recovery, the expense may be well worth it with a case of high or reasonably high value.

> The expense of retaining an attorney is well worth it with a case of high value.

### IF YOU HAVE AN ATTORNEY FEE PROVISION

If you have a written agreement with your opponent stating the winning party will receive an award of attorney fees, seriously consider hiring an attorney to handle your dispute. Even if your attorney fee provision says that only one party is entitled to fees, in many states this one-sided provision is applied to all contracting parties. So don't let a one-sided provision scare you off. If you signed the contract, the fee provision probably applies to you, too.

Is the attorney fees provision missing from your contract? If so, most state law provides that each party pays its own attorney fees, and the winner is not entitled to reimbursement. You've heard the adage that lawyers are the only ones to come out whole in litigation? This is why. Suppose your action is to collect $7,800 for a defective computer system you bought. You pay attorney fees of $4,900 to win your case. The result: without an attorney fee provision you've won $7,800, but your actual gain after attorney fee is only $2,900. You don't even have enough to buy another computer. Thus, it is only beneficial to

> **If your contract has an attorney fee provision, analyze your case both as a winner and as a loser.**

hire an attorney when you have an attorney fee provision or a high case value.

## FEE PROVISIONS CAN WORK AGAINST YOU

Always keep in mind that these provisions work both ways. An attorney fee provision can be as much a downside as an upside. It all depends on who wins. If you lose, such a provision is clearly a handicap. If you thought paying attorney fees is expensive, wait until you have to pay the other side's fees, as well. It's enough to swear off attorney fee provisions forever. But if you're the victor, you'll only feel like one if you have such a provision. Winners want to make sure *every* contract they enter into has an attorney fee provision.

Thus, you need to analyze your case from both perspectives – as a winner and as a loser. Always wear your devil's advocate hat. Ask yourself: "What are my chances of losing – and paying not only my own attorney fees, but my opponent's as well?"

## STEPS TO TAKE BEFORE HIRING AN ATTORNEY

Thus, if you have an attorney fee provision you'll be more inclined to hire an attorney. Before doing so, there are a few steps you should take:

- As always, obtain your feasibility analysis from *The Pocket Lawyer Analyzer* program.

- Review your Legal Evaluation from *The Pocket Lawyer Analyzer* to ensure that you have a high likelihood of prevailing.

- If your likelihood of prevailing is high, evaluate your ability to pay your attorney. Remember that you still have to pay your attorney fees as you go along. You're only entitled to get them back when the case is over. Paying monthly attorney fees can be a very high expense for any budget. You will have to consider whether you can handle this extra stretch.

- Explore contingent-based fee arrangements with your lawyer, which will free you from payment until you win the case. Later in this chapter, we'll discuss fee arrangements and their advantages and disadvantages.

- Finally, review your Collectability Assessment from *The Pocket Lawyer Analyzer*. What are your chances of collecting your attorney fees from your opponent? You don't want a worthless piece of paper that says you get back your attorney fees. You'll still be out the fees you paid.

> **Complete the five step evaluation to determine if you should hire a lawyer.**

Only after you have completed this thorough evaluation will you know whether you should hire a lawyer to represent you in your dispute.

**NOTE:** You rarely get back all the fees you paid your attorney. These provisions generally limit recovery to *reasonable and necessary* attorney fees. The court or arbitrator decides

**Before you hire a lawyer, work through The Pocket Lawyer Analyzer program.**

what is reasonable and necessary. Often, they decide that only half or two-thirds of the fees you paid were appropriate. Sometimes they apply a formula to the result you received. Generally, we find that no one gets paid back dollar for dollar even with an attorney fee provision – the norm is about 65 percent.

## WORK THE POCKET LAWYER ANALYZER BEFORE HIRING YOUR ATTORNEY

If you've discovered that you want to hire a lawyer, make sure you complete *The Pocket Lawyer Analyzer* program first. You'll get some valuable guidance. It will enable you to intelligently discuss your case with your lawyer, and conduct an efficient interview. First, you'll use the program to decide whether it is worth your while to hire a lawyer. Second, *The Pocket Lawyer Analyzer* provides important points to discuss when you interview a lawyer. It will also cut down on your lawyer's time. You will already have the answers to the most important legal and financial aspects of your case:

- Which forum will decide your dispute
- Whether you are entitled to get back your attorney fees
- If there is cause for your damages to be reduced
- Your settlement value

## INTERVIEWING LAWYERS

More and more people are beginning to interview their lawyers in more depth. But many more questions need to be asked and instructions given. This person is going to represent your interests in a very important way. There are three issues to consider to obtain the best lawyer for you and your case:

- **EXPERIENCE:** Find a lawyer well versed in the area of law involved in your matter.

- **EASE OF COMMUNICATING, COMFORT:** Find a lawyer you feel comfortable working with.

- **QUALITY OF WORK:** Find a lawyer who is thorough and competent.

## STEP ONE:
## FINDING A LAWYER EXPERIENCED IN YOUR DISPUTE

Law is highly specialized these days. Lawyers specialize in certain areas of law, as evidenced by listings in your yellow pages. Determine which area of law applies to your dispute. Determine this by reviewing the categories in the yellow pages under "Attorneys."

**PERSONAL REFERRALS:** The very best way to locate a quality lawyer specializing in the area of your dispute is to ask people for referrals. There is nothing as good as a personal referral from someone who has had past dealings with a lawyer. But make sure your friend was pleased with the representation.

> Determine which area of law applies to your case and hire a specialized lawyer.

| Call your bar association for a lawyer referral or simply use the yellow pages. |

Ask some pertinent questions. Some people will refer you to someone they weren't particularly impressed with or someone they've heard about through the grapevine. A bad referral is worse than no referral.

**YOUR BAR ASSOCIATION LAWYER REFERRAL SERVICE:** The second best way to obtain a competent lawyer is to call your local bar association's Lawyer Referral Service. Ask them for referral to a lawyer who handles cases similar to your case. We recommend use of the Lawyer Referral Service because attorneys listed with them generally have undergone a screening process:

- These attorneys have been evaluated. Their prior experience with the subject matter placed them on the appropriate panel. You will generally be referred to a lawyer with training and experience in your particular matter.

- These panel lawyers are typically required to have malpractice insurance.

- Often, you will receive a free one-half hour consultation with these lawyers.

## YELLOW PAGES

Another way of locating counsel is by using the yellow pages and calling attorneys listed under the subject of your dispute. Although this method is not as reliable as the prior two methods, you will find a lawyer who should have significant experience in the area of your dispute. Because law is becoming more competitive, many lawyers now provide information packages to potential clients. These packages consist of biographical information as well as case and client satisfaction statistics. Ask the firm you call if they have such a "new client package" for you.

> Find a lawyer who you are comfortable with, who is competent and has time for your case.

## STEP TWO:
## FINDING A LAWYER YOU CAN WORK WITH

Find a lawyer with whom you feel comfortable. Your participation in your dispute is very important. The more facts you share with your lawyer, the better your representation will be. Thus, you need someone you feel comfortable with and can fully advise of the details of your dispute. In fact, we find that clients who participate most fully with their lawyers do the best, both in their case results and attorney charges. So you do want to feel comfortable with your lawyer. You don't need to like him or her, but you should feel a certain level of comfort.

We find the more involved you become in your case, the more you can control its costs. You want to confer with your attorney about costs and results at each phase of your case. When you feel comfortable with your attorney, you can more fully participate in decision making at each strategic point.

## STEP THREE:
## FINDING A COMPETENT LAWYER

Although you've found a lawyer you're comfortable with who specializes in the topic of your dispute, there's no guarantee that you've found a competent lawyer. You need to interview your candidate to assure competency.

**Review The
Pocket Lawyer
Analyzer with
your lawyer
candidate at
the interview.**

There are many factors which lead to competency. Some lawyers are too busy to be truly competent. Make sure your candidate has time for your case.

Organization is another quality of competency. Is the lawyer organized? Take a look at his office and the desks of his assistants. Is your lawyer candidate clear and straightforward? Is he or she able to communicate with you in a clear way? You will only be able to satisfy yourself as to your candidate's competency through the interview process. After that, you'll find out during your case – which is not the ideal time to learn your lawyer is not as competent as you thought.

### REVIEW THE POCKET LAWYER ANALYZER WITH YOUR CANDIDATE

You are interviewing lawyers now because you *must*. Perhaps your efforts at settlement with your opponent, as recommended in this book, haven't succeeded. Or you have entered the court system as a plaintiff or a defendant, and need assistance through the court maze. Whatever your reason for hiring a lawyer, since you have to do it, let us show you the best way.

We suggest that you review *The Pocket Lawyer Analyzer* with your candidate at the interview. Performing this evaluation with your lawyer achieves two ideal results. First, it answers any questions left unanswered in the program. And you'll confirm your assessment with your lawyer. Second, discussing the issues raised by *The Pocket Lawyer Analyzer* will enable you to assess all three steps of your lawyer selection process – your level of comfort, your lawyer's level of competency, and your candidate's expertise with the area of your dispute.

> Be sure to ask your lawyer all of the questions listed here.

### YOUR LAWYER INTERVIEW CHECKLIST

These are the questions we suggest you ask of your lawyer candidate:

1. How long have you been practicing law?

2. Do you carry malpractice insurance? May I see proof of coverage?

3. Do you encourage clients to consider alternative dispute resolution methods?

4. Have you been trained in dispute resolution?

5. Do you have the time to dedicate to my case?

6. What qualifies you to handle my case, which relates to (subject of your dispute)?

7. Do you have written recommendations from other clients that you can share with me?

8. May I review your resume?

9. If you are unavailable in trial or deposition, who will respond to my inquiries and take care of my case?

10. Are you willing to work with me in tailoring my case to my budget? Of course, I will provide you with written authority if I decide to

**This type of interview goes beyond lawyer biography into legal analysis.**

forego a certain strategy or tactic that you recommend.

11. I am interested in keeping my costs down in this case. Thus, I want to participate in discovery decision making with you, and to undertake some tasks in my case if I am able. Is this agreeable to you?

12. Will you join me in evaluating my case with *The Pocket Lawyer Analyzer* program? (proceed to review the program together)

13. What do you see as the downside of my case?

14. Are you willing to entertain a fee structure different from an hourly charge – such as contingent fee or part contingent fee and part hourly fee?

15. Are you willing to estimate how much my side of the case will cost without considering the other side's strategy?

16. Will you now provide me with an itemized estimate of how much you feel it will cost to prosecute/defend just my side of the case? I will not hold you to the estimate, but I do want to get a reasonable idea of the costs we are talking about.

Once you have explored this checklist with your candidate, you will know whether you want to hire this attorney. This interview process usually takes an hour and one-half to two hours. If your interview takes place with a Lawyer Referral panelist, you will want to pay for the remainder of the interview following any free consultation. This type of interview goes beyond lawyer biography into legal analysis. Thus, you should not expect a free consultation for more than one-half hour at most. Even if you don't hire your candidate, you will presumably obtain a valuable evaluation in your interview process. It will be worth the hour or so of paid attorney time.

> **You can only make informed decisions if you and your attorney communicate clearly.**

## MAKING DECISIONS WITH YOUR LAWYER

You and your lawyer need to discuss the road map of your case and the many ways it can be handled. There is an economical way of representing someone. I call this *basic representation*. Here, you get the legal steps, but no frills. Then there's full charge representation where the cost is usually prohibitive. There's a range in between. You and your attorney should discuss each of these methods and you should provide instruction about which method you want. You can only make an informed decision through clear attorney-client communication.

## CONTINGENT FEE STRUCTURES

With a contingent fee arrangement, you and your attorney share the net recovery in the proportion agreed upon at the beginning of the case. When you are the party seeking a recovery, you should always consider asking your attorney to handle your case on a contingent fee basis. Contingent fee arrangements are fully negotiable between you and your attorney. Though varying widely, contingency works as follows. Generally, you pay the necessary case costs, which typically include case filing, service of process, deposition costs, and expert fees. These costs are reimbursed before net recovery is determined. Net recovery is then split between client and attorney according to their agreement.

## AN EXAMPLE

You come to me and ask me to handle your dispute on a contingent fee basis. We agree to split the net recovery in the following proportions: *30 percent to attorney and 70 percent to client* after costs are reimbursed. Recovery of $45,000 in damages is received in your case. Further, you are awarded attorney fees of $7,000. (Although the fee agreement is contingent, the attorney still keeps track of his time for calculation of the attorney fee award.) Your gross recovery is $52,000. Costs of $2,200 were advanced, leaving $49,800 as a net recovery. Your attorney receives $14,940 as fees and you receive the remaining $34,860. The bottom line is you've recovered about $10,000 less than your actual damages. However, you didn't have to pay attorney fees along the road to your recovery and you recovered a substantial portion of your damages. If you hadn't won the case, you wouldn't pay your attorney anything – a far better result than a party who paid the attorney $7,000 and lost.

## YOUR ATTORNEY SHOULD BELIEVE IN YOUR CASE

Your attorney should believe in your case – or advise you that your case is not very strong. The best way to get your attorney's honest opinion about the merits of your case is to ask the attorney to take it on a contingent fee basis. If they refuse to do so, chances are your case is not a big winner. Otherwise, your attorney would be willing to share in its dividends – unless your attorney has a good reason other than the validity of your case as to why contingent fee is not a preference. You need to come right out and ask.

## DISADVANTAGES OF THE CONTINGENT FEE

For me, I feel there is a conflict of interest inherent in representing clients on a contingent fee basis. This conflict crops up in several ways.

**IMPARTIALITY MAY BE AFFECTED:** A final settlement amount should be decided by the client. Usually, the client's decision is based upon attorney advice. When the attorney fees depend upon the amount of the settlement, the attorney confronts a conflict of interest. His conflict: the more the settlement goes up, the more the attorney will get. If the attorney's desire for higher fees gets in the way of his impartial valuation, he has a conflict of interest.

**CLIENTS MAY HESITATE TO DISMISS A CASE:** A conflict of interest appears when the client decides to give up his case for emotional or financial reasons. For instance, the case has proceeded for a year now. The client feels emotionally and financially drained by the process. He wants to dismiss the case and just move on. Without a contingent fee arrangement, it is entirely up to the client whether to continue to pursue his case. Aware that the lawyer has a share in the ultimate recovery, the client feels far more inclined to proceed forward, despite the emotional and financial factors.

> There can be a conflict of interest in representing clients on a contingent fee basis.

> **With the contingent fee arrangement, no fees are paid if there is no recovery.**

Some contingent fee agreements contain provisions that help avoid such conflicts of interest. They state that if the client dismisses the case without recovery, the client will pay the attorney on an hourly basis. If this is the case, then no conflict of interest occurs. These are important factors which should be considered when entering into any contingent fee arrangement.

### ADVANTAGES OF THE CONTINGENT FEE

One reason why the contingent fee arrangement may be a solution for you, especially if there is no provision for recovery of attorney fees, is that you pay no fees if there is no recovery. In this situation, if you are the loser at the courthouse or at arbitration, your loss ends there. You haven't paid substantial attorney fees just to climb aboard the loser's seat. Losing feels bad enough without paying mounds of attorney fees to get there. If you're the winner, your attorney properly shares in your reward, and generally, his share is more than he would have received if paid by the hour. But your attorney has taken a gamble. Knowing he'd get nothing if you lost, the attorney deserves more for taking this risk.

Although there are downsides and upsides to contingent fee agreements, sometimes they are the ideal answer – especially if you can't afford to pay your attorney as you pursue your dispute.

## THE COMBINATION AGREEMENT

There are many variations to the strict contingent fee agreement. I have some agreements with clients that combine a reduced hourly rate and a contingent fee. For example, one fee agreement calls for half my customary hourly rate and half my customary contingent fee percentage. These agreements are completely negotiable and should be tailored to each individual case. Sit down with your attorney candidate and evaluate the probable outcome of your case. Then work up a mutually agreeable fee arrangement based on that figure.

## THE INCREASED HOURLY RATE CONTINGENT FEE AGREEMENT

This agreement structure is often preferred by both clients and attorneys for contingent fee matters. The attorney's contingent fee compensation is tied to the hours he puts into the case. In this manner, both client and attorney know they're not giving or taking too much. The attorney keeps careful track of his time and receives his total hours multiplied by an increased hourly rate. Since the lawyer is taking a risk – if there is no recovery or no collection on the judgment, he will never be paid – he should be compensated far more than his hourly rate. Typically, attorneys charge 1-½ to 2 times their hourly rate for these contingent fee structures. If the client wins and collects, the attorney gets paid for the time he put in at the increased rate. If there is no recovery, the attorney gets nothing.

> **Attorney fee agreements are completely negotiable and can be tailored to each individual case.**

## FLAT FEE AGREEMENTS

Insist on
obtaining a flat
rate figure from
the lawyer – or
at the very least
a not-to-exceed
estimate.

Lawyer fee structures need to change. Clients need to know the approximate bottom line dollar cost for the service performed. Lawyers should be encouraged to charge fees at flat rates whenever possible – much the same as contractors charge their clients. An experienced lawyer should have a good idea of how long it will take to perform a customary service. These days, largely due to insurance rate increases and competition, lawyers are specializing in certain areas of law. Because of specialization, the lawyer you consult has previously performed the function he or she will provide to you. Thus, the lawyer should have a good idea of how much it is going to cost.

If the lawyer doesn't specialize, or at least focus on the area of law you need, you probably want to go elsewhere. You want a qualified lawyer who has already worked out the quirks. You don't want an inexperienced lawyer trying something new at your expense.

Insist on obtaining a flat rate figure from the lawyer – or at the very least a *not to exceed* estimate. If the lawyer can't provide a specific figure, then you know you're consulting with an attorney who hasn't performed this service before. If your situation is unique or complicated, it may take an initial consultation with the lawyer at his hourly rate to accurately assess an appropriate rate for your transaction. Payment for that time will be well worth your while, because it will give you an opportunity to evaluate the lawyer's capability and strategy, and provide the bottom line cost of his services.

## ESTIMATES FOR LITIGATION

A lawyer will not be able to give you a flat fee for litigation services, because there are too many variables for how much lawyer time your case will require. Unless your case goes to binding arbitration and there is a provision for *no discovery*, there are too many variables that can be used as strategies by your opponents. Will they take depositions? How many? Will they demand document inspections? How lengthy? For the binding arbitration proceeding that has no discovery, however, a lawyer can generally predict the costs and fees.

What your lawyer *can* estimate is how much *your side* should cost based on the discovery decisions you will make together. Will you be taking depositions? How many? You and your lawyer can discuss the legal procedures available, decide which ones you will be using and estimate a cost for each. Through this type of careful analysis, your lawyer can provide you with a rough estimate of the minimum cost for *your* side of the case – not including your opponent's strategies and your responses.

Of course, the one unknown variable will always be the opponent's discovery time for interrogatories and depositions. Some parties want to take depositions of all parties and all possible witnesses. Some attorneys take a deposition in a few hours; others take the same deposition in eight hours. When parties aren't yet represented by counsel, personal style of each party and their attorney is an important unknown in the fee equation. For these reasons, a lawyer cannot predict with accuracy

> For binding arbitration without any discovery, the lawyer can predict what the costs and fees will be.

| Have monthly meetings with your attorney after you receive your bill for each month. |
| :-- |

how much time he will spend, and therefore how much he will charge, on any given case. But he can roughly estimate the fees he will generate for *his* discovery plan.

When you are involved in litigation or arbitration with a provision that allows full discovery, you won't be able to pin down the bottom line for discovery costs and attorney fees. However, you will have a rough estimate for your own plan. There's really nothing more you can do to estimate fees in this situation, except to carefully proceed through every step of the litigation, evaluate the case as you move along and take part in all decisions.

## STRATEGY AND COST CONTROL SESSIONS

You should have monthly meetings with your attorney after you receive your bill to evaluate the services rendered, the amount of attorney fees and costs expended to date, and the potential loss or recovery in the case, given the activity over the past month. Remember that each day you have an opportunity to make a new decision for your case strategy, just as each morning when you wake up you have new opportunities to make changes and direct your day. This is another aspect of taking responsibility for your legal matter by participating fully in the decisions involved in your case.

## CONCLUSION

There will be times when you can't help hiring a lawyer. That's where this chapter comes in. Having expert guidance during darker days makes all the difference. Now that you're in the driver's seat for steering your dispute to resolution, you'll have the right lawyer on board.

\* \* \*

And now, on to our final Chapter 14. What happens when you must enter the court system? How can you best get through it? Read on, to find a life preserver amid the unpredictable seas of litigation: If You Must: Getting the Most from the Courts.

— *Chapter Fourteen* —

# IF YOU MUST:
# HOW TO MAKE THE
# MOST OF THE COURT
# SYSTEM

---

If you haven't been able to resolve your dispute through alternative dispute resolution methods, you'll be entering the court system for solution. This chapter presents four keys to your success. Find out what to expect and how to best set up a savvy litigation plan. This chapter lists the options available to you in the court system, and gives you quick, easy tips for ease and assurance, to achieve the best result in court. But first, at this critical point, your best option is explored: Settlement.

---

## YOUR BEST RESULT: SETTLEMENT

> Knowing the courts are around the next bend is a great settlement motivator for anyone.

It's never too late to make a settlement offer. Why mention this now, when you are poised to enter the court system? It's simple. Throughout this book we strive to present the best possible result you can achieve. Under the circumstances, now that the court system is your forum for justice, your best result is *settlement*. We present several strategies to achieve this end.

## RETURN TO THE POCKET LAWYER ANALYZER AND LAST CHANCE

We presume you've already been through *The Pocket Lawyer Analyzer*. Now is the time to review your results. Look at your case value and feasibility assessment. Then, take your settlement value and proceed back to Chapter 5 *Last Chance*. It's time to conduct your Last Chance session again.

Pull together that settlement you were unable to create before. Why now? You're about to enter the court system and drag your adversary through its gates. Knowing the courts are around the next bend is a great settlement motivator for anyone – almost as powerful as the lawsuit itself.

Follow all the steps in Chapter 5, *Last Chance*. Give your adversary a copy of this book. Ask him to read it – especially this chapter. Sometimes the truth has to come from an impartial source. Set a meeting for a week later. After the pitfalls of the court system come to light, common sense shows that settlement is the only plausible answer.

## If You Must: Making the Most Out of the Court System

If you've fully attempted each of the settlement options above, and are still unable to avoid the court system, you may want to chalk this up to a valuable – or should we say, very costly – learning experience. If not, then the courthouse is your only alternative. This chapter gives you the tools to make the most out of the courts.

> **Because your dispute won't be detoured to out-of-court resolution, get the most out of the court system.**

### You're Not Alone

Nationally, 14.5 million civil lawsuits are filed each year with $88 billion spent on those lawsuits – the vast majority going to lawyers. Now that alternative dispute resolution is fast becoming the way for legal resolution, we expect these numbers to change drastically. But this will take time. Because your dispute is happening *now* and you haven't detoured it for out-of-court resolution, your best move is to get the most out of the court system.

### Attorney Representation

Due to the complexities of the court system we assume you will be hiring an attorney to represent you. Use this chapter in conjunction with Chapter 13, *How to Hire a Lawyer: Insider Tips*. Your choice of lawyer is a key element in pursuing your case in court. Make sure you find someone who meets the criteria in Chapter 13. You want a team member, in every sense of the word. You and your attorney will be a team throughout your case.

> **Court litigation is a very expensive matter – once you have begun, there's no escape, outside of settlement.**

Because civil court actions take 2 to 5 years to get to trial and involve extensive discovery, attorney fees are generally very high. Reminder: always consider whether you have an attorney fee provision in a written agreement between you and your opponent. We may sound like a broken record. But court litigation is a very expensive matter – once you have begun, there's no escape, outside of settlement. Be realistic about the expense you're about to take on.

## THE PITFALLS OF REPRESENTING YOURSELF

In the court system the parties (called litigants) are allowed and encouraged to have attorneys represent them. However, each party is entitled to be self-represented. Because the rules of these courts are many and complicated, you are discouraged from representing yourself. The general court system is simply not set up for self representation. An unrepresented party stands out like a sore thumb. In some attorney circles, unrepresented parties are considered prey and are taken advantage of. For these reasons, self representation just doesn't work in the court system.

## TO HIRE OR NOT TO HIRE A LAWYER

You have determined the value of your case with *The Pocket Lawyer Analyzer*. Does it make sense to hire a lawyer and spend the fees it will take to litigate your case in the court system? If you don't have an attorney fee provision, it may not make economic sense. If you do, it still may not be your wisest choice.

If your case is worth $12,000 and you have to spend $8,000 in attorney fees (only 40 hours of attorney time) to get a $12,000 judgment, is it worth your while? Perhaps, if the court system guaranteed results and if you knew you would be able to collect on your judgment. But the court system, with its many foibles, is known for its unpredictable results. There is no guarantee to your $12,000 judgment.

What about collection? Is there any guarantee that your opponent will pay your judgment? Will you be able to collect through less voluntary means? Even if you have an attorney fee provision and a judgment, you're still out the money unless you collect.

The court system can be a very risky venture. This view of the courts system is what prompted Irish actor Charles Macklin to write: "The law is a sort of hocus-pocus science, that smiles in yer face while it picks your pocket."

> The court system can be a very risky venture. Learn your four keys to success in court.

## YOUR FOUR KEYS TO SUCCESS IN COURT

When you decide the court system is the only way to proceed, the four keys that will assure you of your best success are:

- Keep your costs down
- Continually evaluate your case
- Propose settlement often
- Work closely with your attorney, if you have one

> Keep your attorney's time and discovery to a minimum, while making sure your legal interests are being served.

## SUCCESS KEY 1:
## KEEPING COSTS DOWN

One key to success in the court system is to keep your attorney's time and discovery to a minimum, while making sure your legal interests are being served. Again, have this conversation with your attorney early on and throughout your partnership. You should always keep track of the value of your case and the best and worst bottom line result you'll get at trial. But, equally important, always monitor the amount of attorney fees spent.

**TRACK YOUR ATTORNEY FEES:** Your attorney works on many different cases at a time and cannot keep tabs on these cost factors as well as you can. Also, your attorney is not as motivated as you are to watch costs. It's easy for attorney fees to skyrocket over a short period of time. Attorneys *are* very expensive, and litigation is extremely time-intensive.

One party takes the offensive; the other defends, and vice versa. It's an endless circle. It's nobody's fault; merely conflict following its course. Always watch your costs. Make sure your costs reasonably relate to the potential judgment you seek. As a rule of thumb, try to keep your costs to no more than 1/3 of the amount you're attempting to recover.

Each month when you receive your attorney's billing, calculate the total amount you've paid to date. Some firms provide a running total; some do not. It's only through careful and continual monitoring that you will be aware of how much you have spent, and if it's worth it.

If you find you're getting over a reasonable limit, talk to your attorney. If you have an attorney fee provision, the court is only going to give you what is *reasonable*. Now is the time to pare down and come back in line with what is reasonable. You are the boss – and this is your case.

> **Now is the time to re-evaluate – in terms of case value, liability, and strategy.**

### SUCCESS KEY 2:
### CONTINUALLY EVALUATE YOUR CASE

There are many occasions for evaluation in a case. Each case has a life of its own, and many crossroads along the way. At each juncture, the picture changes. You've just had your deposition taken. Now is the time to re-evaluate – in terms of case value, liability, and strategy. This is where a good relationship with your lawyer pays off. Evaluation and strategy that comes out of mutual effort between attorney and client produce the best result.

Should you take your opponent's deposition? Should you hire an expert? These are decisions you will make as your litigation moves along. These pivotal decisions are best made based on your budget and your case's current strategy. Always update your decisions to correlate to your latest case strategy. Always update your strategy as your case picture changes.

| Whenever the litigation course changes in any significant way, there's another perfect opportunity for settlement. |
| :--- |

### SUCCESS KEY 3:
### CONTINUALLY PROPOSE SETTLEMENT

Any new development in your case should trigger an opportunity for settlement. Here are some of the best occasions:

- Just after the case is filed
- At the ADR status conference
- When depositions are set, before their expense takes hold
- Following the deposition of your opponent
- When you win or lose a motion

Whenever the litigation course changes in any significant way, there's another perfect opportunity for settlement.

### SETTLEMENT OPPORTUNITIES: EXAMPLES

A DEPOSITION HAS JUST BEEN SET: The upcoming expense of depositions presents an optimum settlement opportunity. Your motivating factor – saving money. You'll each spend about $5,000 in the deposition process. $5,000 apiece can get anyone's attention. You write a settlement letter like the one in the Appendix, and attach an arbitration proposal. Have your attorney take a look at it first, to make sure it doesn't backfire on you if your case moves forward. But the proposal should be from you to your opponent. Your proposal will be far more meaningful coming from you, with a powerful objective – to avoid attorney fees and costs.

**A DEPOSITION WAS JUST TAKEN:** You're sick of answering questions. Or your adversary has just had his deposition taken. He didn't like it either. Who does? The post-deposition climate is ideal for proposing settlement.

**ANY CASE CHANGE:** Whenever the picture of your case changes, another unique settlement occasion is at hand. At each of these junctures, you should make a settlement offer. If your proposal is rejected, follow up with a proposal for binding arbitration. Your opponent may not have selected that forum earlier in your dispute, but now he may jump at the chance to leave it all behind.

Many clients stuck in egotistical points of view respond to settlement suggestions with "But won't my opponent think my case is weak?" Our answer is, "No, your opponent will think you're smart – avoiding attorney fees and years of time eaten up by a matter from the past isn't a productive use of time or money." The weak person remains rigidly right, while the wise one proposes solutions.

## SUCCESS KEY 4:
## TEAMWORK WITH YOUR ATTORNEY

One of your most important keys to success is your attorney-client teamwork. Honest and close communication with your attorney and careful planning together guide your case efficiently through the court system. You are a team working closely together toward a common goal – to win or defend your case with the least expense. You can be a most effective team – meeting your financial and emotional needs and obtaining the very best case result. It's

> You and your attorney are a team working toward a common goal – to win or defend your case with the least expense.

**Small Claims Court is the ideal forum for resolving your dispute without attorneys.**

your case. You need to make decisions based upon the informed advice of your team member attorney.

An attorney-client team reaps rewards of its own. Not only does the right relationship bring positive results, but a compatible team can be impressive. Your adversaries will be intimidated by your rapport and the judge and jury will be impressed with your teamwork. A team in synch is a team that tends to win.

## YOUR KEYS TO SMALL CLAIMS COURT SUCCESS

The Small Claims Court system is about as quick and inexpensive as they get. The dollar value limit of cases that qualify for Small Claims Court varies with each state. When you worked *The Pocket Lawyer Analyzer* you determined the limit in your state. If you missed that step, call the Small Claims Court in your district and ask for their case value limit. The limits range from about $1,000 to $7,500 around the nation. The Small Claims dispute limit fluctuates as our standard of living changes. So it is always a good idea to obtain current information.

Small Claims Court was set up for the lay person. It is the ideal forum for resolving your dispute without attorneys and complicated rules. In some states, Small Claims parties are *prohibited* from being represented by counsel. This prohibition against attorneys maintains an equal footing between disputing parties. Neither party has an attorney to manipulate the case.

In states that don't prohibit attorneys, people generally represent themselves anyway, to save costs. You present the facts to the judge or commissioner and he or she applies the law. It's quick, it's easy and it's relatively unemotional. It's all done in an average of fifteen minutes. You receive the judgment by mail.

> **Small Claims appeals are simple, and do not involve the costs and complexities of appeals from higher courts.**

## DRAWBACK TO SMALL CLAIMS: APPEALS

The Small Claims Courts around the nation also vary regarding appeal rights. Most states allow appeals. Generally, appeals are limited to the losing defendant. A minority of states have no appeals. One drawback of appeal rights in Small Claims Courts is that many losing parties exercise their appeal rights, and the cost and stress of your case marches on. In most instances, when an appeal is filed the matter is heard all over again. However, Small Claims appeals are simple, and do not involve the costs and complexities of appeals from higher courts.

Thus, although the appellate process is available after most Small Claims proceedings, its simplicity makes the process just one step more. And for the losing Small Claims party, a different judge hears and decides your appeal. This is a real advantage. Your appellate result will reveal whether the decision made by the Small Claims Court was correct.

> The simple rule for Small Claims Court is to know the law, know the facts, and be prepared to present them in a brief time frame.

## INCREASING THE SMALL CLAIMS LIMIT

One of the answers for our beleaguered court system is to increase the Small Claims limit so more people can handle their own disputes. This would be the ideal answer for the lay person *and* the courts. If the Small Claims limit was increased to $7,500 nationwide, the jammed court system would be relieved of a significant number of its civil actions. The average disputing party could work within this simplified court system on their own.

Raising the qualifying Small Claims limit to $7,500 would increase Small Claims cases and the time necessary to hear them, but the higher courts would nevertheless experience substantial relief. Their cases removed to Small Claims would no longer require the average 20 hours of court time. Instead, they'd receive about an hour. In this manner, only the more expensive cases would be hit with high attorney fees and high court supervision time. The smaller, simpler cases would experience fast turnaround and its partner, reduced expense.

## HOW TO START A SMALL CLAIMS ACTION

The Small Claims Court is set up to serve you. It's easy and it's quick. As long as the value of your case is within its limits, this is your forum. You fill out a simple form or two and you're off to court in a month or less. The whole process couldn't be easier – a significant departure from the complexities of the general court system.

## GET YOUR BEST SMALL CLAIMS RESULT

The simple rule for Small Claims Court is to know the law, know the facts, and be prepared to present them in a brief time frame. You'll have between 10 and 15 minutes to present your side of the case. Have it all written down clearly and concisely. Your statement should consist of:

- A brief summary of the facts
- The law applied
- The damages

If you don't feel comfortable preparing this on your own, consult with an attorney. Our office has provided numerous Small Claims consultations, as will most attorneys. Actually, this type of consultation is most enjoyable to well-intentioned attorneys. It is an opportunity to teach and empower people to handle their own cases. Our office performs a range of services hand-tailored to the client's needs by giving them copies of the law that applies, preparing their written statement for them, and rehearsing their court appearance. The confidence our services provide has made all the difference for our Small Claims clients – both in terms of comfort at the hearing and results!

## PROCEDURE AT THE HEARING

**DOCUMENTS:** At the hearing, provide a copy of your written documents to the judge/commissioner and a copy to your opposing party. Before you start, make sure you let the judge know you have a copy for him or her and you gave a copy to your adversary.

> At the hearing, provide a copy of your written documents and have important witnesses on hand.

**An appeal often allows you to present your case all over again to another judge from start to finish.**

Mark any documents that support your case as Exhibit 1, Exhibit 2, and so on, with extra copies of those as well. In this manner you will be able to briefly summarize your position with all facts and law at your fingertips. Both the judge and your opponent will be impressed.

**WITNESSES:** Have important witnesses on hand. The court will provide you with subpoenas in advance demanding their attendance. Just ask for subpoenas when you file your Claim or Answer to Claim. Most Small Claims Courts also allow written witness statements instead of live testimony as long as they are signed under penalty of perjury. This procedure saves a lot of time at the hearing and makes it far more convenient for your witnesses. With such written witness statements, the witness need not appear.

**RECEIVING YOUR DECISION:** Usually, the judge will take the matter under consideration and mail the decision to you later. In this way, the judge can prepare a decision with a review of your written summary in private.

**SMALL CLAIMS APPEALS:** After receiving the decision, you have a brief time frame to appeal – if appeal is permitted in your state. If appeal is your decision, move forward quickly. Not everyone is allowed to appeal. So check your court rules. An appeal often allows you to present your case all over again to another judge from start to finish. People sometimes hire attorneys to present their appeal. This is where an expense comes in – through the Small Claims Appellate door.

**THE JUDGMENT:** If no appeal is filed, the order you receive is a judgment. This judgment is collectible against your opposing party. And, as with other court forums, your Small Claims Court judgment bears the standard interest rate in your state until paid – in some states as high as 10 percent interest per year. This high interest is clearly an inducement for the losing party to pay your judgment as soon as possible.

> Discovery is your most expensive cost and in many instances, it's a luxury you can't afford.

## YOUR KEYS TO SUCCESS IN THE TRIAL COURTS

Any case above the Small Claims case value limit qualifies for the general trial court system. Some states have a two-tier system, such as Municipal and Superior courts, where cases are divided depending on value and subject. The difference between these systems is not significant. So, we combine them here as the *general trial court system.*

## HOW TO START AN ACTION IN THE TRIAL COURT SYSTEM

You begin your dispute by filing a complaint. Some states now have form complaints, but determining which forms to use is a legal decision in itself, which generally requires legal training. To further confuse the issue, you can't get the forms from the courts. Often you won't know where to obtain the forms. We suggest you start by calling West Publishing Company in Saint Paul, Minnesota at 800-328-9352. You'll probably have to buy a book containing all forms used in your state. But at least you'll have the choices at your fingertips.

## Discovery: Your Largest Expense

Discovery consists of legal methods of discovering facts in cases. The most popular are oral depositions, written questions called interrogatories and demands for document production. Most courts and attorneys encourage discovery. Discovery is your most expensive cost. In many instances, it's a luxury you can't afford. But most people don't know that they don't *have* to afford it.

## Planning for Discovery

Discovery planning is one more reason to have full discussion with your attorney at the beginning of your case. As with everything else, a well thought out plan brings the best result. Sit down with your attorney and discuss the discovery methods available, their costs, and how they apply to your particular case. It's your decision. Do you want to spend $3000 for 10 hours of attorney time and 7 hours of court reporter time taking a deposition to find out what you already know? Put yourself in the drivers seat, make your attorney your co-pilot, and make these preliminary decisions together.

## Plan for Your Side of the Case: The Rest Comes Later

Of course, you can't agree upon a defensive plan before you actually see what your opponent does. But an offensive plan will help you shape your own discovery strategy – and it will put you and your attorney on the same page for estimated costs. Also, with a discovery plan in place, your attorney can propose a joint plan to opposing counsel. Opposing attorneys

---

> An offensive plan will help you shape your own discovery strategy and your attorney can propose a joint plan to opposing counsel.

who work together in representing their clients are far more likely to bring in lower fees than those involved in a power struggle.

## Status Conference: Exploring ADR

A few months after you file your case, most courts hold a status conference. This is a relatively new procedure where the court encourages the parties to agree to a form of alternative dispute resolution. The courts give a clear message: "We're overbooked and don't have time for your case. Which form of alternative dispute resolution will you consider? Mediation or binding arbitration?"

This is your perfect opportunity to once again propose mediation and/or binding arbitration to your opponent. He's had a taste of court and attorney fees. Even if he was against alternative dispute resolution before, the timing is ideal for a change of heart.

## Propose ADR to Your Opponents

A few weeks before this hearing you should begin to propose these alternatives "so we can save on attorney fees." You do the work. Prepare an agreement along the lines explored in Chapter 12 and the Appendix. Write a cover letter to all adversaries pointing out the savings in time and attorney fees if alternative dispute resolution is agreed to by all. See the Appendix for samples.

Your opposing parties are the ones most interested in saving costs and should welcome a proposal with a mutual mission statement – saving attorney fees. If there is an attorney fee

> **Your opposing parties are most interested in saving costs and should welcome a proposal to save on attorney fees.**

> **Jury trials usually take three to four times longer than court trials, all at attorney billable rates.**

provision, point out that they'll have to pay these hardy fees for the next few years until they get to judgment day. Then again, there's no guarantee they'll win. With the unsure court system, it could end up the other way around – and they may be paying your attorney fees.

If there is no attorney fee provision, emphasize how much these cases cost. Recite our statistics. Give them a copy of this book. Do everything you can to get your opponent to agree to a form of alternative dispute resolution.

## TRIAL

Trial is often a long, drawn out affair. In most cases, both you and your adversary have the right to have your case tried by a jury. Either party may claim this important right to trial by jury, even if the other party says they don't want one. Your cost for a jury trial is far greater than a court trial. The jury selection and instruction process takes time. Paperwork needed for a jury trial is voluminous and complex. Trial procedures are also more formalized in jury trials. Jury trials usually take three to four times longer than court trials, all at attorney billable rates.

Because of these expense-creating factors, you and your attorney should carefully consider whether a jury trial is warranted. Assess how much you've already spent in attorney fees. Make a list of reasons why you feel a jury would be better for your case than a judge, and vice versa. Ask your lawyer for an honest opinion about whether a jury is necessary. Evaluate the upsides and downsides. Can a judge alone adequately hear your case? Who is the judge that will hear your case? What is the judge's history? Do you need a panel of 12 peers? Choosing whether or not to have a jury decide your case is a significant decision that should be made by you and your attorney based on careful analysis. Your decision should be based on money and result. The proportions of each will vary with each case and your trial budget.

In planning your trial, you always want to ensure that the expense and the recovery you anticipate correspond. You don't want a full blown five day trial that costs you $10,000 if your case is worth only $17,000. Even if you have an attorney fee provision, the court will find the trial expense was unreasonable and disallow all or a portion of your attorney fees.

Make your jury trial decision early on, after initial discovery has concluded. Court trials often receive priority over jury trials. If you've decided that you will not require a jury, you may get to trial far sooner than the case that requires a jury. It's all a matter of time. When it comes to the court's schedule, there is never enough time.

> It's all a matter of time. When it comes to the court's schedule, there is never enough time.

### WHEN WILL YOU GO TO TRIAL?

The courts have attempted to implement programs to get cases to trial faster. But, for the most part, they haven't hired more judges or built more courtrooms to hear these cases. Generally, cases get to trial three years after filing. Some take five years; some take two. But three years is now the norm nationwide. That's

| Appeal is both a bargaining tactic and a prime settlement opportunity. |

a long time to wait for anything – especially justice.

Most trial dates are continued more than once before they actually go to trial. You show up all ready to go and the judge tells you he doesn't have a courtroom. By law, the criminal cases take priority and they had too many criminal cases this week. When you are stuck in the trial continuance loop, it is perhaps the ideal time to propose binding arbitration. Everyone's there, ready to go. With signatures on an arbitration stipulation, you'll be off to arbitration in a few days or weeks at most – instead of waiting for your next trial date three to six months away with no guarantee you'll go to trial the next time.

### APPEAL

Any party may appeal a judgment from the trial court. It's the best way to register a complaint that the court or jury did something wrong in deciding your case. Appeal is both a bargaining tactic and a prime settlement opportunity. Instead of spending another few years and a further bundle of attorney fees rehashing your case, the appellate process presents another ideal opportunity to settle. A short circuit of the appeal process is clearly in everyone's interest, in terms of time, money, and emotion.

Mediation can also be set up at this point. You've already tried your case through the court system. You'll have to wait another few years for the appellate court to make its ruling. Mediation is the ideal time out between battles. Again, you may want to present your mediation proposal directly to your adversary. You are the parties most motivated to settle, and the source of attorney fees and costs for Round Two. It's well worth your while to enter the mediation forum now.

* * *

It's taken fourteen chapters and a few turns at The Pocket Lawyer Analyzer to conclude this book. We have dedicated The Pocket Lawyer to empowering people beset by legal problems. Have we succeeded? The principle behind this book is as timely today as it was more than two hundred fifty years ago: "Come, agree, the law's costly." Jonathan Swift, Polite Conversation (1738).

# APPENDIX

## MEDIATION AGREEMENT

MINDFUL OF THE HIGH COST OF LITIGATION NOT ONLY IN DOLLARS BUT IN TIME AND ENERGY, THE PARTIES HEREBY ESTABLISH A QUICK, NON-BINDING OUT-OF-COURT DISPUTE RESOLUTION PROCEDURE TO BE FOLLOWED WITH RESPECT TO THE PENDING DISPUTE BETWEEN _____ [NAMES OF ALL PARTIES]_____CONCERNING_____[DESCRIBE DISPUTE FACTUALLY AND CONCISELY]____ .

A. INITIATION: THE DISPUTE SHALL BE REFERRED TO THE NEAREST OFFICE OF THE AMERICAN ARBITRATION ASSOCIATION (AAA) [OR SPECIFY SERVICE OF YOUR CHOICE] FOR MEDIATION. MEDIATION SHALL CONSIST OF AN INFORMAL, NON-BINDING CONFERENCE BETWEEN THE PARTIES AND THE MEDIATOR JOINTLY, THEN IN SEPARATE CAUCUSES WHEREIN THE MEDIATOR WILL SEEK TO GUIDE THE PARTIES TO A RESOLUTION OF THE CASE. THE MEDIATOR SHALL BE APPOINTED BY THE MEDIATION PROVIDER AND SHALL BE AN ATTORNEY OR RETIRED JUDGE EXPERIENCED IN DISPUTES OF THE SAME SUBJECT MATTER. THE MEDIATION PROCESS SHALL CONTINUE UNTIL THE CASE IS RESOLVED OR UNTIL THE MEDIATOR MAKES A FINDING THAT THERE IS NO POSSIBILITY OF RESOLUTION.

B. COSTS AND FEES: THE COST OF SUBMITTING THIS DISPUTE TO MEDIATION AS PROVIDED HEREIN SHALL BE SPLIT EQUALLY BY THE PARTIES.

C. [OPTIONAL] NO ATTORNEY REPRESENTATION: IN THE INTEREST OF COST SAVINGS, THE PARTIES AGREE THAT THEY WILL NOT BE REPRESENTED BY COUNSEL AT THE MEDIATION SESSION. ANY PARTY APPEARING WITH COUNSEL SHALL BE CAUSE FOR CONTINUATION OF THE HEARING.

/S/ DATED AND SIGNED BY THE PARTIES.

# BINDING ARBITRATION AGREEMENT

MINDFUL OF THE HIGH COST OF LITIGATION NOT ONLY IN DOLLARS BUT IN TIME AND ENERGY, THE PARTIES HEREBY ESTABLISH A QUICK, FINAL AND BINDING OUT-OF-COURT DISPUTE RESOLUTION PROCEDURE TO BE FOLLOWED WITH RESPECT TO THE PENDING DISPUTE BETWEEN _____ [NAMES OF ALL PARTIES]_____ CONCERNING _____[DESCRIBE DISPUTE FACTUALLY AND CONCISELY]____ .

A. INITIATION: THE PARTIES HERETO AGREE TO SUBMIT THEIR DISPUTE ABOVE DESCRIBED TO BINDING ARBITRATION ADMINISTERED BY THE AMERICAN ARBITRATION ASSOCIATION (AAA) [OR SPECIFY SERVICE OF YOUR CHOICE]. THE HEARING SHALL BE HELD WITHIN 90 DAYS OF SUBMISSION AND IS TARGETED TO LAST NO LONGER THAN TWO DAYS [OR TIME ESTIMATE FOR YOUR DISPUTE].

B. APPOINTMENT AND POWERS OF ARBITRATOR: THE ARBITRATOR SHALL BE AN ATTORNEY OR RETIRED JUDGE EXPERIENCED IN DISPUTES OF THE SAME SUBJECT MATTER AND SHALL BE CHOSEN BY THE PARTIES FROM AAA'S [OR SPECIFY SERVICE OF YOUR CHOICE] PANEL OF ARBITRATORS. THE ARBITRATOR SHALL HAVE THE AUTHORITY AND POWER TO PROCEED EX PARTE IN THE EVENT THAT ANY PARTY SHALL FAIL, AFTER REASONABLE NOTICE, TO ATTEND THE HEARINGS. THE ARBITRATOR MAY GRANT ANY REMEDY OR RELIEF THAT THE ARBITRATOR DEEMS JUST, INCLUDING, BUT NOT LIMITED TO, INJUNCTIVE RELIEF AND/OR SPECIFIC PERFORMANCE OF A CONTRACT.

C. [OPTIONAL: DO NOT INCLUDE IF PARTIES SELF REPRESENTED] ATTORNEYS FEES: THE PARTIES HERETO AGREE THAT THE PARTY PREVAILING IN THIS DISPUTE SHALL BE AWARDED ATTORNEYS FEES BASED ON THE ACTUAL TIME INCURRED BY THE ATTORNEY FOR THE PREVAILING PARTY FOR THOSE SERVICES NECESSARY TO BRING THE DISPUTE TO JUDGMENT.

D. [OPTIONAL] COSTS: THE PARTIES HERETO AGREE THAT THE PARTY PREVAILING IN THIS DISPUTE SHALL BE AWARDED THE COSTS IT HAS PAID TO THE ARBITRATOR AND TO THE ARBITRATION ADMINISTRATOR PURSUANT TO THIS AGREEMENT.

E. [OPTIONAL] DISCOVERY: THE INTENT OF ARBITRATION IS TO CUT COSTS, PARTICULARLY DISCOVERY COSTS. THUS, THE PARTIES SHALL HAVE ONLY THE FOLLOWING RIGHTS TO DISCOVERY:

1. WRITTEN DISCOVERY. AS TO EACH ADVERSE PARTY, A PARTY MAY USE ANY COMBINATION OF 35 OF THE FOLLOWING:

      A. INTERROGATORIES WITH NO SUB-PARTS.
      B. DEMANDS TO PRODUCE DOCUMENTS OR THINGS.
      C. REQUESTS FOR ADMISSIONS.

2. DEPOSITIONS MAY BE TAKEN ONLY WITH THE CONSENT OF THE ARBITRATOR.

3. ANY AND ALL OTHER DISCOVERY, EXAMINATIONS AND INSPECTIONS MAY BE CONDUCTED ONLY WITH THE CONSENT OF THE ARBITRATOR.

      F. [OPTIONAL] THE AWARD: THE ARBITRATOR SHALL FOLLOW THE FOLLOWING PROCEDURE IN RENDERING THE AWARD: (A) WITHIN 30 DAYS OF SUBMISSION A TENTATIVE AWARD EXPLAINING THE FACTUAL AND LEGAL BASIS FOR THE DECISION WILL BE MADE BY THE ARBITRATOR (B) WITHIN 15 DAYS AFTER MAILING OF THE TENTATIVE AWARD ANY PARTY MAY SERVE WRITTEN OBJECTIONS THERETO. THE ARBITRATOR MAY THEN CALL FOR ADDITIONAL EVIDENCE. (C) IF NO OBJECTIONS ARE SERVED, THE TENTATIVE AWARD BECOMES FINAL AND BINDING. (D) IF OBJECTIONS ARE SERVED, WITHIN 30 DAYS AFTER RECEIPT, THE ARBITRATOR WILL EITHER MODIFY OR CONFIRM THE TENTATIVE AWARD, WHICH AWARD WILL THEN BE FINAL AND BINDING.

      THE AWARD OF THE ARBITRATOR SHALL BE FINAL AND BINDING UPON THE PARTIES WITHOUT APPEAL OR REVIEW EXCEPT AS PERMITTED BY THE ARBITRATION LAWS OF THE STATE WHEREIN THE ARBITRATION IS HELD. APPLICATION MAY BE HAD BY ANY PARTY TO ANY COURT OF GENERAL JURISDICTION FOR ENTRY OF JUDGMENT BASED ON SAID AWARD.

BY SIGNING THIS AGREEMENT YOU ARE AGREEING TO HAVE ANY DISPUTE ARISING OUT OF THE MATTERS INCLUDED IN THIS PROVISION DECIDED BY NEUTRAL BINDING ARBITRATION AND YOU ARE GIVING UP ANY RIGHTS YOU POSSESS TO HAVE THE DISPUTE LITIGATED IN COURT OR BY JURY TRIAL. YOU ARE GIVING UP YOUR LEGAL RIGHTS TO DISCOVERY AND APPEAL EXCEPT AS PROVIDED HEREIN. IF YOU REFUSE TO SUBMIT TO ARBITRATION AFTER AGREEING TO THIS PROVISION, YOU MAY BE COMPELLED TO ARBITRATE. YOUR AGREEMENT TO THIS PROVISION IS VOLUNTARY. I HAVE READ AND UNDERSTAND THE FOREGOING.

/S/ DATED AND SIGNED BY ALL PARTIES.

## Multi-Step ADR Agreement

**Intent of Parties:** Mindful of the high cost of litigation not only in dollars but in time and energy, the parties hereby establish a quick, final and binding out-of-court dispute resolution procedure to be followed with respect to the pending dispute between _____[names of all parties]_____ concerning_____[describe dispute factually and concisely]____ .

### Step 1: Negotiation:

It is the intent of the parties that this dispute be resolved, if possible, informally and promptly through good faith negotiation. The parties therefore agree to meet in person within 30 days of the date of this Agreement to attempt to resolve this matter.

### Step 2: Mediation:

**A. Initiation:** In the event that the dispute is not resolved by Step One, the dispute shall be referred to the nearest office of the American Arbitration Association (AAA) [*or specify service of your choice*] for mediation. Mediation shall consist of an informal, non-binding conference between the parties and the mediator jointly, then in separate caucuses wherein the mediator will seek to guide the parties to a resolution of the case. The mediator shall be appointed by the mediation provider and shall be an attorney or retired judge experienced in disputes of the same subject matter. The mediation process shall continue until the case is resolved or until the mediator makes a finding that there is no possibility of resolution.

**B. Costs and Fees:** The cost of submitting this dispute to mediation as provided herein shall be split equally by the parties.

### Step 3: Binding Arbitration:

Any claim that may be brought within the Small Claims Court is excluded from arbitration. Should any dispute remain between the parties after completion of the resolution processes set forth above, then the parties shall promptly sub-

MIT THE DISPUTE DESCRIBED TO BINDING ARBITRATION ADMINIS-
TERED BY AAA [OR SPECIFY SERVICE OF YOUR CHOICE]. THE HEARING
SHALL BE HELD WITHIN 90 DAYS OF THE MEDIATION SESSION DE-
SCRIBED IN STEP 2 AND IS TARGETED TO LAST NO LONGER THAN TWO
DAYS [OR TIME ESTIMATE FOR YOUR DISPUTE].

A.  INITIATION:  ANY PARTY BOUND BY THIS ARBITRATION
AGREEMENT MAY INITIATE ARBITRATION, AT ANY TIME AFTER NEGO-
TIATION AND MEDIATION PROCEDURES AS ABOVE-DESCRIBED HAVE
BEEN EXHAUSTED, BY SERVING ALL PARTIES WITH NOTICE OF THE NA-
TURE OF THE CLAIM AND A DEMAND FOR ARBITRATION. THE CLAIMANT
SHALL FILE A COPY OF THE DEMAND FOR ARBITRATION AT ANY RE-
GIONAL OFFICE OF THE AAA [OR SPECIFY SERVICE OF YOUR CHOICE],
FOR HEARING UNDER THE RULES APPLICABLE TO THE SUBJECT MAT-
TER OF THIS DISPUTE, TOGETHER WITH THE APPROPRIATE FILING
FEE.

B.  APPOINTMENT AND POWERS OF ARBITRATOR:  THE ARBI-
TRATOR SHALL  BE AN ATTORNEY OR RETIRED JUDGE EXPERIENCED IN
DISPUTES OF THE SAME SUBJECT MATTER AND SHALL BE CHOSEN BY
THE PARTIES FROM AAA'S [OR SPECIFY SERVICE OF YOUR CHOICE]
PANEL OF ARBITRATORS.   THE ARBITRATOR SHALL HAVE THE
AUTHORITY AND POWER TO PROCEED EX PARTE IN THE EVENT THAT
ANY PARTY SHALL FAIL, AFTER REASONABLE NOTICE, TO ATTEND THE
HEARINGS. THE ARBITRATOR MAY GRANT ANY REMEDY OR RELIEF THAT
THE ARBITRATOR DEEMS JUST, INCLUDING, BUT NOT LIMITED TO, IN-
JUNCTIVE RELIEF AND/OR SPECIFIC PERFORMANCE OF A CONTRACT.

C.  [OPTIONAL: DO NOT INCLUDE IF PARTIES SELF REPRE-
SENTED] ATTORNEYS FEES:  THE PARTIES HERETO AGREE THAT THE
PARTY PREVAILING IN THIS DISPUTE SHALL BE AWARDED ATTORNEYS
FEES BASED ON THE ACTUAL TIME INCURRED BY THE ATTORNEY FOR
THE PREVAILING PARTY FOR THOSE SERVICES NECESSARY TO BRING
THE DISPUTE TO JUDGMENT.

D.  [OPTIONAL] COSTS:  THE PARTIES HERETO AGREE THAT
THE PARTY PREVAILING IN THIS DISPUTE SHALL BE AWARDED THE
COSTS IT HAS PAID TO THE MEDIATOR AND ARBITRATOR AND TO THE
MEDIATION-ARBITRATION ADMINISTRATOR PURSUANT TO THIS AGREE-
MENT.

E.  [OPTIONAL] DISCOVERY:  THE INTENT OF ARBITRATION IS
TO CUT COSTS, PARTICULARLY DISCOVERY COSTS. THUS, THE PARTIES
SHALL HAVE ONLY THE FOLLOWING RIGHTS TO DISCOVERY:

1. WRITTEN DISCOVERY. AS TO EACH ADVERSE PARTY, A PARTY MAY USE ANY COMBINATION OF 35 OF THE FOLLOWING:

A. INTERROGATORIES WITH NO SUB-PARTS.
B. DEMANDS TO PRODUCE DOCUMENTS OR THINGS.
C. REQUESTS FOR ADMISSIONS.

2. DEPOSITIONS MAY BE TAKEN ONLY WITH THE CONSENT OF THE ARBITRATOR.

3. ANY AND ALL OTHER DISCOVERY, EXAMINATIONS AND INSPECTIONS MAY BE CONDUCTED ONLY WITH THE CONSENT OF THE ARBITRATOR.

F. [OPTIONAL] THE AWARD:  THE ARBITRATOR SHALL FOLLOW THE FOLLOWING PROCEDURE IN RENDERING THE AWARD: (A) WITHIN 30 DAYS OF SUBMISSION A TENTATIVE AWARD EXPLAINING THE FACTUAL AND LEGAL BASIS FOR THE DECISION WILL BE MADE BY THE ARBITRATOR (B) WITHIN 15 DAYS AFTER MAILING OF THE TENTATIVE AWARD ANY PARTY MAY SERVE WRITTEN OBJECTIONS THERETO.  THE ARBITRATOR MAY THEN CALL FOR ADDITIONAL EVIDENCE.  (C) IF NO OBJECTIONS ARE SERVED, THE TENTATIVE AWARD BECOMES FINAL AND BINDING.  (D) IF OBJECTIONS ARE SERVED, WITHIN 30 DAYS AFTER RECEIPT, THE ARBITRATOR WILL EITHER MODIFY OR CONFIRM THE TENTATIVE AWARD, WHICH AWARD WILL THEN BE FINAL AND BINDING.

THE AWARD OF THE ARBITRATOR SHALL BE FINAL AND BINDING UPON THE PARTIES WITHOUT APPEAL OR REVIEW EXCEPT AS PERMITTED BY THE ARBITRATION LAWS OF THE STATE WHEREIN THE ARBITRATION IS HELD. APPLICATION MAY BE HAD BY ANY PARTY TO ANY COURT OF GENERAL JURISDICTION FOR ENTRY OF JUDGMENT BASED ON SAID AWARD.

BY INITIALING HERE YOU ARE AGREEING TO HAVE ANY DISPUTE ARISING OUT OF THE MATTERS INCLUDED IN THIS PROVISION DECIDED BY NEUTRAL BINDING ARBITRATION PRECEDED BY MEDIATION AND YOU ARE GIVING UP ANY RIGHTS YOU POSSESS TO HAVE THE DISPUTE LITIGATED IN COURT OR BY JURY TRIAL. YOU ARE GIVING UP YOUR LEGAL RIGHTS TO DISCOVERY AND APPEAL EXCEPT AS PROVIDED HEREIN. IF YOU REFUSE TO SUBMIT TO MEDIATION OR ARBITRATION AFTER AGREEING TO THIS PROVISION, YOU MAY BE COMPELLED TO MEDIATE OR ARBITRATE. YOUR AGREEMENT TO THIS PROVISION IS VOLUNTARY. I HAVE

READ AND UNDERSTAND THE FOREGOING. (/S/ INITIALS OF PARTIES.)"

## STEP 4:
## [OPTIONAL] ATTORNEY DEMAND LETTER.

THIS STEP ONLY COMES INTO PLAY WHEN ONE OF THE PARTIES HIRES AN ATTORNEY. AT THAT TIME ATTORNEYS REPRESENTING PARTIES WILL SEND TO THE OTHER PARTIES CORRESPONDENCE SETTING FORTH THE PARTICULARS OF THEIR DISPUTE, THE TERM(S) OF ANY CONTRACT INVOLVED, THEIR RESPECTIVE LEGAL CONTENTIONS, AND A SUGGESTED RESOLUTION OF THE PROBLEM. THE PARTIES WILL THEREAFTER, WITHIN 10 DAYS, SEND WRITTEN RESPONSES TO THE CORRESPONDENCE THUS EXCHANGED. THE PARTIES AGREE THAT THESE WRITTEN SETTLEMENT COMMUNICATIONS ARE CONFIDENTIAL AND EXPRESSLY INADMISSIBLE FOR ANY PURPOSE IN ANY LATER PROCEEDINGS REGARDING THIS DISPUTE.

/S/ DATED AND SIGNED BY ALL PARTIES.

## MEDIATION - BINDING ARBITRATION AGREEMENT

INTENT OF PARTIES: MINDFUL OF THE HIGH COST OF LITIGATION NOT ONLY IN DOLLARS BUT IN TIME AND ENERGY, THE PARTIES HEREBY ESTABLISH A QUICK, FINAL AND BINDING OUT-OF-COURT DISPUTE RESOLUTION PROCEDURE TO BE FOLLOWED WITH RESPECT TO THE PENDING DISPUTE BETWEEN _____[NAMES OF ALL PARTIES]_____ CONCERNING____[DESCRIBE DISPUTE FACTUALLY AND CONCISELY]____ .

### STEP 1 : MEDIATION:

A. INITIATION: THE DISPUTE SHALL BE REFERRED TO THE NEAREST OFFICE OF THE AMERICAN ARBITRATION ASSOCIATION (AAA) [OR SPECIFY SERVICE OF YOUR CHOICE] FOR MEDIATION. MEDIATION SHALL CONSIST OF AN INFORMAL, NON-BINDING CONFERENCE BETWEEN THE PARTIES AND THE MEDIATOR JOINTLY, THEN IN SEPARATE CAUCUSES WHEREIN THE MEDIATOR WILL SEEK TO GUIDE THE PARTIES TO A RESOLUTION OF THE CASE. THE MEDIATOR SHALL BE APPOINTED BY THE MEDIATION PROVIDER AND SHALL BE AN ATTORNEY OR RETIRED JUDGE EXPERIENCED IN DISPUTES OF THE SAME SUBJECT MATTER. THE MEDIATION PROCESS SHALL CONTINUE UNTIL THE CASE IS RESOLVED OR UNTIL THE MEDIATOR MAKES A FINDING THAT THERE IS NO POSSIBILITY OF RESOLUTION.

B. COST AND FEES: THE COST OF SUBMITTING THIS DISPUTE TO MEDIATION AS PROVIDED HEREIN SHALL BE SPLIT EQUALLY BY THE PARTIES.

### STEP 2: BINDING ARBITRATION:

ANY CLAIM THAT MAY BE BROUGHT WITHIN THE SMALL CLAIMS COURT IS EXCLUDED FROM ARBITRATION. SHOULD ANY DISPUTE REMAIN BETWEEN THE PARTIES AFTER COMPLETION OF MEDIATION, THEN THE PARTIES SHALL PROMPTLY SUBMIT THE DISPUTE DESCRIBED TO BINDING ARBITRATION ADMINISTERED BY AAA [OR SPECIFY SERVICE OF YOUR CHOICE]. THE HEARING SHALL BE HELD WITHIN 90 DAYS OF THE MEDIATION SESSION DESCRIBED IN STEP 2 AND IS TARGETED TO LAST NO LONGER THAN TWO DAYS [OR TIME ESTIMATE FOR YOUR DISPUTE].

A.  INITIATION:  ANY  PARTY  BOUND  BY  THIS  ARBITRATION AGREEMENT MAY INITIATE  ARBITRATION, AT ANY TIME AFTER STEP 1 HAS BEEN COMPLETED, BY SERVING ALL PARTIES WITH NOTICE OF THE NATURE OF THE CLAIM AND A DEMAND FOR ARBITRATION. THE CLAIMANT SHALL FILE A COPY OF THE DEMAND FOR ARBITRATION AT ANY REGIONAL OFFICE OF THE AAA [*OR SPECIFY SERVICE OF YOUR CHOICE*], FOR HEARING UNDER THE RULES APPLICABLE TO THE SUB-JECT MATTER OF THIS DISPUTE, TOGETHER WITH THE APPROPRIATE FILING FEE.

B. APPOINTMENT AND POWERS OF ARBITRATOR:  THE ARBI-TRATOR SHALL  BE AN ATTORNEY OR RETIRED JUDGE EXPERIENCED IN DISPUTES OF THE SAME SUBJECT MATTER AND SHALL BE CHOSEN BY THE PARTIES FROM AAA'S [*OR OTHER SERVICE OF YOUR CHOICE*] PANEL OF ARBITRATORS.   THE ARBITRATOR SHALL HAVE THE AUTHORITY AND POWER TO PROCEED *EX PARTE* IN THE EVENT THAT ANY PARTY SHALL FAIL, AFTER REASONABLE NOTICE, TO ATTEND THE HEARINGS. THE ARBITRATOR MAY GRANT ANY REMEDY OR RELIEF THAT THE ARBITRATOR DEEMS JUST, INCLUDING, BUT NOT LIMITED TO, IN-JUNCTIVE RELIEF AND/OR SPECIFIC PERFORMANCE OF A CONTRACT.

C. [OPTIONAL: DO NOT INCLUDE IF PARTIES SELF REPRE-SENTED] ATTORNEYS FEES:  THE PARTIES HERETO AGREE THAT THE PARTY PREVAILING IN THIS DISPUTE SHALL BE AWARDED ATTORNEYS FEES BASED ON THE ACTUAL TIME INCURRED BY THE ATTORNEY FOR THE PREVAILING PARTY FOR THOSE SERVICES NECESSARY TO BRING THE DISPUTE TO JUDGMENT.

D. [OPTIONAL] COSTS:  THE PARTIES HERETO AGREE THAT THE PARTY PREVAILING IN THIS DISPUTE SHALL BE AWARDED THE COSTS IT HAS PAID TO THE MEDIATOR AND ARBITRATOR AND TO THE MEDIATION-ARBITRATION ADMINISTRATOR PURSUANT TO THIS AGREE-MENT.

E. [OPTIONAL] DISCOVERY:  THE INTENT OF ARBITRATION IS TO CUT COSTS, PARTICULARLY DISCOVERY COSTS. THUS, THE PARTIES SHALL HAVE ONLY THE FOLLOWING RIGHTS TO DISCOVERY:

1.  WRITTEN DISCOVERY. AS TO EACH ADVERSE PARTY, A PARTY MAY USE ANY COMBINATION OF 35 OF THE FOLLOWING:
       A. INTERROGATORIES WITH NO SUB-PARTS.
       B. DEMANDS TO PRODUCE DOCUMENTS OR THINGS.
       C. REQUESTS FOR ADMISSIONS.

2. DEPOSITIONS MAY BE TAKEN ONLY WITH THE CONSENT OF THE ARBITRATOR.

3. ANY AND ALL OTHER DISCOVERY, EXAMINATIONS AND INSPECTIONS MAY BE CONDUCTED ONLY WITH THE CONSENT OF THE ARBITRATOR.

F. [OPTIONAL] THE AWARD: THE ARBITRATOR SHALL FOLLOW THE FOLLOWING PROCEDURE IN RENDERING THE AWARD: (A) WITHIN 30 DAYS OF SUBMISSION A TENTATIVE AWARD EXPLAINING THE FACTUAL AND LEGAL BASIS FOR THE DECISION WILL BE MADE BY THE ARBITRATOR (B) WITHIN 15 DAYS AFTER MAILING OF THE TENTATIVE AWARD ANY PARTY MAY SERVE WRITTEN OBJECTIONS THERETO. THE ARBITRATOR MAY THEN CALL FOR ADDITIONAL EVIDENCE. (C) IF NO OBJECTIONS ARE SERVED, THE TENTATIVE AWARD BECOMES FINAL AND BINDING. (D) IF OBJECTIONS ARE SERVED, WITHIN 30 DAYS AFTER RECEIPT, THE ARBITRATOR WILL EITHER MODIFY OR CONFIRM THE TENTATIVE AWARD, WHICH AWARD WILL THEN BE FINAL AND BINDING.

THE AWARD OF THE ARBITRATOR SHALL BE FINAL AND BINDING UPON THE PARTIES WITHOUT APPEAL OR REVIEW EXCEPT AS PERMITTED BY THE ARBITRATION LAWS OF THE STATE WHEREIN THE ARBITRATION IS HELD. APPLICATION MAY BE HAD BY ANY PARTY TO ANY COURT OF GENERAL JURISDICTION FOR ENTRY OF JUDGMENT BASED ON SAID AWARD.

BY INITIALING HERE YOU ARE AGREEING TO HAVE ANY DISPUTE ARISING OUT OF THE MATTERS INCLUDED IN THIS PROVISION DECIDED BY NEUTRAL BINDING ARBITRATION PRECEDED BY MEDIATION AND YOU ARE GIVING UP ANY RIGHTS YOU POSSESS TO HAVE THE DISPUTE LITIGATED IN COURT OR BY JURY TRIAL. YOU ARE GIVING UP YOUR LEGAL RIGHTS TO DISCOVERY AND APPEAL, EXCEPT AS PROVIDED HEREIN. IF YOU REFUSE TO SUBMIT TO MEDIATION OR ARBITRATION AFTER AGREEING TO THIS PROVISION, YOU MAY BE COMPELLED TO MEDIATE OR ARBITRATE. YOUR AGREEMENT TO THIS PROVISION IS VOLUNTARY. I HAVE READ AND UNDERSTAND THE FOREGOING. (/S/ INITIALS OF PARTIES.)"

/S/ DATED AND SIGNED BY ALL PARTIES.

## STIPULATED JUDGMENT

_____ COURT OF THE STATE OF _____

FOR THE COUNTY OF _____

| | |
|---|---|
| (NAME),<br>    PLAINTIFF,<br><br>_____<br><br>VS.<br>(NAME),<br>    DEFENDANT<br><br>_____ | CASE NO. _____<br><br>**STIPULATION FOR<br>JUDGMENT AND JUDGMENT<br>WITH CONDITIONAL STAY** |

THE PARTIES HERETO AGREE TO THE FOLLOWING JUDGMENT AGAINST DEFENDANT (NAME) ON THE FOLLOWING TERMS AND CONDITIONS:

1. THE JUDGMENT: THAT PLAINTIFF (NAME) HAVE AND RECOVER JUDGMENT AGAINST THE DEFENDANT (NAME) THE PRINCIPAL SUM OF (WRITTEN NUMBER IN DOLLARS ($_____)).

2. STAY OF EXECUTION CONDITIONED ON PERFORMANCE: THAT EXECUTION ON THE FOREGOING JUDGMENT SHALL BE STAYED SO LONG AS SAID DEFENDANT PAYS TO PLAINTIFF THE SUM OF $_____ ON OR BEFORE__[DATE]__, AT WHICH TIME PLAINTIFF SHALL FORTHWITH FILE WITH THIS COURT A SATISFACTION OF JUDGMENT IN FULL.

3. TIME IS OF THE ESSENCE: TIME IS OF THE ESSENCE WITH RESPECT TO THIS PAYMENT DATE. IF SAID JUDGMENT AMOUNT IN FULL IS NOT RECEIVED ON___[DATE]___, PLAINTIFF SHALL AUTOMATICALLY AND WITHOUT FURTHER NOTICE TO DEFENDANT AND WITHOUT FURTHER ACTION BY PLAINTIFF, DISCHARGE THE STAY OF EXECUTION DESCRIBED IN PARAGRAPH 2, AND FORTHWITH HAVE JUDGMENT ENTERED AGAINST DEFENDANT IN ACCORDANCE WITH THE TERMS HEREOF IN THE AMOUNT OF $_____.

**4. FULL AND FINAL UNDERSTANDING:** THIS IS THE FULL AND FINAL COMPROMISE AGREEMENT OF THE PARTIES WHICH HAS BEEN EXECUTED CONTEMPORANEOUS WITH A REQUEST FOR DISMISSAL WITH PREJUDICE OF THE ENTIRE ACTION, WHICH REQUEST FOR DISMISSAL SHALL BE FILED IMMEDIATELY.

DATED:_____                          DATED:_____


_____                    _____
(NAME), PLAINTIFF                          (NAME), DEFENDANT


[*SOME COURTS REQUIRE COURT APPROVAL. IF SO, INCLUDE THE FOLLOWING*:]

## ORDER OF COURT

**GOOD CAUSE APPEARING,** THE ABOVE STIPULATED JUDGMENT IS HEREBY ORDERED UPON THE TERMS STATED.

DATED: _____


_____
(NAME)JUDGE OF THE (*COURT NAME*) COURT

# LOSS PREVENTION AGREEMENT

I. ANY AND ALL DISPUTES ARISING OUT OF OR RELATING TO THIS CONTRACT OR ITS SUBJECT MATTER SHALL PROCEED AS FOLLOWS:

STEP 1: THE PARTIES SHALL CONSULT AND NEGOTIATE WITH EACH OTHER, IN GOOD FAITH, AND ATTEMPT TO REACH A JUST AND EQUITABLE SOLUTION SATISFACTORY TO ALL PARTIES. IF THEY DO NOT REACH SUCH SOLUTION WITHIN 45 DAYS, THE NEXT STEP SHALL BE FOLLOWED.

STEP 2: ANY SUCH DISPUTE SHALL BE SETTLED BY BINDING ARBITRATION PRECEDED BY MEDIATION, BOTH ADMINISTERED BY THE AMERICAN ARBITRATION ASSOCIATION [*OR SPECIFY SERVICE OF YOUR CHOICE*], AND JUDGMENT ON THE AWARD RENDERED MAY BE ENTERED IN ANY COURT HAVING JURISDICTION THEREOF. ANY CLAIM THAT MAY BE BROUGHT WITHIN THE SMALL CLAIMS COURT IS EXCLUDED FROM ARBITRATION. THE PREVAILING PARTY IN ARBITRATION SHALL BE AWARDED FEES PAID TO THE MEDIATOR AND ARBITRATOR AND THE MEDIATION-ARBITRATION ADMINISTRATOR.

THE INTENT OF ARBITRATION IS TO CUT COSTS, PARTICULARLY DISCOVERY COSTS. THUS, THE PARTIES SHALL HAVE ONLY THE FOLLOWING RIGHTS TO DISCOVERY.

(1) WRITTEN DISCOVERY. AS TO EACH ADVERSE PARTY, A PARTY MAY USE ANY COMBINATION OF 35 OF THE FOLLOWING:

A. INTERROGATORIES WITH NO SUB-PARTS.
B. DEMANDS TO PRODUCE DOCUMENTS OR THINGS.
C. REQUESTS FOR ADMISSIONS.

(2) DEPOSITIONS MAY BE TAKEN ONLY WITH THE CONSENT OF THE ARBITRATOR.

(3) ANY AND ALL OTHER DISCOVERY, EXAMINATIONS AND INSPECTIONS MAY BE CONDUCTED ONLY WITH THE CONSENT OF THE ARBITRATOR.

BY INITIALLING IN THE SPACE BELOW YOU ARE AGREEING TO HAVE ANY DISPUTE ARISING OUT OF THE MATTERS INCLUDED IN THIS PROVISION DECIDED BY NEUTRAL BINDING ARBITRATION PRECEDED BY MEDIATION AND YOU ARE GIVING UP ANY RIGHTS YOU POSSESS TO HAVE THE DISPUTE LITIGATED IN COURT OR BY JURY TRIAL. YOU ARE GIVING UP YOUR RIGHTS TO DISCOVERY AND APPEAL EXCEPT AS PROVIDED HEREIN. IF YOU REFUSE TO SUBMIT TO MEDIATION OR ARBITRATION AFTER AGREEING TO THIS PROVISION, YOU MAY BE COMPELLED TO MEDIATE OR ARBITRATE. YOUR AGREEMENT TO THIS PROVISION IS VOLUNTARY. I HAVE READ AND UNDERSTAND THE FOREGOING. (/S/ INITIALS OF PARTIES.)"

II. IN ANY PROCEEDING INVOLVING ANY DISPUTE BETWEEN THE PARTIES TO THIS AGREEMENT RELATING TO MATTERS ARISING FROM THIS AGREEMENT OR ITS SUBJECT MATTER, WHETHER IN CONTRACT, TORT OR OTHERWISE, THE PREVAILING PARTY SHALL BE AWARDED ATTORNEY FEES BASED ON THE ACTUAL TIME INCURRED BY THE ATTORNEY FOR THE PREVAILING PARTY FOR THOSE SERVICES NECESSARY TO BRING THE DISPUTE TO JUDGMENT.

/S/ DATED AND SIGNED BY THE PARTIES.

# BINDING ARBITRATION PROPOSAL LETTER

DEAR ADVERSARY:

AN IDEAL TIME TO CONSIDER ALTERNATIVES PRESENTS ITSELF NOW THAT WE'VE ENTERED THE COURT SYSTEM AND PAID HEARTY RETAINERS FOR ATTORNEYS. WITH THIS TASTE OF LITIGATION I BELIEVE MORE THAN EVER THAT IT WOULD BE IN OUR BEST INTEREST TO GET OUR DISPUTE RESOLVED NOW. THERE IS A WAY TO GET THIS DONE WITH THE LEAST AMOUNT OF TIME AND EXPENSE AND THE VERY BEST RESULTS.

## OUR DISPUTE IS ABOUT TO GET VERY EXPENSIVE

THE COST OF THIS DISPUTE WILL BE GREAT. NOW I UNDERSTAND WHY PEOPLE SAY THAT ONLY THE ATTORNEYS COME OUT WELL IN THESE LEGAL DISPUTES. YOU AND I ARE ABOUT TO MAKE TWO MORE ATTORNEYS WEALTHIER. LAWSUITS GENERALLY TAKE 3 TO 5 YEARS TO GET TO TRIAL. THAT IS A LONG TIME TO BE EMBROILED IN THIS DISPUTE, ALL THE WHILE PAYING ESCALATING ATTORNEY BILLS. I THINK I UNDERSTAND WHAT LITIGANTS DESCRIBE AS THE LONG-TERM STRESS OF LEGAL ACTIONS. THE COST AND LENGTH OF THE LEGAL PROCESS ALONE CAN BRING ON PROLONGED HIGH STRESS. BUT I'M CONVINCED WE DON'T HAVE TO GO THROUGH THIS.

## WE CAN RESOLVE OUR DISPUTE QUICKLY AND FAIRLY

WE CAN ROUTE OUR DISPUTE OUT OF THE COURT SYSTEM AND INTO BINDING ARBITRATION. BINDING ARBITRATION IS AN OUT-OF-COURT PROCEDURE WHERE AN ATTORNEY OR RETIRED JUDGE (WELL VERSED IN THE TOPIC OF OUR MATTER) HEARS AND DECIDES OUR DISPUTE. THIS CAN BE DONE IN JUST ONE HEARING SCHEDULED IN A MATTER OF WEEKS. THE COST WOULD BE SO MUCH LESS THAN PAYING OUR ATTORNEYS FOR 3 TO 5 YEARS. TO CUT COSTS FURTHER, WE CAN AGREE IN ADVANCE TO LIMIT THE "DISCOVERY" [FACT FINDING] PROCEDURES AND EXPENSES WE WANT TO INCUR BEFORE THE ARBITRATION HEARING. I'VE HEARD THAT THE RESULTS FROM BINDING ARBITRATION ARE BETTER THAN THE COURTS BECAUSE THESE ARBITRATORS HAVE MORE TIME TO HEAR YOUR CASE. THEY ALSO DO THEIR OWN RESEARCH. THEIR AWARDS ARE RENDERED QUICKLY, EFFICIENTLY AND ECONOMICALLY.

## A BINDING ARBITRATION PROPOSAL FOR YOUR CONSIDERATION

I HAVE ENCLOSED A PROPOSAL FOR BINDING ARBITRATION WITH LIMITED [OPTION: NO] DISCOVERY. IT ALSO INCLUDES A FEW OTHER PROVISIONS. PLEASE FEEL FREE TO STRIKE OUT ANY PROVISIONS WITH WHICH YOU DO NOT FEEL COMFORTABLE. PLEASE CONSIDER THIS PROPOSAL AND RETURN IT TO ME WITH YOUR COMMENTS, SIGNATURE, OR BOTH.

I BELIEVE WE CAN WORK TOGETHER TO ARRIVE AT A FAIR, ECONOMICAL SOLUTION TO OUR DISPUTE. I LOOK FORWARD TO HEARING FROM YOU.

# GLOSSARY

**A**

**ACTUAL DAMAGES:** Generally in a contract action, what you would have gained. In other than contract actions: what you paid or lost. Must be definite and cannot be speculative.

**ADR:** Alternative Dispute Resolution. Out of court methods to solve legal disputes.

**ADVERSARIAL:** Warlike.

**ADVERSARY:** Opponent.

**ALTERNATIVE DISPUTE RESOLUTION:** Out-of-court methods to resolve disputes. Principal methods: arbitration and mediation.

**AMERICAN ARBITRATION ASSOCIATION (AAA):** The largest provider of arbitration and mediation services in the United States, a not-for-profit corporation.

**ARBITRATION [ADVISORY]:** Non-binding proceedings that are not final if the participants object to the award.

**ARBITRATION [BINDING]:** An out-of-court mini-trial by mutual written consent of the parties to a dispute, now a popular ADR method. Parties waive their rights to the court system and appeal. A dispute is brought before an arbitrator for a final, non-appealable award in favor of one party.

**ARBITRATION [JUDICIAL]:** Court-referred arbitration that is not final if one of the participants objects to the award.

**ARBITRATION AGREEMENT [BINDING]:** A written agreement wherein the parties agree to submit their dispute to binding out-of-court arbitration to be decided by an arbitrator whose award is final and binding. No appeal is allowed. The court system is replaced by this ADR procedure.

**ARBITRATION BRIEF:** Submitted by each party to the arbitrator prior to the hearing. Details the facts, law, and issues of the dispute.

**ATTORNEY FEE PROVISION:** A provision that entitles the prevailing party to an award of the attorney fees they incurred in pursuing the dispute.

**B**

**BREACH:** Violation of a duty; failure to adequately fulfill a duty.

## C

**CLAIMANT:** The complaining party in arbitration proceedings.

**COLLECTABILITY:** An indicator of the chances of collecting on a judgment against someone.

**COLLECTABILITY ASSESSMENT:** A determination by *The Pocket Lawyer Analyzer* that indicates your chances of collecting on a judgment against your adversary.

**COLLUSION:** A deceptive scheme.

**COMPLAINT:** A formal document which begins a lawsuit. The plaintiff details the circumstances and allegations surrounding the subject dispute. The defendant must respond within a certain time.

**CONFIDENTIALITY AGREEMENT:** Signed by the parties at mediation to confirm that statements or documents cannot be used in any later proceedings except by the party who made the statement or produced the document.

**CONTINGENT FEE:** A fee arrangement where you split the proceeds from your case with your lawyer in a percentage or amount agreed to. If there is no recovery, there is no payment to your lawyer. These agreements are negotiable.

**CONTINUANCE:** A rescheduling of a legal proceeding.

**COUNTER-ACTION:** Another action filed in the same lawsuit by a defendant who has a claim against his plaintiff or someone else.

## D

**DAMAGES:** A loss suffered as a result of someone's conduct.

**DEFAULT:** Failure to perform an act as agreed.

**DEFENDANT:** The party being complained about in a court action.

**DEFENSE:** A defendant's response to allegations by his plaintiff.

**DEMAND FOR DOCUMENT INSPECTION:** Written demand to a party to produce documents for inspection.

**DEPOSITIONS:** Meetings where attorneys question parties under oath, recorded by a court reporter.

**DISCOVERY:** Legal procedures whereby parties discover facts about their dispute.

**DISPUTANT:** A party in a dispute.

**DOCTORS OF JURISPRUDENCE:** The degree lawyers receive, commonly designated as "J.D."

**F**

**FEASIBILITY:**  Practicability; reasonableness.

**FEASIBILITY ASSESSMENT:**  A determination by *The Pocket Lawyer Analyzer* that indicates whether it is practical and reasonable to proceed with your dispute.

**FORUM:**  A setting in which disputes are heard.

**FORUM INDICATOR:**  Last phase of *The Pocket Lawyer Analyzer* which indicates which court or ADR process will hear your case.

**G**

**GOOD FAITH:**  In honesty, without taking unfair advantage.

**I**

**INTERROGATORIES:**  Written questions posed to a party prior to court trial or arbitration.

**J**

**JUDICIAL ARBITRATION & MEDIATION SERVICE – ENDISPUTE (JAMS):**  Second largest provider of arbitration and mediation services.  Many of their mediators and arbitrators are retired judges.

**JOINT OPEN SESSION:**  The opening session at mediation where introductions are made and parties are encouraged to describe their positions.

**L**

**LAST CHANCE SESSION:**  A settlement method created for this book. With it, you settle your dispute by convincing your opponent that your mutual enemy is the legal system.

**LEGAL CASE EVALUATION:**  Evaluation of the legal liability aspects of your case.

**LEGAL OPTIONS ASSESSMENT:**  An evaluation by *The Pocket Lawyer Analyzer* of the legal options contained in a contract between you and your adversary.  Legal options include attorney fee, binding arbitration and mediation provisions. An action in Small Claims Court is also considered.

**LIABLE:**  Legally responsible.

**LIABILITY:**  Legal responsibility.

**LIMITATION ON DAMAGES PROVISION:**  A written provision that limits or caps damages.  The damaged party recovers his damages but not more than this amount. Proving damages is required.

**LIQUIDATED DAMAGES PROVISION:** A written provision that fixes damages. The dollar amount that will be awarded upon breach by one party. Proving damages is not required.

**LITIGANT:** A party in an action brought in a court.

**LITIGATION:** An action brought in a court for legal determination.

**LOSS PREVENTION AGREEMENT:** A written agreement which includes mediation, arbitration, and attorney fee provisions.

**M**

**MEDIATION:** A voluntary settlement procedure; now a popular ADR method. A trained mediator, usually an attorney or retired judge, facilitates the parties to settlement. No judgment is imposed. Usually precedes court or arbitration. Successful 85% of the **TIME**.

**MEDIATION AGREEMENT:** A written agreement wherein the parties agree to submit their dispute to neutral mediation. The agreement can be signed before or after the dispute begins.

**MEDIATION BRIEF:** Also known as Position Paper. Submitted by each party to the mediator prior to the mediation hearing. Details the facts, law, issues and settlement status of the dispute.

**MEDIATOR:** A specially trained professional, usually an attorney or retired judge, who facilitates mediation hearings toward settlement.

**MULTI-STEP ADR AGREEMENT:** Comprehensive 4-step ADR agreement. Step One is negotiation between the parties. Step Two is mediation. Step Three is binding arbitration. Step Four is optional when a party hires an attorney.

**P**

**PARTIES:** Persons who have signed an agreement; opponents in a dispute.

**PERFORMANCE:** Fulfillment of one's duty. Satisfactory performance is what is expected of a reasonable person.

**PLAINTIFF:** The complaining party in a court action.

**POCKET LAWYER ANALYZER:** The Legal Case Feasibility Evaluation System developed for this book. Available on software through the Order Form.

**POCKET LAWYER ANALYZER FOR DEFENDANTS:** The Legal Case Feasibility Evaluation System developed for defendants in this book. Also available on software through the Order Form.

**PREVAILING PARTY:** The party who wins the case; a defendant or respondent wins the case if no judgment is found against him.

**PUNITIVE DAMAGES:** Damages awarded as a punishment due to intentional or fraudulent conduct.

### R

**RECOVERY:** The compensation a party receives in a lawsuit, binding arbitration or settlement.

**RESPONDENT:** The party being complained about in arbitration proceedings.

### S

**SEPARATE CAUCUSES:** At mediation, confidential sessions held by the mediator with individual parties to elicit settlement offers and demands.

**SETTLEMENT VALUE:** A number determined by *The Pocket Lawyer Analyzer* which is the figure you target for mediation or settlement meetings.

**SMALL CLAIMS COURT:** Courts in each state where opponents can bring their disputes rapidly and inexpensively within a short period of time. Each state has a different Small Claims limit ranging from $1,000 to $7,500. All cases valued under that state's limit can be brought in Small Claims Court.

**SMALL CLAIMS POSITION STATEMENT:** Details the facts, law, issues of the dispute, and attaches exhibits and declarations. Submitted to the judge and opponent at the hearing. Most people do not prepare these. They would do far better if they did.

**STATUS CONFERENCE:** Also known as ADR conference. A hearing held by the court to refer disputing parties to out-of-court ADR procedures for resolution of their disputes. Usually held within a few months of filing a lawsuit.

**STAY:** A delay. (stayed)

**STIPULATED JUDGMENT:** A judgment agreed to by a defendant as an alternative to court or arbitration proceedings, usually coupled with a stay (delay) in collection.

# INDEX

# The Pocket Lawyer

## ORDER FORM

| **Do not include Fax on Demand, which has automated payment.** |
| --- |

_____ Payment enclosed (check or money order only):     $_____

_____ VISA _____ MC  Acct. No. _____-_____-_____-_____

Expiration date _____  Signature _____

Ship to:
Name:_____

Address:_____

**BOOKS ORDERED:  Quantity:** _____ **at $24.95** . . . . . . . . . $_____

| shipping | UPS Ground: $ 5 1st item, $2 each addl. | _____ |
| and | UPS 1 Day:  $20 1st item, $3 each addl. | _____ |
| handling: | UPS 2 Day:  $11 1st item, $2 each addl. | _____ |

## DOCUMENTS/SOFTWARE BY MAIL:
**(complete back of this form)** . . . . . . . . . . . . . . . . . . . . .     $_____

| shipping | Regular Mail: 6% of total | _____ |
| and | UPS 1 Day:  Greater of $17 or 25% of total | _____ |
| handling: | UPS 2 Day:  Greater of $12 or 15% of total | _____ |

**SALES TAX: (shipments within California)** 7.75% of total . . . _____

**TOTAL OF ORDER** . . . . . . . . . . . . . . . . . . . . . . . . . .  $_____

See 0ver ➜

### For Software [3¼" disk] - Specify each:

| **Computer:** | **Word Processing:** | **Spreadsheet:** |
| --- | --- | --- |
| _____ IBM Compatible | _____ Word | _____ Excel |
| _____ Macintosh | _____ WP | _____ Lotus |

[Returns on damaged/defective items only.]

# The Pocket Lawyer

## Document/Software Catalog
### [Please circle your choices]

| No. | Document Name | Hard Copy | Software | Fax on Demand/ E-Mail |
|-----|---------------|-----------|----------|-----------------------|
| 31 | Binding Arbitration Proposal Letter | See 38 | See 38 | $1.00 |
| 32 | Joint Mediation/Arbitration Agreement | " | " | 3.00 |
| 33 | Multi-Step ADR Agreement | " | " | 4.00 |
| 34 | Mediation Agreement | " | " | 1.00 |
| 35 | Arbitration Agreement | " | " | 3.00 |
| 36 | Loss Prevention Agreement | " | " | 2.00 |
| 37 | Stipulated Judgment | " | " | 3.00 |
| 38 | Items 31 to 37 available as a package | $14.00 | $19.00 | n/a |
| 39 | The Pocket Lawyer Analyzer | 10.00 | 34.99 | 10.00 |
| 40 | The Pocket Lawyer Analyzer for Defendants | 10.00 | 34.99 | 10.00 |
| 41 | Book: The Pocket Lawyer | 24.95 | n/a | n/a |
| 42 | Book: The New Home Buying Strategy | 24.95 | n/a | n/a |

➠**Fax-on-Demand orders: (415) 461-7700.** Many documents are available fax-to-fax dialing from the handset of your fax machine. Follow the prompts to order documents, then press the start button on your fax machine. You will immediately receive the documents requested after automated credit card payment. No shipping fees, or sales tax.

☎ **Telephone orders: toll free (800) 843-6700.** Provide name, mailing address, Visa or Mastercard number, expiration date, and items requested.

〰 **General fax orders: (415) 461-4509.** Fax Order Form front and back.

💻 **On-line orders: www.venture2K.com.** Visit our site on the World Wide Web to download the documents you need. No shipping fees or sales tax.

✉ **E-Mail Orders: venture2k@worldnet.att.net.** For computer-to-computer orders. Provide information requested by Order Form, front and back, including mailing or E-mail address, and list documents requested. No shipping fees or sales tax.

📠 **Mail orders:** Venture 2000 Publishers, 100 Larkspur Landing Circle, Suite 112, Larkspur, CA 94939. Send Order Form, front and back. (415) 461-1470

⌘ **Trade orders:** National Book Network, 4720 Boston Way, Lanham, MD 20706 Telephone: (800) 462-6420